D1457238

SOCIOLOGY OF CRIME, LAW AND DEVIANCE   VOLUME 5

TERRORISM AND COUNTER-TERRORISM:
CRIMINOLOGICAL PERSPECTIVES

EDITED BY

MATHIEU DEFLEM

Department of Sociology, University of South Carolina, USA

2004

ELSEVIER
JAI

Amsterdam – Boston – Heidelberg – London – New York – Oxford – Paris
San Diego – San Francisco – Singapore – Sydney – Tokyo

ELSEVIER B.V.	ELSEVIER Inc.	**ELSEVIER Ltd**	ELSEVIER Ltd
Sara Burgerhartstraat 25	525 B Street, Suite 1900	**The Boulevard, Langford**	84 Theobalds Road
P.O. Box 211,	San Diego,	**Lane Kidlington,**	London
1000 AE Amsterdam	CA 92101-4495	**Oxford OX5 1GB**	WC1X 8RR
The Netherlands	USA	**UK**	UK

First edition 2004

Library of Congress Cataloging in Publication Data
A catalog record is available from the Library of Congress.

British Library Cataloguing in Publication Data
A catalogue record is available from the British Library.

ISBN: 0-7623-1040-5
ISSN: 1521-6136 (Series)

⊗ The paper used in this publication meets the requirements of ANSI/NISO Z39.48-1992 (Permanence of Paper). Printed in The Netherlands.

CONTENTS

PART III: COUNTER-TERRORISM, IDEOLOGY, AND SECURITY

PART IV: THE CONSTRUCTION AND REALITY OF TERRORISM

LIST OF CONTRIBUTORS

Gregg Barak	College of Justice & Safety, Eastern Kentucky University, USA
Bonnie Berry	Social Problems Research Group, USA
Donald Black	Department of Sociology, University of Virginia, USA
Kelly R. Damphousse	Department of Sociology, University of Oklahoma, USA
Mathieu Deflem	Department of Sociology, University of South Carolina, USA
Laura Dugan	Department of Criminology, University of Maryland, USA
Aaron E. Kappeler	Department of Anthropology, College of Social and Behavioral Sciences, University of Arizona, USA
Victor E. Kappeler	Department of Criminal Justice and Police Studies, College of Justice and Safety, Eastern Kentucky University, USA
Gary LaFree	Department of Criminology/Democracy Collaborative, University of Maryland, USA
Paul Leighton	Department of Sociology, Anthropology & Criminology, Eastern Michigan University, USA
Willem de Lint	Sociology and Anthropology, University of Windsor, Canada
Richard Rosenfeld	Department of Criminology and Criminal Justice, University of Missouri at St. Louis, USA

Brent L. Smith   Department of Sociology and Criminal
                          Justice, University of Arkansas, USA

Kevin J. Strom   Crime, Justice Policy, and Behavior Program,
                          Research Triangle Institute, USA

Michael J. Thomas   University of Texas at Arlington, USA

Margaret A. Zahn   Sociology and Anthropology, North Carolina
                          State University, USA

INTRODUCTION: TOWARDS A CRIMINOLOGICAL SOCIOLOGY OF TERRORISM AND COUNTER-TERRORISM

Mathieu Deflem

ABSTRACT

Until September 11, 2001, terrorism and counter-terrorism were relatively underexplored topics in the sociology of crime and social control. Since then, however, new ground has been made in the study of terrorism and terrorism-related phenomena across the social sciences, including ground-breaking work from the field of criminological sociology. The chapters in this volume reveal the distinct contribution criminological sociologists have to offer in the study of terrorism and counter-terrorism from a variety of theoretical and substantive viewpoints. The discussions include a usefully broad selection of themes, including conceptual and methodological issues in the criminology of terrorism; ideology and terrorism; and responses to terrorism in domestic and international settings.

Bringing together distinguished scholars from the field of criminological sociology, this volume presents a comprehensive and insightful state-of-the-art overview of terrorism and counter-terrorism scholarship with respect to important concerns of social control, crime, and law. Generally, terrorism has not been central to

Terrorism and Counter-Terrorism: Criminological Perspectives
Sociology of Crime, Law and Deviance, Volume 5, 1–6
Copyright © 2004 by Elsevier Ltd.
All rights of reproduction in any form reserved
ISSN: 1521-6136/doi:10.1016/S1521-6136(03)05001-2

the discourse of criminological sociology (nor criminology in general). Since the terrorist incidents of September 11, 2001, however, terrorism has resolutely moved center stage in sociological and other social-scientific discussions. The contributions in this volume bring out the distinct contribution criminological sociologists have to offer in the study of terrorism and terrorism-related phenomena from a variety of theoretical, methodological, and substantive viewpoints.

TERRORISM, SOCIAL SCIENCE, AND SOCIOLOGY

The history of terrorism and counter-terrorism as topics of sociological reflection is disappointingly straightforward. Until the events of September 11, only very few scholarly studies of terrorism and related issues had been conducted from a distinctly sociological viewpoint, while other social sciences were more prominently represented in the area of terrorism research. Most of the literature on terrorism and counter-terrorism in the social sciences comes from political science, international studies, and law. Political scientists particularly focus on the relationship between terrorism and the planning and implementation of policy programs against terrorism (Heymann, 2003; Laquer, 2003). Terrorism connects intellectually with the interests of international studies scholars who investigate terrorism and counter-terrorism in terms of the manifold interconnections between nations and other localities (Brown, 2002). Scholars of law, finally, approach problems of terrorism and counter-terrorism in the two specialty areas of international law (Lippman, 2003) and criminal law (Demleitner, 2002).

The social-scientific scholarship on terrorism has also focused on the study of counter-terrorism, conceived as the policies and practices defining and responding to terrorism. The literature has focused on counter-terrorism mostly as one aspect of a broader terrorism focus in relation to national legislation and international policy (Crenshaw, 2001; Sterba, 2003). Much less discussed have been the dynamics of the strategies employed to fight terrorism at the level of police organizations (Deflem, 2002, 2004; Henry, 2002).

Insights on terrorism in the social-science disciplines of political science, international studies, and law are highly relevant, but a distinctive tradition of a sociology of terrorism is sadly missing, despite the occasional exceptions (e.g. Deflem, 1997; Gibbs, 1989; Juergensmeyer, 2000; Smith, 1994; Turk, 1982). Since September 11, however, the number of contributions on terrorism and counter-terrorism has expanded exponentially across the social sciences, including sociology and criminology (e.g. Beck, 2002; Etzioni, 2002; Webb, 2002). Providing a clear indication of this sharp rise in attention, a search for terrorism-related articles in the bibliographical database Ingenta uncovered a total of 971 articles on terrorism published since 1997, no less than 785 of which appeared after September 11, 2001 (end-date: October 6, 2003). Likewise, the Library of Congress holds some 31 terrorism-related books published every year from 1990 to 2000, but that number rose to 60 in 2001, 93 in 2002, and already 98 book publications on terrorism by the Fall of 2003 (end-date: October 6, 2003).

Clearly, much valuable research, analyzing the course and conditions of various terrorism issues, is now underway. To ensure more than fleeting interest for the sociology of terrorism and terrorism-related phenomena, it will be important that sociologists build on their proven disciplinary insights in theoretical, method-ological, and other relevant respects. At the same time, given the differential development of terrorism and counter-terrorism across the social sciences, crim-inological sociologists should not be embarrassed to learn from other research disciplines. Then they will be able to provide a distinctive and useful contribution to the scholarship of terrorism and counter-terrorism in the context of important themes related to crime, law, and social control. Indeed, it is the specific province of criminological sociology to study the manifestations of crime and social control, including terrorism and counter-terrorism, in relation to their conditions, processes, and implications at the societal level (Rosenfeld, 2002). The chapters in the present volume seek to contribute to this ambition in a variety of ways.

AN OVERVIEW OF THE CONTRIBUTIONS

The chapters in this volume are presented in four parts. The contributions in Part I discuss important theoretical foundations in the study of terrorism from the viewpoint of criminological sociology. Donald Black's insightful and provocative chapter develops a notion of terrorism as a form of unilateral self-help by organized civilians, involving the covert infliction of mass violence on other civilians. Various characteristics of terrorism are highlighted on the basis of this conception, suggest-ing the violent nature of terrorism, its kinship to warfare, and the ultimate demise of terrorism. In the next chapter, Richard Rosenfeld critically relies on Black's notion of terrorism to argue that terrorism combines elements of predatory and moralistic violence in attacks on societies characterized by capitalism, democracy, and a culture of religious tolerance. Terrorist violence is motivated by an anti-modernist impulse and is only symbolically elevated over other, everyday forms of violence. Gregg Barak extends the theoretical discussion by conceptualizing three forms of terrorist-like behavior: killer boys, suicidal terrorists, and genocidal exterminators. Barak applies the Reciprocal Theory of Violence to broaden our understanding of terrorism in terms of individual, institutional, and structural types of behavior.

In Part II, chapters are brought together that focus on some of the important methodological issues that are to be dealt with in terrorism research. Comparing crime and terrorism with respect to conceptualization, data collection, and research methodology, Gary LaFree and Laura Dugan find that many of these important issues also apply to terrorism research. The authors therefore argue that the application of criminological methods to the study of terrorism would critically contribute to our understanding of terrorism. Kelly Damphousse and Brent Smith suggest the value of the American Terrorism Study as a basis for empirical data to be used to develop and test theories of terrorism. More specifically, Damphousse and Smith find that the data of the American Terrorism Study indicate that terrorist groups have became smaller and that the number of counts per indictment increased after the advent of leaderless resistance in the groups. Likewise, Michael J. Thomas relies on a specific data set to analyze terrorism-related phenomena, critically focusing on the manner in which the United States government categorizes and classifies terrorist groups. Thomas argues that the current systems used by the U.S. government do not comprehensively categorize terrorist groups and do not adequately address the motives of international terrorism. New classificatory schemes would have to be developed to overcome these shortcomings. In the final methodological chapter of this volume, Margaret Zahn and Kevin Strom usefully analyze the investment in terrorism-related research before and since 9/11. Zahn and Strom find that the relative share in federal funds spent on social-science research is still small and that such research has shifted attention from the study of the consequences of the 9/11 attacks to the improved prediction and understanding of terrorism.

Part III of this volume deals with aspects of counter-terrorism policies with respect to important concerns related to ideology and governmental strategies of security. Willem de Lint highlights the role of public relations, secrecy, and executive power in a reconceptualization of autocratic rule that the author refers to as endarkened governance. On the basis of an analysis of the "unlawful combatants" held in Guantanamo Bay, Cuba, de Lint assesses the impact of the events of 9/11 and the political ideology of neoconservativism, which, he argues, is not helpful to build a sound counter-terrorism policy. Bonnie Berry draws parallels between far right terrorist groups and, what she calls, the U.S. right-wing political establishment. The false promise of security, Berry argues, refers to the White House avowal to protect the post-9/11 public without any real or effective measures to ensure public safety. The author concludes that such absence of real security is congruent with a desire to control the public through fear.

In Part IV, finally, we offer chapters that touch on the construction and reality of terrorism in the political and ideological contexts of modern societies. Victor Kappeler and Aaron Kappeler examine the construction of terrorism in the United

States as a moral panic. Focusing on the speeches used by political figures and law enforcement officials, the Kappelers find several rhetorical themes in the discourse on terrorism that are consequential not only for everyday perceptions, but also for the criminology of terrorism. In the final chapter, Paul Leighton argues that criminologists should think about terrorism in a new way by returning to and updating the notion of "The Challenge of Crime in a Free Society" introduced by the President's Commission on Law Enforcement and Administration of Justice in 1967. Without such a rethinking, Leighton fears, criminological research on terrorism will remain involved with technically well-executed, but only marginally relevant work. The chapters in this volume, of course, will hopefully exemplify a different and more profound approach.

REFERENCES

Beck, U. (2002). The terrorist threat: World risk society revisited. *Theory, Culture & Society, 19*(4), 39–55.

Brown, C. (2002). The "Fall of the Towers" and international order. *International Relations, 16*(2), 263–267.

Crenshaw, M. (2001). Counterterrorism policy and the political process. *Studies in Conflict & Terrorism, 24*(5), 329–337.

Deflem, M. (1997). The globalization of heartland terror: Reflections on the Oklahoma City bombing. *The Critical Criminologist, 8*(1), 5.

Deflem, M. (2002). Law enforcement 9–11: Questioning the policing of international terrorism. *Pro Bono, 9*(1), 5–9.

Deflem, M. (2004). Policing global terrorism: The role of Interpol. *Crime & Justice International, 20*, in press.

Demleitner, N. V. (2002). Immigration threats and rewards: Effective law enforcement tools in the "war" on terrorism? *Emory Law Journal, 51*, 1059–1094.

Etzioni, A. (2002). Implications of the American anti terrorism coalition for global architectures. *European Journal of Political Theory, 1*(1), 9–30.

Gibbs, J. P. (1989). Conceptualization of terrorism. *American Sociological Review, 54*(3), 329–340.

Henry, V. E. (2002). The need for a coordinated and strategic local police approach to terrorism: A practitioner's perspective. *Police Practice and Research, 3*(4), 319–336.

Heymann, P. B. (2003). *Terrorism, freedom, and security: Common sense for a democratic society.* Cambridge, MA: MIT Press.

Juergensmeyer, M. (2000). *Terror in the mind of God: The global rise of religious violence.* Berkeley, CA: University of California Press.

Laquer, W. (2003). *No end to war: Terrorism in the 21st century.* New York, London: Continuum.

Lippman, M. (2003). The new terrorism and international law. *Tulsa Journal of Comparative & International Law, 10*, 297–368.

Rosenfeld, R. (2002). Why criminologists should study terrorism. *The Criminologist, 27*(6), 1, 3–4.

Smith, B. L. (1994). *Terrorism in America: Pipe bombs and pipe dreams.* Albany, NY: State University of New York Press.

Sterba, J. P. (2003). *Terrorism and international justice*. New York: Oxford University Press.
Turk, A. T. (1982). *Political criminality: The defiance and defense of authority*. Beverly Hills, CA: Sage.
Webb, G. R. (2002). Sociology, disasters, and terrorism: Understanding threats of the new millennium. *Sociological Focus, 35*(1), 87–95.

PART I:
THEORETICAL PERSPECTIVES IN
THE CRIMINOLOGY OF TERRORISM

TERRORISM AS SOCIAL CONTROL[*]

Donald Black

ABSTRACT

Terrorism in its purest form is unilateral self-help by organized civilians who covertly inflict mass violence on other civilians. Pure terrorism is a distinctive form of social control partly akin to warfare that arises with a particular social geometry: It spans extremely long social distances, reaches upward in social space against a collectivity, and originates in social islands of solidary relationships. The social control of terrorism reflects the same social geometry and therefore extends beyond conventional criminal justice to a strategy also partly akin to warfare. The technological and other contact that gives rise to terrorism – especially international terrorism – ultimately undermines the social distances that separate the adversaries, and the conditions for its existence finally become the conditions for its demise.

THE GEOMETRY OF DESTRUCTION

A bomb explodes on an airplane or a street filled with shoppers. Or several individuals enter a restaurant and spray the room with bullets, indiscriminately killing men, women, and children. Such events are typical examples of terrorism, a

---

[*]This essay was first published in two parts in the American Sociological Association's *Crime, Law, and Deviance Newsletter*. Part I, The Geometry of Destruction, appeared in Spring, 2002, pp. 3–5, and Part II, The Geometry of Retaliation, appeared in Summer, 2002, pp. 3–5. A substantially revised and enlarged version will appear under the title The Geometry of Terrorism in *Theories of Terrorism*, a symposium edited by Roberta Senechal de la Roche, in *Sociological Theory 22* (March 2004), 14–25.

Terrorism and Counter-Terrorism: Criminological Perspectives
Sociology of Crime, Law and Deviance, Volume 5, 9–18
© 2004 Published by Elsevier Ltd.
ISSN: 1521-6136/doi:10.1016/S1521-6136(03)05002-4

phenomenon that proliferated in various parts of the world during the twentieth and early twenty-first centuries. Terrorists have represented diverse groups, including Irish Catholics against Scottish and English Protestants in Northern Ireland, Hindu Tamils against Buddhist Sinhalese in Sri Lanka, and Muslim Arabs against French Catholics in Algeria and Jews in Israel. A sociology of terrorism, however, hardly exists. Specialists in crime, deviance, law, and social control rarely mention the subject. Even a sociological concept of terrorism is difficult to find. Yet how we define terrorism is fateful: A definition is the first step toward identifying the empirical family to which it belongs, the theoretical jurisdiction responsible for its explanation, the social processes it may engender, and possibly some of the practical measures by which it might be counteracted. Here I feature terrorism in its purest form.

What Is Terrorism?

Pure terrorism is unilateral self-help by organized civilians who covertly inflict mass violence on other civilians (see Senechal de la Roche, 1996, pp. 101–105; Ganor, 1998, 2001). Terrorism is social control because it defines and responds to deviant behavior (Black, 1976, p. 105; see also 1984). It therefore belongs to the same family as law, gossip, ostracism, ridicule, and numerous other processes that define and respond to conduct as deviant, express grievances, or handle disputes.

Pure terrorism has several distinguishing characteristics. First, it is a form of *self-help* – the handling of a grievance with aggression (see idem, 1983, 1990, pp. 74–79). It is also *highly violent* – a use of force that injures and kills numerous individuals, or that attempts to do so. It partly resembles lesser forms of violent self-help labeled as criminal in modern societies, including assaults and homicides, which similarly resist or punish someone's conduct as morally wrong (idem, 1983, 1998, pp. xiv–xvi; see also Tucker, 1989; Cooney, 1998). Many homicides are thus instances of private capital punishment, though the state may in turn punish these punishments as criminal.

Unlike most crime that is social control, however, pure terrorism targets those associated with a collectivity such as a particular nationality, race, religion, ethnicity, or political party. Like rioting or feuding, it applies a standard of *collective liability*: Accountability arises from a social location, not wrongful conduct by the specific individuals who are attacked (see Black, 1987, pp. 49–50, 55–57; Senechal de la Roche, 1996, pp. 103–105). Also like feuding, terrorism is *recurrent*, a series of episodes across time. But unlike most feuding, its target is collective. It is *mass violence*. And pure terrorism is *unilateral*, not bilateral – one-sided rather than reciprocal (see Black, 1984, pp. 5–6; 1995, p. 855, note 130; Senechal de la Roche, idem, pp. 101–102).

Pure terrorism is *well-organized*, too – more organized than the crowds involved in riots and lynchings (Senechal de la Roche, idem, pp. 103–105). Terrorism shares with vigilantism its unilateral, recurrent, and organized character, but vigilantism – like criminal justice or lynching – applies a standard of individual rather than collective liability and punishes only those deemed guilty of particular offenses (idem; see also pp. 118–121). Lastly, the *covert* nature of terrorism distinguishes it from most (but not all) vigilantism, rioting, and lynching. Terrorists operate underground, possibly as lone individuals, though their organizations frequently proclaim responsibility for successful attacks.

Because it is a well-organized and highly violent form of self-help that repeatedly attacks mass targets on the basis of their social location, pure terrorism resembles warfare more than other collective violence such as rioting, lynching, vigilantism, or feuding. It also resembles warfare more than mass killings by unorganized individuals (illustrated by the Oklahoma City bombing of a government building in 1995) or individual killings by organized groups (illustrated by assassinations of Spanish government officials by Basque nationalists in the twentieth century). The terrorism of the past likewise resembles warfare in its typically interethnic, sometimes international, character. Yet pure terrorism is not pure warfare. It is a form of *quasi-warfare*.

Unlike pure warfare, terrorism is unilateral and covert rather than bilateral and overt, and it targets ordinary civilians rather than military installations or personnel. Because terrorists wield highly destructive weapons (conceivably biological, chemical, or nuclear) capable of killing and injuring civilians of both sexes and all ages in otherwise peaceful settings, terrorism can be more violent than traditional warfare – and more shocking and infuriating to its enemies. It also lacks the game-like elements found in some forms of warfare (see, e.g. Loy & Hesketh, 1995). It obeys no rules of fair play, such as rules that prohibit particular weapons or rules about the treatment of those who surrender. Former enemies in conventional warfare may resume normal relations much like former opponents in a sports contest, but terrorism is effectively interminable. Terrorists rarely take prisoners, except for ransom, and may kill those they capture. And captured terrorists may wait only for another chance to use their weapons.

More akin to guerrilla warfare, terrorism operates on a small scale and employs hit-and-run or possibly suicidal tactics rather than the sustained application of brute power characteristic of conventional military campaigns for territorial domination. Even so, guerrilla warfare is primarily an embryonic form of territorial struggle that evolves into more conventional warfare as it becomes more successful.

Guerrillas have also historically launched most of their attacks from rural and relatively inaccessible hideouts, while terrorists prefer urban and other active settings in everyday life where they camouflage themselves as ordinary civilians. For definitional purposes, however, a key difference is that guerrilla warfare has military targets, while pure terrorism has civilian targets (see Ganor, 1998). So-called guerrillas may thus engage in terrorism (when they attack civilians), and so-called terrorists may engage in guerrilla warfare (when they attack military installations or personnel).

A classic example of terrorism – the most violent in history – occurred September 11, 2001, when small bands of Arabic men hijacked four passenger airplanes and successfully crashed two into New York City's World Trade Center and one into northern Virginia's Pentagon military complex, killing several thousand civilians (and some military personnel) and destroying property worth billions of dollars. Those involved, including their sponsors, originated in Middle Eastern countries and shared a radical version of Islamic religion and various grievances against the United States, Israel, and other collective entities. Their attacks had all the characteristics of quasi-warfare described above.

The Geometry of Terrorism

Shortly after September 11, many observers (including the American Sociological Association – see 2001) described the events of that day as "criminal acts." But to label terrorism only as crime ignores its moralistic character and its membership in the same family as law and other social control. Terrorism differs substantially from ordinary crime in other respects as well, such as its highly organized and war-like nature. Indeed, to classify terrorism as crime is the surest way to obscure its sociological identity and obstruct its scientific understanding (see Black, 1998, pp. xiv–xvi).

To call something crime implies that its explanation should be criminological: a theory of why people engage in deviant behavior such as robbery, rape, or burglary. Because pure terrorism is social control (though also defined as crime), however, it requires a theory of social control, specifically a theory that explains self-help of this variety – a form of justice pursued by organized civilians who covertly inflict mass violence on other civilians. What might such a theory entail?

Roberta Senechal de la Roche includes a preliminary theory of terrorism as part of a more general theory of social control through collective violence (1996, 2001). She examines terrorism (along with rioting, lynching, and vigilantism) from the standpoint of pure sociology, specifying elements of its social geometry – its multidimensional location and direction in social space (on the geometric logic of pure sociology, see, e.g. Black, 1995, 2000a, b). She features, in particular, the *polarization of the social field* that attracts terrorism and other collective violence: a high degree of relational distance, cultural distance, functional independence, and inequality between the aggrieved and their adversaries (1996, pp. 105–122; see also Black, 1990, pp. 75–79). Terrorism also usually has an upward direction in vertical space, against social superiors (Senechal de la Roche, idem, p. 114). It is a form of what M. P. Baumgartner calls "social control from below" (1984), a much larger subject seldom studied by sociologists.

Senechal de la Roche notes that terrorism typically expresses a "chronic" grievance – one with a long history – such as a demand for political independence or a return of disputed territory, rather than a grievance about a single incident at a single time, such as a theft or sexual assault by a single perpetrator (1996, pp. 118–122). And the offense is collective, not individual. Lastly, terrorism and other collective violence arise with extremely strong partisanship and solidarity among those who participate (idem, 2001). Strong ties among the aggrieved and a lack of ties to their adversaries make a highly moralistic, explosive, and lethal combination (idem; see also Baumgartner, 1988, pp. 85–100; Black, 1998, pp. 125–132, 149–150, especially note 10; Cooney, 1998, Chapter 4). Terrorism thrives in small, island-like, close-knit, and homogeneous units of larger organizations. These small groups are mainly brotherhoods of young men, often weakly connected to primordial families and largely segregated from women and children. Their enemies are physically close but socially distant in the outer reaches of social space. Most if not all terrorists also have contact with partisans who support their operations with financial and other resources. Terrorists likewise enjoy popular support, possibly acclaim, from those whose grievances they pursue. In short, terrorists are not mere individuals. They are agents of a multidimensional location in social space – and agents of social control.

THE GEOMETRY OF RETALIATION

The Social Control of Social Control

The social control of terrorism is an instance of *the social control of social control* – justice in response to something that is itself a form of justice. Understandably, therefore, terrorists define the social control of terrorism as deviant behavior, a further offense that makes their enemy all the worse. And while pure terrorism – by civilians against civilians – is crime as well as social control, it is difficult to deter with punishment or other social control, much as it is difficult to deter other modes of justice such as rioting or feuding (Black, 1983, p. 39). Many terrorists are willing to die as martyrs, and some even use suicidal methods of attack (see Ganor, 2000; Schweitzer, 2000). In turn, the social control of terrorism is considerably more aggressive and severe than an ordinary system of criminal justice. Social geometry again explains why.

The geometry of terrorism, particularly the high degree of social polarization between the adversaries, is not conducive to social control through law. Law is scarce at the extremes of relational and cultural distance – in the closest conflicts (such as those within the same household) and in the most distant conflicts (such as those between different nations or tribes): *Law is a curvilinear function of social distance* (see Black, 1976, pp. 40–46, 73–78). Thus, just as a polarized structure of extremely distant adversaries attracts the quasi-warfare of terrorism (see Senechal de la Roche, 1996, pp. 115–122), so it attracts quasi-warfare against terrorism – especially international terrorism. The upward direction of terrorists' complaints (idem, 114), often against an entire nation-state, is inimical to law as well (Black, 1976, pp. 21–28). Although nation-states may use law against terrorists, their enormous social superiority also produces highly violent self-help, including war-like attacks against terrorists and their supporters (see idem, 1998, pp. 144–145, 149–153). The sheer destructiveness of terrorism, like that of invasions and other acts of warfare, is yet another element attracting more social control than law normally provides. Just as terrorism is not merely a form of crime, then, so the social control of terrorism is not merely a form of criminal justice. To expect otherwise would be sociologically unrealistic.

Beyond the Case

Warfare differs drastically from criminal justice because it reaches beyond particular cases of deviant behavior by individual offenders. Instead it wields massive force to achieve the total neutralization – possibly annihilation – of a collective enemy. Might makes right. And warfare begets warfare. The cycle commonly ends only when one side incapacitates the other or surrenders, though an explicit or implicit truce ending hostilities is another possibility (see Collins, 1990, especially pp. 76–81).

Because terrorism in its pure form – by underground civilians – is more elusive than the usual targets of conventional warfare, however, its social control includes no clash of armies or navies, no battlefields, fortresses, or fleets. Quasi-warfare against terrorism is frequently as covert as terrorism itself. The secret identities of terrorists and their unwillingness to end hostilities in a public fashion also make it difficult if not impossible to establish their defeat. The social control of terrorism nevertheless exhibits several elements of conventional and guerrilla warfare:

Armed forces seek to kill, injure, immobilize, capture, or otherwise neutralize members of terrorist organizations, their partisans, and possibly other civilians associated with terrorists. As in warfare, too, collective liability begets collective liability in the manner of a vicious circle. Although terrorist acts sometimes arise partly in response to violence against civilians, each instance of terrorism is likely to ignite more violence, which may in turn bring still more terrorism, more reprisals, and so on. Terrorism may likewise beget terrorism in a reciprocal exchange of civilian death and destruction. In fact, existing theory suggests that terrorism may be effectively countered by answering it in kind – a policy of "tit for tat" – with equal violence against civilians associated with the terrorists (see generally Axelrod, 1984). Greater violence may be even more effective. But a negotiation of peace is conceivable as well. What actually happens depends on the social geometry of the conflict (see Black, 1990, pp. 83–88).

Another departure from a case-oriented model of social control is *prevention* (see idem, 1984, pp. 8–9). Much social control of terrorism pertains to the future – to what might happen where – rather than to what has already occurred. Target-oriented prevention protects potential targets from terrorist attacks with such measures as armed guards in public places, surveillance systems for the detection of bombs and other weapons, and restricted entry into vulnerable settings. Terrorist-oriented prevention employs various methods of information gathering (possibly including torture) to locate and incapacitate terrorists before they strike. It may entail special surveillance and travel restrictions for individuals socially similar to terrorists as well.

Terrorists might also conceivably defeat their adversary and win their demands. Hence, still another departure from a case-oriented model in the social control of terrorism, unlikely in reality, is *reform*: a reorganization of the existing world to redress the grievances of the terrorists (idem). Hypothetical examples in the twenty-first century might be the abandonment of Northern Ireland by the United Kingdom and possibly its unification with the Republic of Ireland, or the creation of a Palestinian state encompassing much or possibly all of Israel. Yet while historically violence has occasionally achieved social change, including major political reform, terrorists have so far had limited success. And their demands may be difficult to meet. How, for instance, might the United States have satisfied those who killed thousands of Americans September 11, 2001? At least part of their grievance seemed to be the American way of life itself, such as the freedom of women and the flamboyant and sensual nature of its popular culture. Also relevant was the religiously heathen character of the American people from the standpoint of the Islamic terrorists. Perhaps they would have ended their aggressive plans for the future had the United States agreed to become a radically different civilization, its citizens converted to Islam and prepared to submit to a clerical dictatorship, its women banished from most public life and covered in veils when not confined to their homes. Instead the terrorists provoked quasi-warfare aimed at their total elimination.

The Evolution of Terrorism

Pure terrorism is largely if not totally a phenomenon of the modern age, particularly the twentieth century and beyond. Far from being primitive or uncivilized, it is virtually unknown in tribal societies and post-tribal societies at a medieval or early modern stage of development. Terrorism by and against civilians arises and flourishes with high levels of technology, including rapid transportation, electronic communications, and new weapons of mass destruction. Modern technology permits contact between people widely separated in physical space, but social distances remain: differences in religion, language, customs, and modes of livelihood. Civilizations constantly collide in electronic media such as television, movies, and computers. Social geology shifts, and the ground trembles.

Witness the rise of international terrorism, dramatized by the events of September 11, 2001 – surprise attacks by alien warriors crossing national boundaries in search of justice. Technology twists the shape of global space, spreading a social virus at the speed of light and initiating an age of international rebellion with war-like slaughters of prosperous foreigners at home and abroad. Witness the new architecture of death, unwittingly designed by engineers of modern efficiency – shopping malls, office buildings, buses, and airplanes that collect and confine swarms of civilians unable to defend themselves against invisible enemies blending into the crowd.

International terrorism erupts from below like a volcano. Millions watch the carnage and take sides, many mourning and many celebrating, everyone certain of who is right and who is wrong. The warriors are champions of lost land and possibly lost causes, defenders of traditions contaminated by modernity, fighting an irreversible infection of an irresistible way of life that seeps electronically into the social atmosphere of their changing societies. Executioners are everywhere, and everyone is guilty, liable at any moment to mutilation and oblivion. Isomorphic with its social field, international terrorism is a prism flashing its origins, the fragmentation of bombs and shredding of bodies reflecting and recapitulating the disintegration of dying civilizations invaded by the present (see Black, 1990, pp. 90–92).

Yet terrorism in its pure form is a rare species of social control, its lifespan limited to the time of shocking implosions of social space during the twentieth and twenty-first centuries. The conditions of its existence ultimately become the conditions of its decline. The intermingling of peoples and cultures, electronically and otherwise, inexorably destroys most of the differences now polarizing populations and collectivizing violence. As the social universe shrinks, right and wrong lose the clarity that comes only with enough distance in social space. Partisanship weakens. Enemies disappear. Along with the extermination of tribes and villages, the bombing of cities, the genocides, the torture of countless prisoners – all in the name of morality – terrorism finally becomes merely an interesting specimen from an earlier stage of social evolution. Its inevitable fate is sociological death (see generally idem, 1998, Chapters 7–8, especially pp. 154–155).

ACKNOWLEDGMENTS

For comments on earlier drafts, I thank M. P. Baumgartner, Roberta Senechal de la Roche, Christopher David Stevens, and James Tucker. I also thank Gary Jensen for originally inviting me to write a brief essay on this subject.

REFERENCES

American Sociological Association (2001). Statement of the American Sociological Association on Terrorist Attack, September 11, 2001. www.asanet.org/media/terrorstmt.html. Updated September 21.

Axelrod, R. (1984). *The evolution of cooperation*. New York: Basic Books.

Baumgartner, M. P. (1984). Social control from below. In: D. Black (Ed.), *Toward a General Theory of Social Control*,Vol. 1: *Fundamentals* (pp. 303–345). Orlando: Academic Press.

Baumgartner, M. P. (1988). *The moral order of a suburb*. New York: Oxford University Press.

Black, D. (1976). *The behavior of law*. New York: Academic Press.

Black, D. (1983). Crime as social control. *American Sociological Review, 48*, 34–45. Longer version reprinted in Black (1998).

Black, D. (1984). Social control as a dependent variable. In: Black (1998), 1–26.

Black, D. (1987). Compensation and the social structure of misfortune. In: Black (1998), 47–64.

Black, D. (1990). The elementary forms of conflict management. In: Black (1998), 74–94.

Black, D. (1995). The epistemology of pure sociology. *Law & Social Inquiry, 20*, 829–870.

Black, D. (1998). *The social structure of right and wrong*. San Diego: Academic Press (revised edition; first edition, 1993).

Black, D. (2000a). Dreams of pure sociology. *Sociological Theory, 18*, 343–367.

Black, D. (2000b). The purification of sociology. *Contemporary Sociology, 29*, 704–709.

Collins, R. (1990). Violent conflict and social organization: Some theoretical implications of the sociology of war. *Amsterdams Sociologisch Tijdschrift, 16*, 63–87.

Cooney, M. (1998). *Warriors and peacemakers: How third parties shape violence*. New York: New York University Press.

Ganor, B. (1998). Defining terrorism: Is one man's terrorist another man's freedom fighter? International Policy Institute for Counter-Terrorism: Online Article Series. September 23. www.ict.org.il/articles/articledet.cfm?articleid=49.

Ganor, B. (2000). Suicide terrorism: An overview. International Policy Institute for Counter-Terrorism: Online Article Series. February 15. www.ict.org.il/articles/articledet.cfm?articleid=128.

Ganor, B. (2001). Terrorism: No prohibition without definition. International Policy Institute for Counter-Terrorism: Online Article Series. October 7. www.ict.org.il/articles/articledet.cfm?articleid=393.

Loy, J. W., & Hesketh, G. L. (1995). Competitive play on the plains: An analysis of games and warfare among Native American warrior societies. In: A. D. Pellegrini (Ed.), *The Future of Play Theory: A Multidisciplinary Inquiry into the Contributions of Brian Sutton-Smith* (pp. 73–105). Albany: State University of New York Press.

Schweitzer, Y. (2000). Suicide terrorism: Development and characteristics. International Policy Institute for Counter-Terrorism: Online Article Series. April 21. www.ict.org.il/articles/articledet.cfm?articleid=112.

Senechal de la Roche, R. (1996). Collective violence as social control. *Sociological Forum, 11*, 97–128.

Senechal de la Roche, R. (2001). Why is collective violence collective? *Sociological Theory, 19*, 126–144.

Tucker, J. (1989). Employee theft as social control. *Deviant Behavior, 10*, 319–334.

TERRORISM AND CRIMINOLOGY

Richard Rosenfeld

ABSTRACT

Donald Black's explanation of terrorism as a form of self-help represents an important starting point for the development of a criminology of terrorism. However, Black's theory neglects the predatory character of terrorist violence and the institutional conditions under which terrorism emerges and is sustained. As a form of violence, terrorism combines elements of predatory and moralistic violence. As a form of political grievance, contemporary terrorism represents a utopian counter revolt against the institutional triumvirate of modernity: free markets, a democratic polity, and religious tolerance. Intellectual responses to terrorism that locate its "root causes" in economic deprivation and political oppression misunderstand the anti-modernist impulse that motivates terrorist violence. Social responses that symbolically elevate terrorism over equally deadly sources of risk denigrate the everyday violence faced by millions of Americans.

INTRODUCTION

Criminology has no theory of terrorism – with one exception: Donald Black's explanation of terrorism as a form of *self-help* (Black, 2004).[1] Black explains terrorism as he does all other forms of moralistic violence. Terrorism arises from a specific set of structural relationships among individuals and groups. However, terrorist violence is not caused by and therefore cannot be explained by the attributes of individuals or groups. "Structures kill and maim," Black explains,

Terrorism and Counter-Terrorism: Criminological Perspectives
Sociology of Crime, Law and Deviance, Volume 5, 19–32
Copyright © 2004 by Elsevier Ltd.
ISSN: 1521-6136/doi:10.1016/S1521-6136(03)05003-6

"not individuals or collectivities" (p. 6). Black's explanation of terrorism, like his theory of law, derives from his strategy of "pure sociology," which explains all of human behavior with reference to its geometry in multidimensional social space. Pure sociology ignores thoughts, feelings, goals, and purposes. It is free of psychology and teleology; it is free of *people* (3; see also, Black, 2002c).

Black's explanation of terrorism offers a provocative starting point for understanding the relationship between terrorism and modernity. His perspective has significant advantages over "people-based" explanations of terrorism. But it suffers from its determined inattention to the predatory character and institutional context of terrorist violence. Terrorism is moralistic or justice-oriented violence accomplished by predatory or "criminal" means. The genesis of terrorist violence lies within a particular configuration of social institutions at odds with the institutional triumvirate of modern society: free markets, liberal democracy, and religious tolerance. Terrorism represents a grievance against modernity. Incorporating in Black's theory a conception of the institutional sources of terrorism not only enriches its explanation of terrorism but other forms of violence as well.

TERRORISM AS SELF-HELP

Black defines terrorism in its "pure" or ideal-typical form as "self-help by organized civilians who covertly inflict mass violence on other civilians" (Black, 2004, p. 6). This definition is vastly superior to the bureaucratic and normative definitions of terrorism that have proliferated in recent years (see Martin, 2003, pp. 31–54). It avoids the ambiguity of terms such as "force," "coerce," and "intimidate" found in official definitions, such as those of the U.S. Department of Defense and FBI, which can be construed as encompassing non-violent but forceful or "intimidating" political acts such as protest demonstrations and acts of civil disobedience. For Black, terrorism requires violence, by civilians against other civilians, clearly distinguishing it from non-violent political action. One may quarrel with other aspects of Black's definition, such as its exclusion of violence by the state or unorganized individuals, but not with its analytical precision.

The precision of Black's definition of terrorism results from another distinguishing feature, its connection to a well-articulated *theory* of social behavior. Terrorism is a form of *social control*, a response to deviant behavior. It belongs to a subclass of social control Black terms "self-help," "the handling of a grievance with aggression" (Black, 2004, p. 6; see, generally, Black, 1998). It is distinguished from other forms of self-help, such as homicide and assault, by its organized and collective character, and from still others, such as warfare, because it is unilateral, covert, and targets civilians. Terrorism is "quasi-warfare" (Black, 2004, pp. 7–9).

Terrorism also differs from other forms of moralistic violence in its distinctive social geometry, its location and direction in social space. Terrorism arises from extreme "social polarization" between groups, meaning great cultural distance, relational distance, inequality, and functional independence (Black, 2004, pp. 11–12). In addition, terrorist violence is directed upward at social superiors, one reason why Black's definition of terrorism excludes state violence. The great social distance separating terrorists from their targets explains not only the occurrence of terrorism but also the extremity of terrorist violence. The more distant and less intertwined the social actors, the fewer restraints on the level and means of violent aggression. However, terrorism also has a physical geometry that explains its relative rarity. Until very recently, would-be terrorists were as physically distant from the objects of their grievance as they were socially distant, often literally "across the world." With the advent of modern technologies of communication, transportation, and mass destruction, terrorists can more easily reach their enemies (Black, 2004, pp. 14–18).

But the same technologies that increase the opportunities for terrorism, according to Black, inevitably erode the social distance between enemies. Conflict and violence may remain, but the distinctively destructive, inter-collective, and civilian-oriented character of terrorism diminishes: "The intermingling of peoples and cultures, technologically and otherwise, inexorably destroys the differences now polarizing populations and collectivizing violence . . . .. Partisanship weakens. Enemies disappear" (Black, 2004, pp. 22–23). Modernity, which makes terrorism possible, will eventually destroy it.

TERRORISM AS CRIME

For Black, then, terrorism is collective moralistic violence requiring the co-existence of a grievance, high social distance, and low physical distance. If any of these conditions is missing, terrorism will not occur. The contribution to criminology of Black's explanation of terrorism is the same as that of his broader theory of social control: Terrorism is a social response to perceived deviance that emerges under specific, observable structural conditions. The theory predicts where and when we should find terrorism and where and when it should be absent. It may be wrong in specific respects, but it is testable, and it avoids the individualistic bias that pervades contemporary criminological theory and research (see Messner & Rosenfeld, 2004).

Black himself views criminology as an inhospitable intellectual home for his explanation of terrorism, preferring instead his own brand of "pure sociology." That is unfortunate, because criminology has much to contribute to the study of terrorism, including Black's own explanation of terrorist violence. Black's rejection of criminology as a home for terrorism is based on a too narrow reading of the discipline's subject matter. He characterizes criminology as the study of "why people engage in deviant behavior such as robbery, rape, or burglary – often behavior with no moralistic element at all" (Black, 2004, p. 9). The etiology of criminal behavior is an important but certainly not the sole subject matter of modern criminology. The field also encompasses the origins and application of legal rules and the sources and consequences of informal social control. In Edwin Sutherland's classic definition, criminology is the study of rule making, rule breaking, and the social response to rule breaking. It is difficult to think of a more appropriate scientific arena for Black's theory of moralistic violence. Or a more useful one, because Black's explanation of terrorism and violent social control more generally would benefit from accommodating non-moralistic or "predatory" as well as moralistic violence.

TERRORISM AS VIOLENCE

Criminology offers a dual conception of violence that helps to explain the uniquely "terrifying" quality of terrorism. Some violence, the type Black refers to as "moralistic," is provoked by the victim, at least in the offender's eyes, and its purpose is deterrence, retribution, or self-defense. Familiar examples include the father who spanks his child for disobedience or the would-be victim who fights off an attacker, thereby converting the attacker into a victim. Another type of violence, often termed "predatory," is not provoked by the victim, and has no moralistic purpose. Even from the offender's perspective, the victim of predatory violence is innocent of wrongdoing. The classic example is the typical street robbery.[2] What separates terrorism from other forms of violence is that it targets innocents to advance a moral claim. *Terrorism uses the means of predatory violence to accomplish the goal of moralistic violence.* Terrorism is in this sense deviant violence. It crosses the boundary between so-called criminal and justice-oriented violence, which is why it so often seems incomprehensible (Rosenfeld, 2002). Black calls it "quasi-warfare," but a more precise term is "criminal warfare." Terrorism is the nexus of warlike aims and criminal (i.e. predatory) means. That is the fundamental reason for the official ambivalence and conflict over whether terrorism should be regarded as a criminal justice or military problem, as crime or war: It is both (cf. Dworkin, 2003).

By neglecting the criminal or predatory component of terrorist violence, Black's (2004) explanation of terrorism is unable to account for its key distinguishing and defining characteristic, the mixing of moralistic goals and predatory means. By neglecting non-moralistic violence per se, Black prematurely rules out the possibility that it, too, is meaningfully and predictably distributed in multidimensional social space. Both Black's pure sociology and traditional criminological theories of violence likely would be enriched by research on the social geometry of predatory violence (Rosenfeld, 2001).

THE INSTITUTIONAL CONTEXT OF TERRORISM

Black's (2004) explanation of terrorism is limited not only by its conception of the *form of* but also the *motivation for* terrorist violence. He says little about the social origins or distribution of the *grievances* that motivate terrorism, presumably because pure sociology ignores the purposes and rationales for social action. However, a complete explanation of terrorism must account for the nature of the terrorist's grievance: Without a grievance, there would be no terrorism. And, like the social and physical distance between the terrorist and his enemies, grievances are socially organized. The grievances motivating contemporary terrorism emerge in and are sustained by a distinctive configuration of social institutions, and the target of those grievances is the institutional arrangement that defines modern society: free markets, democracy, and religious tolerance.

Social distance and physical proximity between terrorists and their enemies may explain the opportunity for terrorist violence, but not its motivation. Enemies are not created by social distance per se – or are they? Black seems to think so. In a fascinating essay on making enemies, Black (1998, pp. 144–157) defines "moralism" as the tendency to treat people as enemies. "Moralism," he argues, "is a product of its social environment" (p. 144). Specifically, moralism arises from extreme social distance and social superiority: The greater the social distance between parties, the more likely the superior party will treat the inferior party as an enemy. Evidently, nothing else is required, no history of conflict, competition over resources, culture of aggression, or imperial design. "Social superiority and distance make enemies, regardless of conduct.... When social conditions are right, enemies will be found" (Black, 1998, p. 153).

The argument that enemies require only social distance and superiority begs the question of who or what generates social distance and superiority. Black takes cultural distance (e.g. differences in values, beliefs, language, religion), relational distance (degree of intimacy or connectedness), vertical distance (differences in wealth, power, prestige), and every other kind of social distance for granted. They are exogenous to his general theory of social control and to his specific explanation of terrorism. Put another way, Black has a theory of social control but no corresponding theory of social space. Without a theory of social space – a theory that explains *why* two or more parties occupy specific social locations and are arrayed in particular relations to one another – we cannot adequately explain why grievances arise, enemies are made, social control is applied, and terrorism occurs.

As Black recognizes, social distance and relations of superiority and inferiority are not fixed or timeless. They are variables.[3] The question is, what aspects of groups explain their distance from one another along the multiple dimensions of social space? The answer, I propose, lies in the institutional arrangements of the particular groups under consideration in the analysis of a specific conflict. Contemporary terrorism is an attack in the name of premodern institutional arrangements on the institutions that have come to define modern societies. *Institutional-anomie theory* is a criminological perspective that places the nature of and relations among social institutions at the center of the analysis of crime (Messner & Rosenfeld, 2001a, b). It explains the dominant patterns of crime in any society according to the prevailing *institutional balance of power* within the society. The institutional balance of power in modern Western societies is dominated by the free-market economy, more or less constrained by a democratic polity, a highly complex formal educational system, and a flexible, thin family system. Religious institutions in such societies tend to be fragmented and comparatively weak. They must accommodate to strong norms of universalism and tolerance that emanate from and are sustained by more powerful economic and political institutions. Contemporary terrorism represents a contrasting institutional balance of power dominated by family, ethnicity, and religion. Therein lies the institutional source of the vast social distance between terrorists and modern societies and the terrorists' call to arms against the West.

Crime and the Institutional Balance of Power

Institutional-anomie theory was originally developed to explain the high levels of economically motivated predatory crime in the United States (Messner & Rosenfeld, 2001a). Under conditions of free-market dominance, the social controls imposed by other institutions atrophy, and criminal behavior of all kinds increases. Moreover, the no-holds bared, bottom-line ethic of market relations exerts a strong influence on social relations generally, and offers cultural encouragement for the achievement of goals, monetary goals in particular, "by any means necessary" (cf. Schwartz, 1994). The result is especially high levels of acquisitive crime accompanied by force. The crime of armed robbery is perhaps the quintessential "anomic crime" (Messner & Rosenfeld, 2001b, pp. 154–155).

However, economic dominance is only one manifestation of institutional imbalance, and distinctive patterns of crime also characterize societies dominated by the state and those in which the so-called primordial institutions of civil society, the kinship system and religion, are dominant. State-dominated societies tend to be characterized by widespread moral cynicism, the lack of personal agency on the part of citizens, weakened civil institutions, and correspondingly high levels of corruption. Now consider the institutional sources of crime in societies in which the primordial institutions are dominant.

Terrorism and Ethno-Religious Dominance[4]

Whereas economic dominance is associated with the cultural condition of anomie, and state dominance with moral cynicism and withdrawal, the dominance of family and religion leads to a kind of extreme moral vigilance or hyper-moralism. Individuals develop a strong sense of interpersonal obligation, but one that is restricted to persons with whom they share particular social statuses or identities, often based on kin, ethnic, or religious affiliation. In the absence of strong social support for universalistic rules of conduct, a sense of identity with or obligation to others who are outside of the relevant social groups is virtually non-existent. In other words, kin or ethno-religious dominance breeds social distance.

The supremacy of civil institutions encourages crimes in defense of the moral order itself, or self-help. Such offenses include vigilantism, hate crimes, and violations of human rights that might not be crimes in a legalistic sense but are widely regarded as crime-equivalents (cf. Michalowski & Kramer, 1987). Because perceived disturbances in the sex-role system are viewed as striking at the heart of civil society, women have been disproportionately victimized by such crimes of social control. The Taliban's reign in Afghanistan offers a nearly perfect example (*New York Times*, 1997; Rashid, 2000). A Taliban decree issued in 1996 after the capture of Kabul reads in part (grammar, punctuation, and spelling as in the original translation):

> Women you should not step outside your residence. If you go outside the house you should not be like women who used to go with fashionable clothes wearing much cosmetics and appearing in front of every men before the coming of Islam . . . . If women are going outside with fashionable, ornamental, tight and charming clothes to show themselves, they will be cursed by the Islamic Sharia and should never expect to go to heaven (Rashid, 2000, p. 217; see Borger, 1997; Herbert, 1997, for examples from other societies).

Terrorism is also nourished under the dominance of the primordial institutions in a world in which contrasting institutional arrangements have been on the ascendance for two centuries. The contemporary terrorist fights a rearguard battle against cultural contamination by the powerful forces of economic and political freedom. The terrorist attacks not only the "Infidel" populations of modern societies but also the modernizing elements within traditional societies. Terrorism emerges not only in traditional societies but also in the premodern backwaters of modern societies. There, too, religious and ethnic solidarity, real and imagined, figures prominently as a protest ideal against the rationalism and universalism of the modern world. In Benjamin Barber's (1996) provocative phrase, the contemporary terrorist is engaged in a "Jihad vs. McWorld": a struggle to maintain or restore a social order based on the fundamentals of faith, family, and community against a rootless world order of abstract markets, mass politics, and a debased, sacrilegious "tolerance."

In keeping with Barber's generic use of the term "jihad," the grievances of the contemporary terrorist are bred in a "fundamentalist" institutional climate and are not associated with any particular ethno-religious preserve. "The struggle that is Jihad is not then just a feature of Islam but a characteristic of all fundamentalisms" (Barber, 1996, p. 206). Nor, it should be clear, is terrorism a product of religion as such, any more than individualistic predatory crime is a product of markets or corruption a product of states. Terrorism, predatory crime, and corruption are produced by differing forms of *institutional imbalance*.

The three forms of institutional imbalance discussed earlier are each "incomplete" in an important sense. They fail to incorporate elements of the moral codes associated with other institutions. A market economy tends to foster respect for individual rights and for voluntary personal choices. Markets also are "universalizing" institutions; they encourage people to venture beyond the confines of local social settings and ties in search of more customers, higher incomes, lower costs, or better jobs. These moral orientations associated with markets do not in themselves produce crime. To the contrary, when properly joined with sentiments of mutual obligation, they bolster the norm of reciprocity that connects the expectations of some roles to the obligations of others (borrower to lender, landlord to tenant, student to teacher) and thus serve to inhibit criminal victimization. The institutions of civil society and the state foster such sentiments of mutual obligation, the former promoting a sense of interpersonal trust (Putnam, 2000), the latter sentiments of national solidarity or patriotism. However, the institutions of civil society do not embody the universalism of the market, nor does the state promote values of individual autonomy.

A full understanding of the social and cultural sources of crime, corruption, or terrorism, then, must consider not only the values and beliefs that are favored when a particular institution dominates the institutional balance of power but also the social consequences when alternative cultural prescriptions are renounced or insufficiently developed. The market promotes crime when the freedom of action that it encourages is left unchecked by considerations of collective order and mutual obligation. These political and social values, likewise, assume degraded forms in the absence of attention to individual rights and liberties, which typically accompany market arrangements. It follows that crime, corruption, and terrorism are likely to be minimized when the respective cultural orientations of the three institutional complexes are balanced such that each serves as a continuous reminder of the indispensability of the others.

WITHER TERRORISM?

Although he pointedly rejects all teleological arguments as unscientific, Black's explanation of terrorism is premised on a theory of history. Terrorism's days are numbered. "The conditions of its existence," Black argues, "ultimately become the conditions of its decline."

> The intermingling of peoples and cultures, technologically and otherwise, inexorably destroys the differences now polarizing populations and collectivizing violence. ... terrorism finally becomes merely an interesting specimen from an earlier stage of social evolution. Its inevitable fate is sociological death (Black, 2004, pp. 22–23).

Terrorism, Black believes, follows the historical decline of social distance in a world made smaller by advanced communication and transportation technologies and the interdependence of once separate activities. Terrorism will be extinguished along with the "dying civilizations" from which it sprang (p. 22).

What convinces Black that social distance is shrinking, civilizations are dying, and terrorism is headed toward extinction? Little in his strategy of pure sociology or his theory of social control prepares the way for such claims. One would think he would have little patience with a culture-laden concept such as "civilization," much less with organic metaphors for explaining social change (cf. Black, 2002c). In his conviction that terrorism cannot last, Black betrays the modernist conceit that the world is converging, in fits and starts to be sure, on a single model of social order built on markets, democracy, and tolerance. In this inspirational tale, modernism grinds down the sharp edges of traditional society and its primordial institutions, and reduces the dangers posed by the terrorism committed in their name.

We always should be suspicious of theories of historical inevitability, especially when they have "our side" coming out ahead, as they so often do. Consider the common assumption, shared by most political conservatives as well as liberals in the West, that sooner or later we will have to address the "root causes" of terrorism (sooner for the liberals, later for the conservatives). And what are the root causes of terrorism? Poverty and oppression. As Austin Turk (2002, p. 349) has written: "[Terrorism] can over time be ended through prevention if its roots are eliminated, which means removing the deprivations and injustices that create the environments in which people's fears and hopelessness make terrorism appear to be their only option." The notion is that terrorists and their supporters are in some sense "frustrated" and "alienated." They have been left out of the modern world and will feel better once their material and political circumstances improve.

But what if the root causes of terrorism lie not in deprivation and exclusion but in hostility to modernism itself? What if terrorism and the fundamentalist sentiments fueling it are continuously replenished by modernism? If that were so, then every well-intentioned effort to ameliorate the root causes of terrorism might only feed them, and the so-called war on terrorism will indeed be never-ending. The triumphs of modernism and its forcible expansion across the globe are undeniable. But they leave in their wake terrible yearnings for traditional values and ways of life. The terrorist seizes on those yearnings, transforms them into battle cries of the dispossessed, and using the sophisticated tools of modernity, takes the battle to the enemy.

Social distance is not necessarily reduced when cultures collide. The exact opposite may occur. Cultural distance grows with the development of new doctrines that demonize the encroaching enemy. Relational distance grows with the promulgation of new edicts specifying where one may work, how one must dress, and whom one may marry. New boundaries are enforced. Walls are built. Contact ends.

The idea that technological advance and social contact inevitably reduce social differences and make enemies obsolete ignores the plain fact that social distance contracts and expands according to historical circumstance. After the abolition of slavery in the United States, the segregation and disenfranchisement of African-Americans grew over the next forty years (Woodward, 1966). Residential segregation of the races has not abated in recent decades (Massey & Denton, 1993). The Jews in Hitler's Germany were demonized and destroyed by policies of social distance. Japanese Americans were "distanced" through internment during World War II. The collapse of the Soviet empire revived former ethnic and religious antagonisms, tore apart nations, created new enemies, and produced new exterminations. The end of European colonialism has had the same consequences throughout the world. History is not kind to intellectual doctrines that dismiss the role of human agency in the continuous destruction and recreation of social distance.

THE SOCIAL RESPONSE TO TERRORISM

Only the most selective reading of recent history sustains the fiction of the inevitable taming of anti-modernist impulses. If terrorism is inspired by visions of ethno-religious dominance and triggered by a fundamentalist counter-revolt against modernism, the prudent conclusion is that terrorism will last as long as modernism upends traditional status hierarchies, threatens sacred verities, destroys traditional livelihoods, breaks apart communities, and uproots whole populations: Terrorism will last as long as modernism itself. Meanwhile, the guardians of modern societies have little choice but to apply a judicious mixture of criminal-justice and warlike strategies in combating terrorist violence, "judicious" in the sense of preserving civil liberties while engaging in preemptive intelligence gathering and target hardening. Because protecting liberty and safeguarding security are inherently contradictory objectives, tradeoffs between them are inevitable and will continue to fuel public debate over desirable and effective responses. But reconciling the conflicting claims of liberty and security is not unique to the problem of terrorism. That conflict underlies all responses to crime and violence in a democratic society.[5] Just as criminology offers distinctive insights into the nature of terrorist violence and the institutional sources of terrorist grievances, it also contributes a valuable object lesson to the war on terrorism.

Criminologists have contributed more than their fair share of criticism of the war on drugs.[6] Some of those criticisms apply just as well to the war on terrorism. Although the analogy is far from perfect, many parallels exist between the drug war and the war on terrorism (Massing, 2001). Both are *moral crusades*, campaigns to change the moral status of given acts, persons, or groups (Gusfield, 1963). Moral crusades tend to resolve the heterogeneity of a problem area into a single, dramatic image. The drug war chose for special condemnation a single type of drug – crack cocaine – and a single category of user and purveyor – young, inner-city males – and filled the prisons with them (Miller, 1996; Tonry, 1995). Other aspects of the problem received correspondingly less attention, and it is far from clear that the actual dangers of inner-city crack use and selling merited such an overwhelmingly punitive response. Finally, no one has demonstrated that the war on drugs has had any effect on overall levels of drug abuse.

So, too, in the war on terrorism. Prior to September 11, 2001, references to terrorism in the U.S. media and academic literature were as likely to refer to domestic as foreign or international groups and events. Foreign sources now dominate public debate and government policy regarding terrorism. But the threat of domestic terrorism has not disappeared. Consider the case of "Project 7."

Early in 2002 a tip from a defector led the sheriff's department of Flathead, Montana to two trailers in which they found: "30,000 rounds of ammunition, a broad array of small arms, body armor, pipe bombs, exploding booby traps, bomb-making chemicals" and other dangerous materials. These items had been amassed by a militia group calling itself "Project 7" that, according to the defector, was planning to assassinate some twenty or so local law enforcement officials early in the summer, in the hopes that this would provoke the state to send in the National Guard. They would then take on the National Guard which, they believed, would bring in NATO troops, triggering "all-out revolution" (Harden, 2002).

The reporter who covered the story for the *New York Times* characterized the plot as having all the elements of a "Monty Python sketch." But is it any more farfetched than a small band of terrorists armed with box cutters commandeering commercial aircraft and flying them into the World Trade Center and Pentagon to promote world-wide Jihad? The post 9–11 "crusade" against terrorism – a term the President continued to use even after being informed of its historical meaning – has focused media and public attention not on terrorism as such but on a particular source and form of terrorism that marginalizes the dangers posed by groups such as Project 7. That may be a perfectly understandable national response to the 9–11 attacks; in fact, thinking of responses to terrorism as moral crusades helps to make them understandable. But moral crusades prefigure policy responses in such a way that some evils are symbolically elevated over others that pose the same or even greater objective dangers.

The myopic view of risk underlying the war on terrorism can lead to responses that, at best, are wasteful and ineffective and, at worst, denigrate more prosaic but equally deadly sources of intentional violence. The FBI took special pains in its *Uniform Crime Reports* for 2001 to distinguish the homicides resulting from the terrorist attacks on the Pentagon and New York City from the other approximately 16,000 homicides that occurred that year (http://www.fbi.gov/ucr/01cius.htm). The reported homicide count and rate for New York City for 2001 exclude the 2,823 World Trade Center victims.

How would New York's picture of lethal violence have appeared had those deaths been included in the city's homicide rate? Obviously, the picture would have been far worse. The city's official rate of 9 per 100,000 population would have increased nearly five-fold to a rate of 44 per 100,000 – about the same as the homicide rates in New Orleans, Detroit, and Washington, DC, but lower than Gary, Indiana's rate of 79 per 100,000 (http://bjsdata.ojp.usdoj.gov/dataonline). Criminology's most important contribution to public debate over the risk posed by terrorism is the reminder that millions of Americans live with rates of violence rivaling the worst terrorist attack in our history. Who crusades for them?

NOTES

1. This discussion of Black's theory is based on his forthcoming article "The Geometry of Terrorism" (2004). Professor Black generously shared a prepublication manuscript of his essay. Page citations in this chapter are to the prepublication manuscript. An earlier version of the essay was published in two parts in the *Crime, Law, and Deviance Newsletter* of the American Sociological Association (2002a, b).

2. The distinction between predatory and moralistic or justice-oriented violence is discussed in Tedeschi and Felson (1994).

3. Pure sociology is nothing if not scientific, from Black's perspective, and science is the "study of variation" (Black, 1998, p. 158). Black defines "social life" as variation in multiple dimensions of social space (vertical, horizontal, cultural, etc.). "Each differs from one setting to another . . .," according to Black, and "each predicts and explains the behavior of social life" (p. 159). Black avoids, except by way of the occasional anecdote, discussing the social sources of variation in the dimensions of social space, presumably because doing so would require him to examine the behavior of persons and groups, a task that is outside the scope of pure sociology.

4. Parts of this section are adapted from Messner and Rosenfeld (2001b, pp. 155–156).

5. See Dworkin (2003) for a thoughtful discussion of the tradeoffs between liberty and security in responding both to terrorism and conventional crime.

6. An early but still relevant statement is Alfred Blumstein's 1992 presidential address to the American Society of Criminology (Blumstein, 1993).

REFERENCES

Barber, B. (1996). *Jihad vs. McWorld*. New York: Random House.

Black, D. (1998). *The social structure of right and wrong* (Rev. ed.). San Diego, CA: Academic Press.

Black, D. (2002a). The geometry of destruction. *Crime, Law, and Deviance Newsletter* (Spring), 3–5.

Black, D. (2002b). The geometry of retaliation. *Crime, Law, and Deviance Newsletter* (Summer), 3–5.

Black, D. (2002c). The purification of sociology. *Contemporary Sociology, 29*, 704–709.

Black, D. (2004). The geometry of terrorism. *Sociological Theory, 22* (forthcoming).

Blumstein, A. (1993). Making rationality relevant – The American Society of Criminology 1992 Presidential Address. *Criminology, 31*, 1–16.

Borger, J. (1997). Women are killed for family honor. *St. Louis Post-Dispatch* (November 6), A11.

Dworkin, R. (2003). Terror and the attack on civil liberties. *New York Review* (November 6), 37–41.

Gusfield, J. R. (1963). *Symbolic crusade*. Urbana, IL: University of Illinois Press.

Harden, B. (2002). A far-right Militia's far-fetched plot draws some serious attention. *New York Times* (www.nytimes.com, accessed March 3, 2002).

Herbert, B. (1997). Algerian terror. *New York Times* (November 9), 15.

Martin, G. (2003). *Understanding terrorism*. Thousand Oaks, CA: Sage.

Massey, D. S., & Denton, N. A. (1993). *American apartheid: Segregation and the making of the underclass*. Cambridge, MA: Harvard University Press.

Massing, M. (2001). Home Court Advantage: What the war on drugs teaches us about the war on terrorism. *American Prospect* (December 3), 24–27.

Messner, S. F., & Rosenfeld, R. (2001a). *Crime and the American dream* (3rd ed.). Belmont, CA: Wadsworth.

Messner, S. F., & Rosenfeld, R. (2001b). An institutional-anomie theory of crime. In: R. Paternoster & R. Bachman (Eds), *Explaining Criminals and Crime* (pp. 151–160). Los Angeles: Roxbury.

Messner, S. F., & Rosenfeld, R. (2004). 'Institutionalizing' criminological theory. *Advances in Criminological Theory* (forthcoming).

Michalowski, R. J., & Kramer, R. C. (1987). The space between laws: The problem of corporate crime in a transnational context. *Social Problems, 34*, 34–53.

Miller, J. G. (1996). *Search and destroy: African-American males in the criminal justice system*. New York: Cambridge University Press.

New York Times (1997). The Taliban's War on Women (November 5), A26.

Putnam, R. D. (2000). *Bowling alone: The collapse and revival of American community*. New York: Simon & Schuster.

Rashid, A. (2000). *Taliban*. New Haven, CT: Yale University Press.

Rosenfeld, R. (2001). The role of third parties in violent conflict: A comment on Cooney's theory of third parties. *Theoretical Criminology, 5*, 261–265.

Rosenfeld, R. (2002). Why criminologists should study terrorism. *The Criminologist* (November/ December), 1, 3–4.

Schwartz, B. (1994). *The costs of living: How market freedom erodes the best things in life*. New York: Norton.

Tedeschi, J., & Felson, R. B. (1994). *Violence, aggression, and coercive actions*. Washington, DC: American Psychological Association.

Tonry, M. (1995). *Malign neglect: Race, crime, and punishment in America*. Oxford University Press.

Turk, A. T. (2002). Confronting enemies foreign and domestic: An American dilemma? *Criminology and Public Policy, 1*, 345–350.

Woodward, C. V. (1966). *The strange career of Jim Crow* (2nd Rev. ed.). New York; Oxford.

A RECIPROCAL APPROACH TO TERRORISM AND TERRORIST-LIKE BEHAVIOR

Gregg Barak

ABSTRACT

In the context of a general discussion of terrorism and through the use of narrative descriptions, I examine some of the properties and pathways common to three forms of "terrorist-like behavior." Specifically revealed in this chapter are the underlying tensions and dynamics involved in the actions of "killer boys," "suicidal terrorists," and "genocidal exterminators." The intentions here are to share some of the insights of Barak's recently developed Reciprocal Theory of Violence and to broaden the understanding of terrorism as it relates to individual, institutional, and structural behavior.

INTRODUCTION

Elsewhere I have written extensively on the reciprocity of violent and nonviolent relationships and about the properties of violence and nonviolence (Barak, 2003). I have also introduced a "reciprocal theory of violence" which argues, among other things, that despite the diversity of violent and nonviolent expressions found throughout families, neighborhoods, classrooms, workplaces, country clubs, or in a variety of other settings and groupings, there are established pathways to violence and nonviolence that cut across the interpersonal, institutional, and structural

Terrorism and Counter-Terrorism: Criminological Perspectives
Sociology of Crime, Law and Deviance, Volume 5, 33–49
Copyright © 2004 by Elsevier Ltd.
All rights of reproduction in any form reserved
ISSN: 1521-6136/doi:10.1016/S1521-6136(03)05004-8

spheres of social and cultural organization. According to this theory, violence or abuse, and nonviolence or non-abuse, are viewed as operating along a two-sided continuum where the actions of individuals, organizations, or nation-states are capable of stimulating, accommodating, or resisting various pathways to either violence or nonviolence. Contextualized in this fashion, violent and nonviolent reciprocal relations consist of connecting and overlapping patterns that involve the repetitious or habitual acts of perpetrators, victims, and agents of social control. Hence, there may exist within and across different forms of violent and nonviolent behavior, similar and dissimilar states or "mind sets" of emotional being.

In this chapter, I examine some of the properties and pathways common to three forms of "terrorist-like behavior" in the context of terrorism more generally. In doing so, I dwell longer with killer boys than with suicidal terrorists or genocidal exterminators because the former cases are the least likely of the three examples to conjure up images of terrorist-like behavior. Before turning to these acts of terrorism, consider briefly, acts of sexual coercion as illustrative of the sameness and difference involved in various acts of terrorist-like behavior.

Heterosexual rape, child molestation, and gender harassment, for example, are among the most common forms or expressions of this kind of violence. Though different in many respects, these three forms of violence may, indeed, each correspond to the same kind of related and underlying tension or dynamic that underpins many forms of terrorism. In each of these types of sexual coercion, the perpetrators share a common need to compensate for a lack of an adequately secure sexual identity. Varying only by degree, heterosexual rapists, child molesters, and gender harassers, whether diagnosed as "normal" or "pathological" actors, are persons who consciously and unconsciously use their situations or relative positions of power to control, force, trick, or pressure relatively weaker persons through fear, intimidation, and what often amounts to a sexual terror of other human beings so that they may feel some kind of temporary relief or release from their sexuality anxiety. Terrorists, too, may share this need to overcome anxiety, sexual or otherwise, in the pursuit of pride and self or collective respect.

This pathologic or sympathetic interpretation and analysis of these perpetrators' sexuality as "sick" or compulsive, or of their behavior as the product of weakness, vulnerability, repressed rage, unacknowledged shame, and underdevelopment (i.e. the perpetrators are also victims), is one viable view, among others, of what motivates these offenders. Other viable analyses include the idea that the different pathways of these coercers originate in a need for sexual gratification, control, domination, or some combination of these. From this latter perspective, the ordinary occurrences of acquaintance, date, and marital rape, for example, are viewed as extensions or exaggerations of conventional sexual relations and power differentials between men and women, boys and girls. These violations are not the result of some kind of aberration or deviant response on the part of so many normative "offenders." According to this view, rape is not about pathology, it's "a form of socially conditioned sexual aggression that stems from traditional gender socialization and sexual learning" (Berger, Free & Searles, 2001, p. 250). In the end, there is plenty of data to support the positions that both "mentally ill" and "culturally normative" offenders and victims comprise the perpetrators of sexual violence.

Acts of sexual misuse or abuse are primarily committed by men against women and children, and secondarily by women against children. Those who perpetrate these kinds of sexual activities were often victims of child abuse themselves. As children, their acquired abilities to trust, empathize, and identify with others were undeveloped as a consequence of their abuse or neglect. As adults, if alienation from both self and others continues, this is enough to "help" violators disassociate from their victims or suppress any ability they might have to mutually identify with others. With respect to the weakening institutions of patriarchy and the legacy of a "double standard" of sexuality, however, coercive activities by men may still be associated with the abuse of prostitutes and a misogynist culture more generally. After all, sexual harassment sometimes includes rape, as does child sexual abuse, and prostitution often involves rape and sexual harassment (Grauerholz & Koralewski, 1991).

In similar fashion, there is no single variable or set of variables that can account for the full range of other forms of violence, such as homicide, terrorism, penal abuse, economic slavery, and so on. In short, because all of the factors that contribute to violent behavior reside in such diverse realms as biology, psychology, or culture, their complex, multidimensional, and interactive pathways are in need of sorting out. In short, whether the manifestations of violence in general or of sexual violence in particular are reflected or not in various internal and external factors, there are pathways or developmental themes that can be identified and used to reveal overlapping etiologies among the varieties of violence. The same is also true of the diverse yet similar pathways to terrorism.

In an effort to reveal the reciprocal social relations linking the properties and pathways of various forms of terrorist behavior, most of this essay will consist of providing narrative descriptions of the similar tensions or underlying dynamics involved in the actions of "killer boys," "suicidal terrorists," and "genocidal exterminators." In each of these different but related scenarios of interpersonal, institutional, and structural terrorism, the perpetrators and victims – young or old – were all dealing one way or the other with issues of shame, esteem, loss (or lack), and repressed or suppressed anger. In the first instance, the stories of boys that kill consist of histories of abandonment or of disconnected youths who have been victimized in one form or the other as infants and young children, by their parents and/or their communities. These stories are also about youths who have lost their childhood and who have, at a very early age, been exposed to, rather than protected from, the dark side of violent realities. Last but not least, these stories of violent boys are about the efforts of youths to overcome their feelings of humiliation and rejection, even when they are a product of functional families and communities.

In the second example, the nature of suicidal terrorists is shown to involve scenarios that have to do with the exclusion from or disaffection with political and economic participation. This occurs primarily among young adult males. The pathways taken to these particular forms of lethal violence are numerous and emanate from larger histories of religious, ethnic, and cultural conflicts involving an array of secular and nonsecular groups. In the process, these acts of violence have often served as a means of establishing the terrorist as a martyr who has been victimized by some greater social evil or injustice.

In the third example, genocide has to do with an entire people's or tribal-nation's cultural disassociation from and rationalization of the mass extermination of groups of different human beings. Rather than the Holocaust, for example, being the product of a perverted, pathological, or diseased handful of collaborators suffering from despair and acting in isolation, this episode of systematic and planned execution was more accurately the product of exterminators who belonged to supportive groups of well-wishers and sympathizers, who were seeking individually and collectively to reassert their cultural pride and dignity. The collective emotions of onlookers and bystanders, all of whom possessed degrees of prejudice, bigotry, and hostility toward non-Aryan races as well as generations of repressed patriarchal hostility, were not only enduring elements of the normal state of affairs; these sentiments of insensitivity to other humans were quite often celebrated by nonviolent, law-abiding citizens, responding to their uniquely shared humiliation and defeat as a nation during the years immediately following the first World War.

Before turning to these three forms of terrorism, some kind of discussion is called for on the meaning of the word *terrorism* and on the way in which below I conceptualize these case studies as exemplifying commonly shared characteristics and experiences of terrorist-like behaviors of shame, rage, and revenge (Scheff & Retzinger, 1991).

TERRORISM AND TERRORIST-LIKE BEHAVIOR

There are numerous definitions of terrorism and characterizations of terrorists. Many of these definitions of terrorism are one-sided, biased, or politically and legally restrictive, indicting some behaviors and ignoring others. In other words, some forms of terrorism have been illegitimated and others have been legitimated. Terrorist violence of the first kind involves kidnapping, torturing, and killing; terrorist violence of the second kind involves freedom fighting, national liberation, and social justice (Barak, 1991). Hence, there has been a fair amount of disagreement about the accuracy and application of these terms: "one's man terrorist is another man's freedom fighter." If one is looking for a definition that "works" universally over time, then one needs to refer to those definitions of terrorism and terrorist violence that try to employ standards that show no political favoritism, do justice to the social relations of inequality, and are inclusive of all forms of terrorism, "retail" and "wholesale," without regard to victims or perpetrators.

Some of these forms of generic terrorism are of the more traditional violent actions aimed as inducing fear of similar attack in as many non-immediate victims as possible so that those so threatened accept and comply with the demands of the terrorists; some are of the more contemporary vintage like suicide bombers or bio-terrorists who are not necessarily negotiating demands but who are, instead, attempting to create widespread panic and despair, or who are engaging in a totally new kind of terrorism as warfare. What both of these "old" and "new" forms of terrorism committed by "wholesalers" and "retailers" alike, share in common with the terrorist-like behaviors discussed shortly, is "the use and/or threat of repeated violence in support of or in opposition to some authority" (Rosie, 1987, p. 7).

There are traditionally three basic types of terrorism or terrorists: religious, political, and racial or ethnic. Each of these may express different and overlapping kinds of grievances, real or imagined. Terrorist motivations are too numerous to count. Generally, the motivations of most terrorists have been separated into "rational/irrational," "psychological," and "cultural" ones. With rare exceptions, most terrorists (and counter-terrorists) believe their "cause," or the actions that flow from it, are not only morally good or justified, but that they are necessary means for achieving some end that will better society. Whether these forms are about inducing fear and panic or securing negotiations of some kind, there is typically some underlying ideological belief system driving the behavior. In contrast, some terrorist-like behavior such as the killings of relatively anonymous people by adolescent males, are less about, if not at all, ideology than they are about personal vengeance and redemption. In other words, their terrorist-like behaviors are more social than necessarily religious, political, or ethnic as traditionally classified.

When examining the various kinds of terrorism and terrorist violence, it helps to think about whether these acts are domestic- or foreign-based (or both) and whether they are carried out by governments or by citizens (or both). Historically, when terrorism is carried out from above in some kind of systematic way, it has been labeled as wholesale or state terrorism. This is the type of governmental abuse and terror perpetrated by traditional dictatorships, from Europe to Central and South America, that in the popular vernacular has often been referred to as a "reign of terror." By contrast, when terrorism is carried out from below in quasi-organizational cells or sporadic outbursts, it has been labeled retail terrorism, or guerrilla warfare, and is often referred to as a "state of siege" (Falk, 1988). When terrorism becomes a joint venture carried out both simultaneously or dialectically from "above" and "below" perhaps this should be referred to as "civil war."

From what has been defined and characterized as terrorism and terrorist behavior, thus far, one could create a taxonomy or a classification scheme as follows.

A TAXONOMY OF TERRORISM

Categorical Types	Organizational Types	Motivational Types	Objective Types
Ethnic	Domestic-based State, Wholesale	Cultural	Control & Domination
Political	Domestic-based Nonstate, Retail	Psychological	Intimidation, Fear & Negotiation
Religious	International-based State, Wholesale	Rational	Panic, Crisis & Desperation
Social	International-based Nonstate, Retail	Irrational	Retaliation & Vengeance

At the same time, a reciprocal approach to terrorist-like behavior views such taxonomies, on the one hand, as useful for descriptive and analytical purposes, and, on the other hand, as unfortunately divisive of the existing, overlapping, and accumulating social relations of terrorist-like behavior that cut across interpersonal, institutional, and structural orders of society. If one uses this taxonomy to describe, for example, the terrorist organization Al Qaeda, the following types are applicable: categorical – ethnic, political, and religious; organizational – international, nonstate retail and state wholesale; motivational – cultural, psychological, and irrational; and objective – panic, crisis, and desperation and retaliation and vengeance.

KILLER BOYS: A CASE OF LOST CHILDHOOD

In both the rash of relatively unusual rural and suburban school shootings across America in the 1990s and the more steadily occurring and common inner-city drive-by shootings committed in association with gang activities during the late 1980s and early 1990s, there are profound emotional and psychological similarities that link these acts of lethal violence. In the scheme of socialization and social relationships, gender, far more than either race or class, is etiologically connected to these expressions of violence. As there are shared pathways between these forms of youthful killing, there are also different, and overlapping, pathways. Familial and/or social abandonment, for example, may be experienced by adolescent boys, leading to multiple pathways to killing. Those who experience only the former or only the latter types of abandonment will differ from those who accumulate both types of experience.

From the beginning of life and even possibly before birth, human development has required the interplay of biology and culture. Child development, for example, is about "the characteristics children bring with them into the world *and* the way the world treats them, nature *and* nurture" (Garbarino, 1999, p. 72: italics in the original). By combining the perspectives of exchange theory, resource theory, ecological theory, and sociobiology, it can be argued that children "face different opportunities and risks for development because of their mental and physical make up *and* because of the world they inhabit *and* because of how well their inborn traits match up with what their social environment offers, demands, rewards, and punishes" (Garbarino, 1999, p. 72: italics in the original). What this kind of developmental model assumes about lethal youth violence is that natural or biological predispositions to aggression will only translate into behavior when they occur in social situations that allow or promote their expression. In other words, social contexts matter very much in the impact, expression, and mediation of temperamental characteristics associated with violence.

Developmentally, whether a baby is characterized as "difficult" or "easy" or predisposed to be "hyper," "hypo," or somewhere in the middle of a continuum of temperament, all newborns possess essentially the same needs. On their own, without social interaction, human infants can neither survive physically nor develop normally. "To begin the process of human development, a child needs not so much stimulation as responsiveness; children need to make connection through entering into a relationship" (Garbarino, 1999, p. 38). Making a connection or an attachment with another human being during the first year of life is a critical step in the process of human development.

During infancy, according to most psychological models of development, we are all natural narcissists – it's a matter of survival. If we are not to become sufferers of classic narcissism, a personality disorder in which the symptoms include lack of empathy, grandiose fantasies, excessive need for approval, rage, social isolation and depression, psychoanalytic theory informs us that we must more or less successfully negotiate the uneven transition from the natural narcissism of infancy to a more realistic view of our place in the world by the age of 4 years. The psychological adjustment away from narcissism begins around month 3, when most babies come to know and love the people who care for them. By 9 months, most babies have formed a specific attachment to one or more caregivers.

Attachment is a mixture of at least two properties, *knowing* and *feeling*. Positive connections are supposed to exist when infants know their caretakers in their particularity as individuals and when they are able to feel for them as special individuals. When both of these conditions occur, there is said to be a sense of affirmative connection and a foundation for sound emotional development. When one, the other, or both of these properties are missing from early childhood development, there is a greater likelihood of detachment, disconnection, disassociation, and/or denial. Although there are varieties of attachment, it is generally concluded that in the presence of their "objects" of attachment and desire, infants become free to explore and to develop their skills in mastering the world. Conversely, it is also concluded that

> In the absence of the beloved object, they become wary and withdrawn, defensive rather than exploratory, captured by their anxiety. This relationship becomes one of the important mediators between a child's temperament and the challenges of entering and mastering the world outside the family. Good attachment does not inoculate a child against later misfortune, but it does get the child off on the right foot (Garbarino, 1999, p. 39).

In terms of human development, then, what does get the child off on the wrong foot, or on a pathway to violence? It should be clear by now that there is no one thing, but rather a series of things: an accumulation of things that are both inside and outside a young person's head. At the interpersonal level, these may include early childhood trauma, abuse, neglect, or family disruption. At the institutional or structural levels, these may include toxic environments, economic deprivations, communities of violence, racism, and other systems of cultural discrimination and oppression, such as the intense pressure that most boys feel, by virtue of the dictates of masculine socialization, to be tough, to suppress tender emotions, and to be powerful.

Interpersonally, youths suffering from abuse, neglect, or disruption are more likely to experience shame, rejection, alienation, rage, and a bloated sense of self-centeredness. On top of this, if they are experiencing the damage or injury inflicted by living in the ecological communities most victimized by other forms of institutional and structural violence, these youths (especially males) are more susceptible or vulnerable to victimization and to longer careers of violence, to committing lethal violence, and to being institutionalized first as juveniles and then as adults, for life. By contrast, those young males who have been supported by a parent or significant other and insulated from institutional and structural forms of violence tend to be relatively protected from the darker sides of life, at least during their early infancy and toddlerhood. Having bonded, attached, or connected in their formative social relationships, these individuals are more likely to empathize and relate with other people in a positive fashion. Young people who have been deprived politically and economically, but not socially or emotionally, are also less likely to experience desensitization and to dehumanize others near and far, making them less likely to engage in violence throughout the life cycle, with most violent activity on their parts peaking (if it exists significantly at all) during late adolescence and, shortly after that, disappearing altogether.

As for killer boys, although most will have a history of victimization, this need not be the case. Some boys who mange to kill have not been obvious victims of physical abuse, emotional neglect, or environmental toxins. However, through "normal" human developmental processes these boys end up feeling terribly inferior, rejected, and/or humiliated, even when they have grown up in the ideal family setting. Whether based on reality, fantasy, or some combination of the two, killer boys, from the school corridors to the ghetto streets, engage in toughness and aggression as a means of adaptive survival or as a defense mechanism against overwhelming feelings of personal vulnerability. Whether these killer boys are withdrawn or acting out, most of them have experienced overwhelming feelings of abandonment and intense bouts of depression that they typically do their emotional best to suppress, deny, and avoid altogether.

Psychoanalytically, of course, such feelings stem from the shared fear of mother-child abandonment common to all newborn humans. If these feelings of abandonment do not dissipate normally, or if they remain as unresolved issues of rejection (e.g. when a boy concludes that his addicted mother chose crack and other drugs over him), then strong feelings of humiliation are often the result:

> What shame a boy feels when he is abandoned by his mother! What lengths he will go in order to defend himself against these feelings. Inside, he "forgets" so that he doesn't have to feel. Outside, he punishes the world so that he feels avenged. Shame at abandonment begets covert depression, which begets rage, which begets violence. That is one of the powerful equations of life for lost boys (Garbarino, 1999, p. 44).

At the same time, not knowing your biological father can also lead to severe feelings of abandonment associated with the usual feelings of shame, rejection, and negative self-worth.

Where repressed feelings of early childhood coalesce in a context of persistent poverty and deprivation, accompanied by feelings of alienation from society's broader institutions, such as schools and law enforcement, then a "code of the street" often develops as a means of psychological adaptation. Organized around a desperate search for "respect" and a credible threat of vengeance, this code credits the possession of both respect and credibility with the ability to shield the ordinary person from the interpersonal violence of the street. In the form of a kind of "people's law," or "street justice," the code involves a "primitive form of social exchange that holds would-be perpetrators accountable by promising an 'eye for an eye,' or a certain 'payback' for transgressions. In service of this ethic, repeated displays of 'nerve' and 'heart' build or reinforce a credible reputation for vengeance that works to deter aggression and disrespect, which are sources of great anxiety on the inner-city street" (Anderson, 1999, p. 10).

In sum, whether the killer boys are lost in early childhood due to parental abuse, neglect, or maltreatment, or in early adolescence due to economic deprivation, racial prejudice, and/or societal stigmatization, the interactive search for individual and social respect may, sooner or later, erupt into lethal violence that, although it appears random and senseless to most law-abiding citizens, has an intrinsic logic of its own. This logic is rarely understood by victims, victimizers, or society at large, which are all too often too busy dismissing these violent deeds as the inexplicable acts of crazy or evil people.

SUICIDAL TERRORISTS: A CASE OF SECULAR DESPAIR

As suggested above, terrorism, terrorists, and terrorist-like behavior, come in all sizes, shapes, and forms. For example, there are neighborhood terrorists, political terrorists, religious terrorists, ethnic terrorists, ecoterrorists, narcoterrorists, state terrorists, counterterrorists, and international terrorists, to identify the socially most prominent. These different terrorist groups may consist of street gangs, political anarchists, religious extremists, nationalist-separatists, governmental agents, hired mercenaries, and/or organized criminals. While there are no "terrorist personalities" or even "terrorist mind sets" per se, there are subcultural worlds of terrorism that are motivated by political calculus, by nationalist fervor, or by religious hate. These different subcultural groups of terrorists, such as those involved in suicidal terrorism, have their own unique social psychologies and dynamics that help to reinforce a pattern of one-dimensional groupthink. This form of thinking does not accommodate the other person's point of view and often amounts to little more than clichés to express one's own "point of view," which is more often than not simply the reflection of a social construction of reality capable of engaging in what Arendt (1963) referred to as "the word-and-thought-defying banality of evil."

Historically, those who become members of violent sectarian groups or extremist cults have been mostly young adult males. Suicidal, homicidal, or both, in the case of suicidal terrorists who kill themselves and others, the composition of these subcultural organizations varies from nation to nation according to social conditions, religious traditions, and historical factors. In Europe of the 19th and 20th centuries, for example, there were working-class and elite-born terrorists, respectively. In the Muslim world of today, terrorists are likely to come from two classes. Either they are unemployed and from poor families, or they have been educated at universities or seminaries but are also unemployed. What is shared by Western and Eastern terrorists across the modern periods are collective feelings: of betrayal by authorities and elders; of social, psychological, and political, if not spiritual, despair; and of shame and humiliation at their own inefficacy to alter or transform their situation.

Terrorists, secular and nonsecular, East and West, are generally not psycho- or sociopaths, but they are often persons with unresolved psychological tensions, unfulfilled spiritual yearnings, and feelings of isolation and loneliness. Joining a terrorist subculture provides members with self-confidence, certainties, and a sense of belonging to a closely knit, exclusive community engaged in a "righteous" struggle against some omnipresent enemy. What these subcultural terrorist groups possess in common are fantasies of evil and dreams of victory over conspiring evil agents, whether they are political, religious, ideological, or cultural.

Often these beliefs in conspiracies, intensified by a group mentality, border on paranoid delusions capable of facilitating fanaticism, self-deception, and violent behavior. Every religion has had its share of fanatic proponents, especially during its formative stages. But the spirit of fanaticism has not been confined to the religious sphere only:

> Fanaticism was one of Adolf Hitler's favorite terms, and it appeared again and again in his speeches. It has appeared in every religious and political creed, especially the radical ones, in one way or the another. It is not the same as fundamentalism, because the fundamentalist is (or anyway should be) bound by the holy texts, whereas the fanatic frequently feels free to provide his own interpretations. Fanaticism can turn inward and express itself in asceticism or self-flagellation, as it still does, for example, among the Shiites. But in our day and age it shows itself more frequently as hostility toward an outside enemy, an unwillingness to compromise, and an eagerness not just to defeat the enemy but to destroy him. The modern fanatic is more eager to castigate the flesh of others than his own (Laquer, 1999, p. 98).

Although the century that has just ended and the one that has just begun has not experienced a rise in Christian or Islamic fundamentalism per se, there has been, especially in the autocratically ruled countries of Central Asia and elsewhere, a revival of Zoroastrian and Manichean theology. Dating back to the third century and to the ancient religions of the Middle East that believed in an eternal struggle between divine powers of good and evil, both of these early religious traditions profoundly influenced the extreme warrior visions of Islamic and Judeo-Christian thought alike (Warner, 2001).

In a way that is not dissimilar to the code of the street subscribed to by youthful killers of the inner cities, members of secular and nonsecular terrorist subcultures also subscribe to the code of their sect or cult. Perhaps what differentiates terrorists who kill from kids who kill is the degree to which the former are able to better compartmentalize and control their violence. What these offensive and defensive fanatics, religious zealots, political soldiers, and gangbangers all share in common is "an absolute certainty as to the justness of their cause, legitimacy of their leader, the inability to recognize other moral values and considerations, and the abdication of critical judgment" (Laquer, 1999, p. 99).

Historically, suicide has played an important role in a number of religious sects and terrorist groups. These acts, committed by both individuals and groups en masse, may stem from a variety of psychological sources, rational and irrational. A tradition of collective suicide in the history of religious sects can be traced back to a wing of the Donatists, a fourth-century Christian sect in North Africa, and it has continued into the present day. At their extremes, these suicidal sects have regarded life on earth as relatively unimportant, a prelude to life after death – to paradise, a place of material and sexual fulfillment where as martyrs the sect members will be reunited with their families and stand in front of God as innocent as newborn babies. Hence, their suicides are often thought of as joyful occasions. It is not unusual for living family members to be proud of and to even celebrate their dead relative's suicidal-homicidal exploits.

In 2004, in the West Bank or Gaza Strip, suicidal terrorists may be protesting the Israeli occupation, showing their hate and contempt for the USA and for Jews, and trying to liberate all of Palestine, but they may also be on a pathway to paradise. Other Palestinian candidates for suicide may be more fatalistic, less theological, about dying, maintaining that since they are bound to die violently sooner or later, they might as well die sooner for a good cause. In the case of the World Trade Center, the U.S. Pentagon Building, and the crashed jet airliner in Western Pennsylvania on September 11, 2001, it is claimed that suicidal terrorists like Mohamed Atta and several of his coconspirators were said to be driven and incensed by an American-backed repressive Egyptian regime, the Gulf War, and the Oslo peace accords. More generally, when it comes to suicidal bombers, it is often difficult, if not impossible, to disentangle religious from nationalist motives.

GENOCIDAL EXTERMINATORS: A CASE OF CULTURAL DENIAL

On the dark side of cultural existence, anything is possible, even the mass exterminations of fellow human beings.

> During the Nazi period of the 1930s and 1940s, millions of people (particularly, but not exclusively, Jews) were systematically rounded up and shipped to concentrations camps, where they were worked to death, starved to death, tortured to death, or simply executed. Three decades later, the Khmer Rouge Party, under the leadership of Pol Pot, did much the same thing to the people of Cambodia. Just after the turn of the [20th] century, the Turks attempted to exterminate the Armenian people (Garbarino, 1999, p. 112).

Genocide usually involves the cultural denial that any "real harm" is being done. Mass killings of "other" human beings are socially rationalized as necessary either to overcome evil of some kind or to accomplish some greater collective good for those who are not being eliminated. Generally, genocidal killings represent extreme forms of hate and intolerance. By comparison, institutionalized discriminations such as "redlining" geographical areas as uninsurable or selective employment practices represent moderate forms of hate and intolerance. Individual bigotries, in the form of expressed ideologies, written, spoken, or portrayed, represent mild forms of hate and intolerance.

Histories of genocide, past and present, reveal that the buildup of a collective or cultural denial of other groups' right to exist requires not only generations of family and community members passing along or instilling, at both the conscious and unconscious level, attitudes conducive to actions of intolerance, but a shared need for vengeance and retaliation, aimed at real or symbolic enemies that represent the objects of repressed shame and anger. Stories of genocide also disclose, for example, that the denial of persecuted personhoods require the cultural support and accumulation of prejudice and hatred across the spheres of interpersonal, institutional, and structural violence. In the case of the Nazi era of the 1930s, tens of thousands of German citizens reacted to Hitler's interpretation of a terrible economic and political situation by helping to transform both their collective humiliation and historical sympathy for anti-Semitism into mass murder (Goldhagen, 1996).

However, cross-national comparisons reveal that in the late 19th and early 20th centuries, there were variations in the degree and types of anti-Semitism across Europe, for example. Some countries such as Bulgaria had traditions of religious tolerance and diversity and were thus less susceptible to anti-Jewish policies and practices, even during hard economic times. In other countries such as Romania, Great Britain, Italy, and France, between 1879 and 1939, when economic prosperity was deteriorating and the level of immigration of Eastern European Jews was increasing, anti-Semitism grew. It all depended "on the extent to which Jews were perceived as a threat to non-Jews" (Levin, 2001, p. 149). In Poland, for example, evidence was recently revealed that a massacre of Jews in the town of Jedwabne, in 1941, involved ordinary farmers who herded 1,600 of their Jewish neighbors into a barn and set it on fire (Stylinski, 2001).

The point is that the policies and practices of genocide were carried out and encouraged not by ideological fanatics and schizophrenics, but by ordinary citizens. In other words, histories of cultural hate that culminate in genocide have not depended on individual pathology or abnormal psychology. Rather, these genocides are simply the extreme manifestations of the shared normative and traditional values of hatred and intolerance. The combination of a long history of anti-Semitism and a strong desire or need to protect the Fatherland as each of these were connected to one's individual self-interest accounted for the creation and enactment of the "final solution" in Nazi Germany:

> Hitler's condemnation of the Jews reflected not only his personal opinion, but also the beliefs of hundreds of thousands of German and Austrian citizens. While the police looked on approvingly, university students joined together to beat and batter their Jewish classmates. Faculty members and students voiced their demands to rid the universities of Jews and cosponsored lectures on "the Jewish problem." Because of their genuine conviction, thousands of German soldiers and police helped to murder Jews. Civil service bureaucrats aided in doing the paperwork to expedite carrying out Hitler's extermination program. Many important business, banking, and industrial firms cooperated in the task of enslaving and murdering Jewish citizens. Thousands of German physicians cooperated in sterilizing or eliminating the "undesirables." Finally, whereas the church in other European countries denounced racist anti-Semitism, Germany's religious leaders (both Catholic and Protestant) failed to protest the final solution (Levin, 2001, p. 47).

Hence, genocidal exterminators refer not only to those folks who constructed the ovens and filled them with people and gas, but to the hundreds of thousands of civilians and noncivilians alike who aided and abetted, or did not resist, the extermination of whole groups of people.

Collectively, genocide represents the familiar, subcultural, and cultural depersonalization and desensitization of others, to the extent that the perpetrators fail to see the individuality and humanity of their victims. That is, to the extent that the genocidal exterminators lack the ability to empathize, they lose their ability to control their inhumanity. They also become objects and subjects of unlimited possibilities for violence. The same kinds of reciprocal relations of violence, for different as well as for overlapping reasons, engulf killer kids and suicidal terrorists, as these too have become vulnerable to interpersonal and subcultural forms of depersonalization and desensitization.

IMPLICATIONS

In this chapter I have used the reciprocal theory of violence – which argues that both the properties of and pathways to violence or nonviolence, across the spheres of interpersonal, institutional, and structural relations as well as across the domains of family, subculture, and culture, are cumulative, mutually reinforcing, and inversely related – to explore the common pathways and properties of terrorist-like behavior in three forms: youthful homicide, suicidal bombing, and mass genocide. Common to each of these forms of terrorist-like behavior were constellations of reciprocal properties of and pathways to lethal violence that included, among other things: personal and social histories of humiliation, shame, depersonalization, desensitization, and dissociation of one kind or the other.

Perhaps, on a deeper psychoanalytic level not really explored here, the experiences and memories of humiliation shared by those engaged in terrorist-like behavior make the perpetrator feel entitled to discharge aggression in destructive acts (Margalit, 2003). What emerges, then as a precursor to much violent behavior in general and to terrorist-like behavior in particular, is a psychic formation of reciprocal relationships that entrap those who would "blow us up" in a peculiar kind of motivated irrationality. For example, on the surface, persons engaged in these terrorist-like behaviors believe because of their personal, group, or nation's humiliation and suffering, that they are entitled to their acts of hatred and violence. Beneath the surface, the situations are often the reverse. Because they find enjoyment in destructive hatred, these persons actually become attached to their sense of individual and/or collective humiliation. Dialectically, one might conclude: terrorists and those engaged in terrorist-like behavior, on the conscious level, may hate or despise their sense of humiliation; on the unconscious level, however, they may take pleasure in and hold onto it with all their might.

Like Anthony Giddens' (1984) structuration theory more generally, the reciprocal theory of violence or of terrorist-like behavior does not treat individual action and social structure as separate and dualistic phenomena. On the contrary, the interpersonal, institutional, and structural levels of society are, indeed, part and parcel of the same set of inclusive cultural relations. Thus, to "bring off" terrorist interactions, most individuals, groups, or nation-states make use of their knowledge of cultural behavior in such a way as to render their interchanges "meaningful." Similarly, to reduce such behavioral patterns as terrorism and terrorist-like behavior, social policies are called for that not only transcend the "necessity" of counter-terrorist violent strategies in the short-run, but which ultimately require that the etiology of such developmental behavior be addressed at its political, economic, and cultural intersections.

In sum, just as the behavioral actions of sexual misuse, abuse, or terrorism are matters of both character and social structure, so too, ultimately, are the behavioral actions of both terrorism and counter-terrorism. That is to say, none of these behaviors can be separated from issues of personality and individual development, on the one hand, or from the social legacies of inequality and privilege, on the other hand. Thus, the various forms of interpersonal expressions of self-esteem, pride, anger, and humiliation must all be addressed within the larger cultural and institutional contexts of expressed masculinity, misogyny, and patriarchy.

Finally, not to acknowledge these relationships or to do anything less in the struggle to reduce terrorism and terrorist-like behavior, according to the reciprocal theory of violence and nonviolence, will in all probability only beget more not less terrorism. In other words, anti-terrorist practices such as acts of counter-terrorism or war will not serve as any kind of permanent or lasting deterrent against terrorism. As an alternative to resisting the likely reproduction of terrorism and terrorist-like behavior and as an effort in the creation of empathetic pathways between individuals and nation-states alike, strategies involving mutualistic practices such as altruistic humanism or positive peacemaking are called for that strive to reproduce patterns of nonviolent interaction. These nonviolent and cooperative means of socially interacting hold out the possibilities of transforming interpersonal, institutional, and structural relations away from the globally dominant paradigm of adversarialism and toward the globally subordinate paradigm of mutualism (Fellman, 1998).

REFERENCES

Anderson, E. (1999). *Code of the street: Decency, violence, and the moral life of the inner city.* New York: W. W. Norton.

Arendt, H. (1963). *Eichmann in Jerusalem: A report on the banality of evil.* New York: Viking.

Barak, G. (Ed.) (1991). *Crimes by the capitalist state: An introduction to state criminality.* Albany, NY: SUNY.

Barak, G. (2003). *Violence and nonviolence: Pathways to understanding.* Thousand Oaks, CA: Sage.

Berger, R. J., Free, M. D., & Searles, P. (2001). *Crime, justice, and society: Criminology and the sociological imagination.* Boston: McGraw-Hill.

Falk, R. (1988). *Revolutionaries and functionaries: The dual face of terrorism.* New York: E. P. Dutton.

Fellman, G. (1998). *Rambo and the Dalai Lama: The compulsion to win and its threat to human survival.* Albany, NY: SUNY.

Garbarino, J. (1999). *Lost boys: Why our sons turn violent and how we can save them.* New York: Anchor.

Giddens, A. (1984). *The constitution of society: Outline of the theory of structuration.* Cambridge, UK: Polity.

Goldhagen, D. (1996). *Hitler's willing executioners: Ordinary Germans and the Holocaust.* New York: Basic Books.

Grauerholz, E., & Koralewski, M. A. (1991). *Sexual coercion: A sourcebook on its nature, causes and prevention.* Lexington, MA: D.C. Heath.

Laquer, W. (1999). *The new terrorism: Fanaticism and the arms of mass destruction.* New York: Oxford University Press.

Levin, J. (2001). *The violence of hate: Confronting racism, anti-semitism, and other forms of bigotry.* Boston: Allyn & Bacon.

Margalit, A. (2003). *The ethics of memory.* Cambridge, MA: Harvard University Press.

Rosie, G. (1987). *The directory of international terrorism.* New York: Paragon House.

Scheff, T. J., & Retzinger, S. M. (1991). *Emotions and violence: Shame and rage in destructive conflicts.* Boston: Lexington Books.

Stylinski, A. (2001, March 16). *Polish role is admitted in 1941 massacre.* Boston Globe, p. 15.

Warner, M. (2001, December 16). *Ideas and trends: Fantasy's power and peril.* New York Times, §4, p. 5.

PART II:
METHODOLOGICAL ISSUES IN
TERRORISM RESEARCH

HOW DOES STUDYING TERRORISM COMPARE TO STUDYING CRIME?[☆]

Gary LaFree and Laura Dugan

ABSTRACT

Although the research literature on terrorism has expanded dramatically since the 1970s, with few exceptions little of this work has been done by criminologists or has appeared in criminology journals. This is surprising because breaking of laws and reactions to the breaking of laws have long been central concerns of criminology and terrorism is closely related to both of these concerns. In this paper we compare crime and terrorism in terms of conceptualization, data collection and methodology. In general we find many similarities and even though there are important conceptual and methodological differences, many of these are similar to the familiar tension that exists between general criminology and specialized areas of study such as organized crime, hate crime or juvenile gangs. In short, we conclude that criminological theory, data collection, and methodological approaches are highly relevant to terrorism research and that applying criminological methods to the study of terrorism could rapidly increase our knowledge of terrorism and our understanding of its causes and consequences.

Although the research literature on terrorism has expanded dramatically since the 1970s (for reviews, see Babkina, 1998; Kennedy & Lum, 2003; Mickolus &

[☆]An earlier version of this paper was presented at the annual American Society of Criminology meetings, Chicago, Illinois, November 2002.

Terrorism and Counter-Terrorism: Criminological Perspectives
Sociology of Crime, Law and Deviance, Volume 5, 53–74
ISSN: 1521-6136/doi:10.1016/S1521-6136(03)05005-X

Simmons, 1997; Prunkun, 1995; Schmid & Jongman, 1988), with few exceptions (Chauncey, 1975; Landes, 1978; Smith & Damphousse, 1996, 1998) little of this work has been done by criminologists or has appeared in criminology journals. This may at first seem surprising, given that the most widely accepted definition of criminology (Sutherland & Cressey, 1978, p. 3) includes the study of "... the breaking of laws and reactions to the breaking of laws": both of which would seem to fall unambiguously under the subject heading of terrorism. Speaking of how criminologists have generally neglected the study of terrorism, Richard Rosenfeld (this volume) points out that much criminological theory appears to be relevant to terrorism research and argues that criminologists should take a more active interest in studying terrorism. We strongly agree with this assertion and are convinced that terrorism should be an important area of study for criminologists.

However, there are also obvious differences between terrorism and common forms of crime. If criminologists are going to make a contribution to the study of terrorism, it seems important to keep in mind both ways in which terrorism and crime are similar and different. In this paper we explore similarities and differences between crime and terrorism with regard to conceptualization, data collection, and research methods.

CONCEPTUALIZING TERRORISM AND CRIME

In this section we examine a set of conceptual similarities and differences between terrorism and crime. We also include several areas in which terrorism and crime are partly similar but partly different. We can in no way claim that this list is exhaustive – other similarities and differences can no doubt be generated. However, we have summarized some of the more obvious similarities and differences. As our presentation unfolds, it will be clear that most of the similarities and differences we list are not absolute. In large part this is because of the diversity of behavior included under the terms "crime" and "terrorism." In general, problems of conceptualizing terrorism are more similar for some crimes (e.g. hate crimes; organized crime; gang violence) than they are for others (e.g. murder, robbery, rape).

Conceptual Similarities

S1: The Study of Terrorism, Like the Study of Crime, has been Intensively Interdisciplinary
Researchers who have studied terrorism, like those who have studied crime, come from a range of disciplines, including sociology, political science, psychology,

history, economics, anthropology and philosophy. On the positive side, this inter-disciplinary focus has stimulated research and pushed the study of both terrorism and crime well beyond the bounds of a single discipline. On the negative side, the fact that both areas of research are intensively multidisciplinary likely encourages theoretical confusion and makes the adoption of a general theory more difficult.

S2: Both Terrorism and Crime are Social Constructions

The fact that this statement is trite does not make it less important. Forty years ago labeling theorist Howard Becker (1963) argued that deviance and crime are not objective properties of certain actions or behavior, but rather definitions constructed through social interaction. In Becker's words (1963, p. 9), "deviance is not a quality of the act the person commits, but rather a consequence of the application by others of rules and sanctions to an 'offender.' " While many specific predictions from labeling theory have been tested and rejected, this part of the argument remains hard to refute. Few criminologists would maintain that all guilty parties are arrested and convicted for their crimes or that every individual convicted of crime is in fact guilty. The conclusion that a crime occurred must always be based on evidence that may be imprecise, inexact, or incorrect. Those actually apprehended and convicted for engaging in a particular form of crime undoubtedly bear an inexact relationship to all those who have actually committed the crime in question.

Similarly, whether a case is classified as terrorism ultimately depends on a process of social construction. That is, terrorism is not simply "out there" to be counted in the same way that we might count rocks, trees, or planets (Turk, 2002). But rather, to qualify as terrorism a particular act must be recognized and defined as such. And in fact, no matter how seemingly heinous an act, there are invariably at least some individuals who will not see it as terrorism. This fundamental reality is recognized by the common truism that "one man's terrorist is another man's freedom fighter." Examples are legion. Menachem Begin, former Israeli prime minister, was well known in the late 1940s as a leader of the notorious Irgun Zvai Leumi, a terrorist group that worked to speed the departure of the British from Palestine. Similarly, while many consider Yasir Arafat a terrorist, many others see him as a legitimate leader of the Palestine Liberation Organization.

S3. For Both Terrorism and Crime There are Major Differences Between Formal Definitions and How These Definitions are Applied in Actual Practice

Researchers in criminology have long appreciated the fact that the actual application of law bears only a faint resemblance to legal statutes. Thus, early work by Roscoe Pound (1930) distinguished "law on the books" from "law in action." Criminologists (e.g. Sutherland, Cressey & Luckenbill, 1992, p. 4) point out that

while compared to other sets of rules for human conduct, criminal law is noteworthy for its uniformity and specificity. Nevertheless, these ideal characteristics of
the criminal law are rarely features of the criminal law in action. For example, in
analyses of how legal agents make decisions in rape cases (Koski, 2003; LaFree,
1989) it is common to find extra legal variables like victim or defendant race or
marital status playing a major role in predicting criminal justice outcomes.

Similarly, governments do not consistently apply their own definitions of
terrorism in individual cases. Thus, the U.S. State Department (2001) defines
terrorism as: "premeditated, politically motivated violence perpetrated against
noncombatants targeted by sub national groups or clandestine agents, usually
intended to influence an audience." But in certain instances, the U.S. government
resists applying this definition. For example, McCauley (1991, p. 129) points
out that for many years the U.S. State Department did not define the Nicaraguan
Contras as engaging in terrorist activity against the leftist Sandinistas, even though
the Contras were arguably a "sub national group" "using politically motivated violence" "against noncombatants." Likewise, many governments were ambivalent
about labeling the actions of the African National Congress in its conflict with both
white and black enemies in South Africa as terrorism – in spite of the fact that some
actions of the ANC seemed to clearly fit under common definitions of terrorism.

Of course, the use of unwritten rules to classify cases as terrorism is not just a
problem of governments. Individuals and groups that have collected data on terrorist activities also invariably struggle to consistently apply their formal definitions
to specific cases. For example, after providing a formal definition of terrorism in
its report, the Global Pinkerton Intelligence Services (1998, p. 1) notes that "other
forms of political violence . . . are included on a selective basis."

S4. Terrorism, Like Common Crime, is Disproportionately Committed by Young Males

In the U.S. in 2001, males accounted for 87.5% of all murder, 89.9% of all
robbery, and 86.4% of all burglary arrests (Uniform Crime Reports, 2002). Age
is so consistently associated with criminal behavior across different nations and
over time that criminologists Gottfredson and Hirschi (1990, p. 124) have argued
that "the age effect is everywhere and at all times the same." Similarly, terrorism
is predominantly the work of young men (Laqueur, 1977, p. 21; McCauley &
Segal, 1987, pp. 232–233; Russell & Miller, 1983); usually in their twenties and
often in their early twenties.

S5. Sustained Levels of Terrorism, Like Sustained Levels of Crime, Undermines Social Trust

In an earlier work, LaFree (1998, p. 71) argues that trust between individuals in
society increases predictability by allowing people to act based on their perception

that others are likely to perform particular actions in expected ways. Crime represents a particularly serious form of unpredictability and thus an important threat to trust. These connections can be seen clearly in the legendary low crime rates found in post-World War II Japan. Low crime rates in Japan allow the Japanese, even in large cities, to feel comfortable being away from their homes, in public places at night. They also allow individuals to show less concern about protecting their private property. Bicycles and other easy-to-steal items that are carefully guarded in many societies are frequently left unprotected in Japan. These characteristics make even urban Japan a relatively crime free, mostly predictable place. This in turn fosters high levels of trust, even among strangers.

By contrast, predictability and trust are seriously undermined in societies experiencing high levels of street crime. Thus, rapidly rising street crime rates in the United States during the 1960s and early 1970s had a devastating effect on relationships of trust between people, particularly in the high crime areas of inner cities (Fukuyama, 1995; LaFree, 1998). More recently, in many of the struggling democracies of Latin America, alarming increases in rates of violent crime have fractured civic life and driven frustrated citizens to seek more punitive forms of social control and weaken or suspend altogether civil-liberty safeguards (Fajnzylber, Lederman & Loayza, 1998). Likewise, threats of crime in the transitional democracies of Eastern Europe have raised major challenges to democratization and have resulted in calls for restraints on freedom and civil liberties in the name of maintaining social order (Hraba et al., 1998).

Similarly, Crenshaw (1972, p. 388) argues that terrorism upsets the social framework upon which members of a society depend and undermines predictability in social relations. Because no one can be sure of what behavior to expect of others, levels of trust are reduced and individuals turn inward, concentrating more on their own survival. Thus, as with societies experiencing high levels of crime, societies undergoing sustained terrorist attacks are likely to experience lower levels of social solidarity, reduced cooperation and interdependence, and declining levels of trust.

Conceptual Differences

D1. While Terrorist Activities Typically Constitute Multiple Crimes (e.g. Murder, Kidnapping, Extortion), for Many Nations, a Specific Crime of Terrorism does not Exist

One of the most basic differences between terrorism and common crimes is that terrorism in most nations is behavior that violates a number of existing criminal statutes but is not defined as a specific separate category under criminal law. For example, suspected terrorists in the United States are typically prosecuted for a

variety of criminal offenses rather than terrorism. Thus, in a study of federal prosecution of terrorists in the U.S. from 1982 to 1989, Smith and Orvis (1993, p. 669)
show that the most common subjects of terrorist prosecutions have been racketeering (30.2% of the total), machine guns, destructive devices and other firearms
(16.7%), and conspiracy (9.3%). This situation began to change in the United
States after the mid-1990s, and especially after the terrorist attack of September
11, 2001. Nevertheless, even today, most persons suspected of terrorism in the U.S.
are being prosecuted not for terrorism per se, but for a range of crimes commonly
associated with terrorism.

Legal prohibitions specific to terrorism are even less well defined at the international level. An early attempt at constructing an internationally acceptable
definition of terrorism was made by the League of Nations in 1937, but was never
ratified by member states (United Nations, 2002). The United Nations has still not
developed a unified legal definition of terrorism, but instead has adopted 12 related
conventions and protocols.

An important research implication of this situation is that it is much more difficult
to develop national or international counts of terrorism than it is to develop total
counts for most crime types. Thus, to study the prosecution of terrorist cases in
the United States, Smith and Orvis (1993) had to begin with annual reports on
terrorism provided by the Federal Bureau of Investigation, then request from the
FBI an unpublished list of persons omitted from their reports that were nevertheless
indicted as a result of terrorism and terrorist-related activities. They then asked
the Department of Justice to match the resulting list with federal court docket
numbers assigned throughout the United States and Puerto Rico. Even with these
procedures, the authors estimate (p. 666) that they missed 29% of the known,
officially labeled, federally indicted terrorists for the period included in their study.
The task of developing an international list of those prosecuted for terrorism would
of course be considerably more complex.

*D2. The Response to Common Crime Rarely Moves Beyond Local Authorities
Whereas the Response to Terrorism Usually does*
For most crimes committed around the world, criminal justice issues are handled
by local authorities and never gather international or even national attention. By
contrast, terrorist acts are frequently reported outside of the local area where they
occur and typically gather national and often international attention. This means
that the type of data available on common crimes and terrorist acts are likely to be
quite different. In most jurisdictions, common crimes result in an overwhelming
amount of local processing information generated by police, prosecutors, courts,
probation offices, prisons and other parts of the criminal justice bureaucracy. These
same local agencies develop little information on terrorism. By contrast, much of

the terrorist information that exists is limited to international incidents. Thus, terrorist information collected by the U.S. State Department is limited to cases of international terrorism and excludes terrorism within nations.

This means that available data for common crimes and terrorist acts occupy opposite ends of the local-international spectrum. Thus, it is often impossible to develop cross-national estimates of common crimes because local, regional and national differences in laws make it difficult to compile international estimates. By contrast, it is difficult to obtain data on domestic terrorism.

D3. While Those Who Commit Common Crimes are Usually Trying to Avoid Detection, Those Who Commit Terrorism are Often Seeking Maximum Attention and Exposure

While common criminals are usually struggling to avoid a large audience, terrorists are often seeking a large audience. Hoffman (1998, p. 131) argues that all terrorist groups strive to get maximum publicity for their actions and points out that because of this fact (p. 132) the modern news media plays "a vital part in the terrorist's calculus." Because a common goal of terrorism is to gain media attention, terrorist events are often carefully staged. This is much less common with other crimes – although it does happen occasionally, as in the case of hate crimes or serial homicides or rapes.

D4. Terrorism, Unlike Common Crime, is Typically a Means to Broader Political Goals

Most street crimes do not have larger political purposes. By contrast, the overriding objective of terrorism and its ultimate justification is the furtherance of a political cause. Hoffman (1998, p. 41) argues that the criminal frequently employs violence as a means to obtain some material goal, such as money or material goods, or to kill or injure a specific victim. Thus, criminals often have selfish, personal motivations and their actions are not intended to have consequences or create psychological repercussions beyond the criminal act. By contrast, the fundamental aim of terrorists is often a political motivation to overthrow or change the dominant political system. Crenshaw (1983, p. 2) points out that "the intent of terrorist violence is psychological and symbolic, not material." Nevertheless, terrorist groups do face the ongoing challenge of generating support for their operations and indirectly at least, this requires money and material support.

D5. Terrorists are More Likely Than Common Criminals to See Themselves as Altruists

Although common criminals vary widely in terms of how they perceive their activities (cf. Anderson, 1999; Black, 1998; Katz, 1988), few criminals see their crimes as altruistic behavior. By contrast, many terrorists see themselves as altruists. Hoffman (1998, p. 43) claims that terrorists frequently believe that they are serving a cause that will achieve a greater good for some wider constituency.

D6. Terrorists are More Likely Than Common Criminals to Innovate
Policy recommendations in criminology are generally based on the assumption that the past informs the future. Thus, best practices evaluations in criminology (Sherman et al., 1997) tell us what worked in the past and extrapolate from this to make predictions about what will work in the future. But with terrorist activities the relationship between past and future behavior may be much less certain. Consequently, terrorism is likely to depend more than common crime on innovation.

Conceptually Mixed

M1. Terrorism, Like Some Forms of Crime, Typically Includes an Organizational Structure and Advocates Who Show Varying Levels of Commitment and Support for Terrorist Activities
Most definitions of terrorism include the requirement that it be committed not by a lone operator but by an organized group. For example, we have seen above that the U.S. State Department (2001) definition includes the requirement that terrorism involve "sub national groups." Thus, terrorist activity implies membership and at least a loosely articulated ongoing organizational structure. By contrast, such organizational structures are rare in many forms of common crime. It is hard to imagine, for example, a group of offenders organizing to support murder or robbery. But there are major exceptions. For example, organized crime activities frequently do have an ongoing organizational structure (Maltz, 1994). Similarly, hate crimes and gang activities may be at least loosely connected to support groups (Maguire & Pastore, 1996, p. 349; Short, 1997).

M2. Terrorist Acts, Like Some Crimes, are Typically Part of a Sustained Program of Violence
As a result of the foregoing (an organizational structure and political goals), terrorism, unlike most common crime, is usually part of a sustained program of violence. Thus, most definitions of terrorism exclude single, unplanned acts of violence (Crenshaw, 1972, p. 384). For this reason Senechal de la Roche (1996, p. 118) points out that terrorism typically expresses a "chronic" grievance. By contrast, single, unplanned acts of violence are common among criminals. But again, some forms of crime, notably organized crime, gang activities, and serial

crimes, can resemble terrorism in terms of representing a relatively sustained program of violence.

M3. Terrorists, Like Criminals, Vary in Terms of the Extent to Which They Select Victims in a Random, Indiscriminate Way

Criminologists (Gottfredson & Hirschi, 1990; Katz, 1988) have long noted that a high proportion of all criminal offenders target victims that are previously known to them. Nevertheless, many criminals also target strangers. Similarly, terrorists frequently target specific individuals for assassination or hostage taking. But at the same time many other terrorist activities pay little attention to the specific identity of the victims of their actions. As Aron (1966, p. 170) notes, it is this indiscriminate nature of terrorism that helps to spread fear; if no one in particular is a target, no one can be safe.

DATA COLLECTION SIMILARITIES
AND DIFFERENCES

Data Sources

Traditionally, crime data come from three sources, corresponding to the major social roles connected to criminal events: "official" data collected by legal agents, especially the police; "victimization" data collected from crime victims; and "self-report" data collected from offenders. In the United States, the most widely used form of official crime data has long been the Federal Bureau of Investigation's Uniform Crime Report. Major official sources of data on international crime include the International Criminal Police Organization (Interpol), the United Nations crime surveys, and for homicides only, the World Health Organization (for a review, see LaFree, 1999). Since 1973, the major source of victimization data in the United States has been the National Crime Victimization Survey. For international data, the International Crime Victimization Survey has now collected several waves of data from samples of individuals in several dozen nations around the world (van Dijk, Mayhew & Killias 1989). Compared to the collection of victimization data in the United States, the collection of self-report survey data has been more sporadic. Nevertheless, several major large-scale national self-report surveys now exist (Elliott, Huizinga & Menard, 1989; Johnston, Bachman & O'Malley 1993). Similarly, several waves of an international self-reported crime study have been undertaken (Junger-Tas, Terlouw & Klein, 1994).

In general, terrorism data from these three sources is either entirely lacking or faces important additional limitations. Although some countries do collect official data on terrorism, these data face at least two major difficulties. First, data on terrorism collected by government entities are inevitably influenced by political considerations. Of course, to some extent, this is also a problem with official data on common crimes. Police, courts and correctional officers frequently face political pressure to present their crime data in particular ways (McCleary, Nienstadt & Erven, 1982). However, the political pressure is likely to be especially acute with regard to terrorism. Beginning in 1961, the U.S. State Department has produced a chronology of "significant terrorist incidents" and it now provides an annual Patterns of Global Terrorism Report that reviews international terrorist events by year, date, region, and terrorist group and includes background information on terrorist organizations. However, as noted above, the State Department faces tremendous political pressure to interpret terrorism in particular ways.

Second, while huge amounts of detailed official data on common crimes are routinely produced by the various branches of the criminal justice system in most nations, this is rarely the case for terrorism. For example, as noted above, most suspected terrorists in the United States are not legally processed for their acts of terrorism, but for other related offenses. It is true that this situation continues to evolve. For example, in the United States in 1995, Chapter 113B of the Federal Criminal Code and Rules added "Terrorism" as a separate offense and the Antiterrorism and Effective Death Penalty Act was signed into law by President Clinton in 1996. Among other things, the 1996 act attempts to cut fundraising by those affiliated with terrorist organizations, enhances the security measures employed by the aviation industry, and expands the reach of U.S. law enforcement over selected crimes committed abroad. Similarly, the U.S. Patriot Act, passed in 2001, strengthens criminal laws against terrorism by adding to the criminal code terrorist attacks against mass transportation systems, domestic terrorism, harboring or concealing terrorists, or providing material support to terrorists (115 Stat. 374, Public Law 107–56 – October 26, 2001). Nevertheless, it still remains the case that most of those persons who are officially designated as terrorists in the annual reports produced by the FBI are prosecuted under traditional criminal statutes. So, there is no easy way to gather official data on those arrested, prosecuted or convicted of terrorist activities unless you do as Smith and his colleagues have done (Smith & Orvis, 1993), and assemble the data on a case by case basis. And of course the ability to use official data to study terrorism in many other nations is even more complex.

Victimization data, which have played an increasingly important role in the study of crime, are almost entirely irrelevant to the study of terrorist activities. Several features of terrorism mean that victimization surveys are unlikely to ever have widespread applicability. To begin with, for most nations and at most points in time, terrorism is much rarer than other criminal acts. This means that even with extremely large sample sizes, few individuals in most countries will have been victimized by terrorists. Moreover, because one of the hallmarks of terrorism is that victims are often chosen at random, victims of terrorist events frequently have few details to report. And finally, in many cases, victims of terrorism are killed by their attackers.

Self-report data on terrorists has been more important than victimization data, but it too faces serious limitations. Most active terrorists are unwilling to participate in interviews. And even if willing to participate, getting access to known terrorists for research purposes raises obvious challenges. As terrorism researcher Ariel Merari (1991) has put it, "The clandestine nature of terrorist organizations and the ways and means by which intelligence can be obtained will rarely enable data collection which meets commonly accepted academic standards." Still, we can learn a good deal from direct contact with terrorists or former terrorists. A good example is the recent work by McCauley (2003) based on an examination of the notebooks and letters left behind by the 9/11 suicide bombers.

Because of the difficulties with the use of official data, victimization data and self-report data, most research on terrorism has been based instead on secondary data sources: the media (or media derived data bases), books, journals, or other published documents. In a review by Silke (2001), nearly 80% of all terrorism research reviewed was based on secondary data sources rather than on primary contact with suspected or actual terrorists, terrorist victims, or legal agents investigating terrorists. Most of the documents analyzed in these studies are open access and are not classified. Thus, a research source that is rarely used in criminology research is a mainstay of research on terrorism. Nevertheless, over time researchers have begun to put together these secondary sources into increasingly rigorous terrorist event data bases. In the next section, we briefly review these developments.

Terrorism Event Data Bases

Table 1 summarizes eight terrorism event data bases. According to Table 1, the Pinkerton Global Intelligence Services (PGIS) data have by far the largest number of events of any of the other data sets – about 7 times more events than the next three largest – ITERATE, the U.S. State Department and Tweed. From 1970 to 1997, PGIS trained researchers to identify and code all terrorism incidents they could identify from wire services (including Reuters and the Foreign Broadcast Information Service), U.S. State Department reports, other U.S. and foreign government reporting, U.S. and foreign newspapers (including the *New York Times*, the *British Financial Times*, the *Christian Science Monitor*, the *Washington Post*, the *Washington Times*, and the *Wall Street Journal*), information provided by

Table 1.   Major Archival Databases on Terrorist Incident Reports.

Author	Scope	Period	Number of Incidents
PGIS	Domestic & International	1970–1997	73,931
ITERATE	International	1968–2000	10,837
TWEED (Europe)	Domestic	1950–1999	10,498
US Dept. of State	International	1980–2001	10,026
RAND	International	1968–1997	8,509
TRITON	Domestic & International	Mid-2000 to mid-2002	2,452
RAND-MIPT	Domestic & International	2001–2002	2,261
COBRA	International	1998–1999	1,041

PGIS offices throughout the world, occasional inputs from such special interests as organized political opposition groups, and data furnished by PGIS clients and other individuals in both official and private capacities. In more recent years, PGIS researchers also relied on the Internet. Similar coding forms were used during the entire 28 years of data collection. Although about two dozen persons were responsible for coding information over the years spanned by the data collection, only two individuals were in charge of supervising data collection during the entire period.

Based on coding rules originally developed in 1970, the persons responsible for collecting the PGIS data base sought to exclude criminal acts that appeared to be devoid of any political or ideological motivation and also acts arising from open combat between opposing armed forces, both regular and irregular. The data coders also excluded actions taken by governments in the legitimate exercise of their authority, even when such actions were denounced by domestic and/or foreign critics as acts of "state terrorism." However, they included violent acts that were not officially sanctioned by government, even in cases where many observers believed that the government was openly tolerating the violent actions. Because the goal of the data collection was to provide risk assessment to corporate customers, the data base was designed to error on the side of inclusiveness. The justification was that being overly inclusive best serves the interest of clients – an employee of a corporation about to move to Colombia would be concerned about acts of violence against civilians and foreigners, even if these acts were domestic rather than international, threatened rather than completed, or carried out for religious rather than political purposes.

The ITERATE (International Terrorism: Attributes of Terrorist Events) data, originally collected by Edward Mickolus (1982), has probably been the most widely used archival source of terrorism data in terms of empirical research (e.g. Enders & Sandler, 1993). The ITERATE data contains two different types of files:

quantitatively coded data on international terrorist incidents; and a qualitative description of each incident included in the quantitative files. The quantitative data are arranged into four files, containing: (1) basic information on the type of terrorist attack, including location, name of group taking responsibility, and number of deaths and injuries; (2) detailed information on the fate of the terrorists or terrorist group claiming responsibility; (3) detailed information on terrorist events involving hostages; and (4) detailed information on terrorist events involving skyjackings.

In addition to PGIS, three of the other data sources listed in Table 1 are private risk assessment companies: Cobra, Triton and Tweed. All of these companies have taken an increasing interest in terrorist risk in recent years. Tweed prepares an annual register that details political, economic and social events related to terrorist activities; Triton prints a list of current global activities of specific terrorist groups; and the Cobra Institute is currently developing a chronology of world terrorism events and detailed information about known terrorist groups.

The U.S. State Department provides a chronology of "significant terrorist incidents," beginning in 1961. Each report includes a brief description of all events. The State Department also provides an annual Patterns of Global Terrorism Report, which reviews international terrorist events by year, date, region, and terrorist group. The Report includes background information on terrorist organizations, U.S. policy on terrorism, and progress on counter terrorism.

RAND has collected a detailed set of secondary data on international terrorist events from 1968 to 1997. In addition, RAND in collaboration with the Oklahoma City National Memorial Institute for the Prevention of Terrorism is currently developing a very detailed secondary data base on both international and national terrorism since 1998. RAND may be unique among groups collecting data on terrorism through its use of a special "vetting" committee to determine whether a particular incident qualifies as terrorism. Cases that are suspected to be terrorism are brought to this group of experts which study each case before adding it to the terrorism event count data base.

The main reason why the PGIS data base is so much larger than the other secondary data bases is that PGIS gathered information on all terrorist events – both domestic and international. To underscore the importance of this difference consider that two of the most noteworthy terrorist events of the 1990s – the March 1995 nerve gas attack on the Tokyo subway system and the April 1995 bombing of the federal office building in Oklahoma City – both lack any known foreign involvement and hence were pure acts of domestic terrorism. Note also that many of these data bases only track very recent events. For example, Cobra, Triton and RAND's new data system all begin after 1998.

Another reason for the larger number of cases in the PGIS data base is that PGIS (1998, p. 1) employed a broader definition of terrorism than the one used by most of the other major data bases: "the threatened or actual use of illegal force and violence to attain a political, economic, religious or social goal through fear, coercion or intimidation." Neither the State Department nor the FBI definition of terrorism includes threats of force. Yet as Hoffman (1998, p. 38) points out, "terrorism is as much about the threat of violence as the violent act itself." In fact, many, perhaps most, hijackings involve only the threatened use of force (e.g. "I have a bomb and I will use it unless you follow my demands"). Similarly, kidnappers almost always employ force to seize the victims, but then threaten to kill, maim or otherwise harm the victims unless demands are satisfied. Also, the State Department definition is limited to "politically motivated violence." By contrast, the PGIS definition also includes economic and religious objectives. These characteristics of the PGIS data have encouraged us to begin a project to computerize and analyze these data (LaFree & Dugan, 2002).

METHODOLOGICAL SIMILARITIES AND DIFFERENCES

While we have identified some important differences between terrorism and crime with regard to conceptualization and data collection, it also seems clear that most of these differences can be resolved with research methods currently available to criminologists. In fact, we strongly believe that the experiences of criminologists in analyzing crime data might make a real contribution to the study of terrorism. We begin this section by considering two key differences between crime and terrorism and some of the methodological implications of these differences. We then summarize several areas in which methods now being used in criminology might usefully be applied to the study of terrorism.

Methodological Differences

Compared to common crimes, most terrorist events have at least two characteristics that raise special methodological issues. First, while criminals usually commit crimes without considering how policy makers will respond to their activities, terrorists often attack in order to generate a policy response from authorities. This implies that when determining causal relationships between policy and violence, compared to those studying common crimes, those studying terrorism need to more thoroughly address issues of simultaneity between violence and government action. For example, temporal ordering of attacks might suggest a drop in terrorism after a specific policy was adopted. However, the terrorist group may have intentionally heightened their violent activity to generate this policy response. Thus, the drop in violence following the policy may simply be a regression to their average level of activity.

One methodological strategy for addressing issues such as these is to employ game theory methods. For example, Bueno De Mesquita and Cohen (1995) demonstrate that noncooperative game theory can be used to predict citizens' choices between socially acceptable behavior or criminal activity depending on their beliefs about how governments will respond (see also, Cohen & Machalek, 1988; Krebs, Costelloe & Jenks, 2003). Similarly, research by Tauchen, Witte and Long (1991) uses noncooperative game theory to determine which variables best determine the equilibrium of family violence between spouses. With the sequential ordering of each group's terrorist attacks and the government's policy responses, game theoretical methods could be used to identify variables that influence the behavioral choices of terrorist organizations.

Second, while most violent crime is committed by individuals, most terrorist activity is committed by groups of individuals whose membership is dynamic. This means that while the unit of analysis for most criminological research is the offender, concentrating on individual offenders is more complex and may be entirely counterproductive in terrorism research. But again, it is possible to identify methodological solutions to this problem within criminology. To begin with criminology researchers studying gangs and organized crime networks (Howell, 1998; Howell & Decker, 1999; Rosenfeld, Bray & Egley, 1999) face similar problems. While most of the current gang research examines individuals (Battin, Hill, Abbott, Catalano & Hawkins, 1998; Rosenfeld et al., 1999), there is growing interest in studying the dynamics of group membership using network analysis (Rosenfeld, White & Phillips, 2003). These newer analysis methods could help us better understand how relational factors, such as social ties among peers, can influence terrorist group membership and subsequent terrorist attacks. Moreover, as in criminology, terrorism researchers can easily replace studies of individual offenders with studies of incidents or activity across geographical units.

Methodological Similarities

Methodological similarities between studying terrorist violence and common crime become apparent when we step back and recognize that criminal events and terrorist attacks look much the same regardless of the motivation behind them: both are events that can be counted and both display non-random temporal and spatial patterns that are likely associated with endogeneous and exogenous characteristics of offenders, targets, and situations. There are also substantial investigatory and forensic similarities. Thus, the same basic investigatory methods are relevant whether tracing money laundering in general or money laundering that is supporting terrorism; the same forensic methods used for crime scene investigation are equally useful for investigating terrorist violence. Although a full explication of common criminology methods that could be applied to terrorism data is well beyond the scope of the current paper, in the sections that follow, we offer several concrete methodological applications that seem promising.

Analysis of Distributions and Trends

As in the study of crime trends, analysis of terrorism trends can be easily disaggregated across several dimensions, including modes of terrorism (e.g. bombings, hijackings, assassinations); terrorist targets (e.g. embassies, factories, military facilities, public officials); and costs of terrorism (e.g. number of casualties, ransom dollars paid). Further, because terrorist groups often strike repeatedly, terrorism distributions can also be compared across types of groups such as ethnic separatists, left wing radicals, survivalists, or religious extremists. Because much criminological research emphasizes the understanding of crime patterns across several dimensions, criminologists should be able to offer related strategies for studying patterns of terrorism over space and time (Bureau of Justice Statistics, 2001).

Geographic Mapping

An important strategy used by criminologists to study spatial and temporal patterns of events employs geographic mapping techniques (Cohen & Tita, 1999; Messner, Andelin, Baller, Hawkins, Deane & Tolnay, 1999; Rosenfeld, Bray & Egley, 1999) Just as these scholars have imbedded crime incidents into maps of counties and cities, terrorism researchers can create regional and world-wide maps depicting numbers and rates of terrorist activities around the globe. Point maps will make obvious the location of incidents and the groups responsible for carrying out attacks, as well as how locations evolve over time.

Recently introduced exploratory spatial data analysis techniques (ESDA) provide researchers with important new tools for distinguishing between random and non-random spatial patterns of events (Anselin, 1998). While most of these ESDA methods are cross-sectional, Cohen and Tita (1999) have devised methods for extending static cross-sectional views of the spatial distribution of homicides to consider dynamic features of changes over time in spatial dependencies. This methodology can be used to identify innovative forms of terrorist activity and to demonstrate patterns of adoption by other terrorist organizations.

In criminology these methods have also been used to distinguish *contagious diffusion* of homicide between adjoining units and *hierarchical diffusion* of homicide that spreads broadly through commonly shared influences (Cohen & Tita, 1999). By applying these methods to terrorism data, we should be able to distinguish between terrorist organizations or cells that grow through direct recruitment of individuals living in neighboring territories (contagious diffusion) and groups that form instead through commonly shared influences that are geographically dispersed (hierarchical diffusion). For example hierarchical diffusion might be based on reactions to favorable media portrayals of terrorists (see Enders & Sandler, 1999 for a discussion of "copycat" terrorist incidents).

Time-Series Analysis
Econometric time-series methods can also be used to describe important features of terrorist event trends globally and across geographic units. One of the authors has recently applied these methods to investigate booms and busts in homicide rates across 34 nations over a 43 year period (LaFree & Drass, 2002). These techniques were originally developed by economists to study business cycles by decomposing activity into two components: a trend component (that is, a general, long-term increase or decrease in the level of a variable over time), and a cyclical component that represents short-term, yet noticeable, deviations from the general trend (Stock & Watson, 1988). Attention to trend components is especially important here because earlier research suggests that terrorist activity is cyclical in nature (Enders & Sandler, 1995, 2000). As with crime trend analysis, once trend components are isolated, scholars can address questions about similarities and differences in characteristics of terrorism (e.g. hijackings, politically or religiously motivated events) and cycles across geographic units (i.e. cities, nations, or regions).

Causal Analysis
The predominant goal of studying crime is to identify variables that cause either increases or contribute to crime desistence. Research methods used to isolate potential causal influences of crime can also be used to estimate the effects of political, economic and social variables on the likelihood and frequency of terrorist activity. Further, because terrorism data can be structured with repeated measures of geographic units over time, standard methods of longitudinal analysis can be used to estimate the impact of variables while controlling for unobservable within state time-invariant effects that vary across geographic boundaries (Hausman & Taylor, 1981 for a description of estimation methods using panel data). In addition to longitudinal methods, effects of repeated measures can be estimated by modeling terrorism data hierarchically. This strategy has been used by criminologists and others to estimate coefficient parameters while documenting within-time and across-time variation (Bryk & Raudenbush, 1992; Lawton, Taylor & Perkins, 2003; for an overview of multi-level linear models, see Goldstein, 1987).

An important consideration when investigating terrorist attacks is to disentangle simultaneous relationships. In criminology, neighborhood disorder and decline can lead to crime and crime can lead to disorder and decline (Skogan, 1990). Similarly, terrorist activity could both be caused by and provoke political, economic, and social instability (Enders & Sandler, 1993). By disentangling these effects using methods common to criminologists, such as tests of Granger causality, generalized method of moments, and two-stage least squares, it should be possible to more clearly understand how terrorism is both influenced by and can lead to regional changes in political, social, and economic conditions (Arellano & Bond, 1991; Granger, 1969; Green, 2003; Pindyck & Rubinfeld, 1998).

Life-Course Analysis

An important current interest among criminologists is to examine patterns of criminal behavior over the life course (Moffitt, 1993; Nagin & Land, 1993; Sampson & Laub, 1995). Ideas and strategies developed by these scholars can also be applied to the study of the life-course of terrorist groups. For example, Nagin's (1999) trajectory analysis has been used to sort individuals into groups based on their offending behavior over time. With slight modification, this method can identify developmental trajectories of terrorist organizations over time from their inception. Trajectory analysis can also be expanded to group geographic regions by their patterns of terrorist violence. For example, criminologists (e.g. Weisburd, Bushway, Yang & Lum, 2003) have recently used trajectory analysis to analyze crime trajectories of street segments in Seattle over a 14-year period.

CONCLUSION

This paper strongly advocates that criminologists join with others in advancing the study of terrorism. While we readily acknowledge important differences between common crime and terrorism, the similarities in conceptualization, data collection, and research methods suggest that the existing knowledge-base of criminology can quickly expand what is known about the patterns, causes, and consequences of terrorism. In general, many of the differences between terrorism and common crime are no more challenging than differences between common crime and more specialized crimes, such as youth-gang activity, organized crime, hate crime, or domestic violence. Each has distinctive features that require an investment of time and effort to better understand the substantive dynamics. One important role of criminology has been to inform policy makers about how to best evaluate common and specialized crime intervention. A distinctive advantage of criminology in terms of terrorism research is that framing issues in criminal rather than political terms tends to downplay the legitimacy of terrorist claims. Moreover, framing terrorism as a crime reinforces the idea that terrorism is a common problem that should be considered along side other common problems when allocating resources or considering the relevancy of civil rights issues. By focusing on the obvious connections between terrorism and crime, we may be able to not only contribute to a better understanding of terrorism, but also to help formulate more rational policies for combating it.

ACKNOWLEDGMENT

We would like to thank Clark McCauley for his very helpful comments.

REFERENCES

Anderson, E. (1999). *Code of the street: Decency, violence and the moral life of the inner city*. New York: W. W. Norton.

Anselin, L. (1998). Exploratory spatial data analysis in geocomputational environment. In: P. Longley, S. Brooks, R. McDonnell & B. Macmillian (Eds), *Geocomputation: A Primer*. New York: Wiley.

Arellano, M., & Bond, S. (1991). Some tests of specification for panel data: Monte Carlo evidence and an application to employment equations. *Review of Economic Studies, 58*, 277–297.

Aron, R. (1966). *Peace and war*. London: Weidenfeld & Nicolson.

Babkina, A. M. (1998). *Terrorism: An annotated bibliography*. Commack, NY: Nova Science Publishers.

Battin, S. R., Hill, K. G., Abbott, R. D., Catalano, R. F., & Hawkins, J. D. (1998). The contribution of gang membership to delinquency beyond delinquent friends. *Criminology, 36*, 93–115.

Becker, H. S. (1963). *The outsiders*. New York: Free Press.

Black, D. (1998). *The social structure of right and wrong*. San Diego: Academic Press.

Bryk, A. S., & Raudenbush, S. (1992). *Hierarchical linear models. Advanced quantitative techniques in the social sciences series*. Newbury Park, CA: Sage.

Bueno De Mesquita, B., & Cohen, L. E. (1995). Self-interest, equity, and crime control: A game-theoretic analysis of criminal decision making. *Criminology, 33*, 483–518.

Bureau of Justice Statistics (2001). *Sourcebook on Criminal Justice Statistics*. Washington, DC: Office of Justice Programs, U.S. Department of Justice.

Chauncey, R. (1975). Deterrence: Certainty, severity, and skyjacking. *Criminology, 12*, 447–473.

Cohen, J., & Tita, G. (1999). Spatial diffusion in homicide: An exploratory analysis. *Journal of Quantitative Criminology, 15*, 451–493.

Cohen, L. E., & Machalek, R. (1988). A general theory of expropriative crime: An evolutionary ecological approach. *American Journal of Sociology, 94*, 465–501.

Crenshaw, M. (1972). The concept of revolutionary terrorism. *Conflict Resolution, 16*, 383–396.

Crenshaw, M. (Ed.) (1983). *Terrorism, legitimacy and power*. Middleton, CT: Wesleyan University Press.

Elliott, D. S., Huizinga, D., & Menard, S. (1989). *Multiple problem youth: Delinquency, substance abuse, and mental health problems*. New York: Springer-Verlag.

Enders, W., & Sandler, T. (1993). The effectiveness of anti terrorism policies: A vector-autoregression intervention analysis. *American Political Science Review*, *87*(4), 829–844.

Enders, W., & Sandler, T. (1995). Terrorism: Theory and applications. In: K. Hartley & T. Sandler (Eds), *Handbook of Defense Economics* (pp. 213–249). Amsterdam: North-Holland.

Enders, W., & Sandler, T. (1999). Transnational terrorism in the Post-Cold War Era. *International Studies Quarterly*, *43*, 145–167.

Enders, W., & Sandler, T. (2000). Is transnational terrorism becoming more threatening? *Journal of Conflict Resolution*, *44*, 307–332.

Fajnzylber, P., Lederman, D., & Loayza, N. (1998). *Determinants of crime rates in Latin America and the world: An empirical assessment.* Viewpoint series. Washington, DC: World Bank.

Fukuyama, F. (1995). *Trust: The social virtues and the creation of prosperity.* New York: Free Press.

Goldstein, H. I. (1987). *Multilevel models in educational and social research.* London: Oxford University Press.

Gottfredson, M. R., & Hirschi, T. (1990). *A general theory of crime.* Stanford, CA: Stanford University Press.

Granger, C. W. J. (1969). Investigating causal relations by econometric models and cross-spectral methods. *Econometrica*, *37*, 424–438.

Green, W. H. (2003). *Econometric analysis* (5th ed.). Upper Saddle River, NJ: Prentice-Hall.

Hausman, J. A., & Taylor, W. E. (1981). Panel data and unobservable individual effects. *Econometrica*, *49*, 1377–1398.

Hoffman, B. (1998). *Recent trends and future prospects of terrorism in the United States.* Santa Monica: Rand.

Howell, J. C. (1998). *Youth gangs: An overview.* U.S. Department of Justice, National Institute of Justice, Office of Juvenile Justice and Delinquency Prevention, Washington, DC.

Howell, J. C., & Decker, S. H. (1999). *The youth gangs, drugs, and violence connection.* U.S. Department of Justice, National Institute of Justice, Office of Juvenile Justice and Delinquency Prevention, Washington, DC.

Hraba, J., Bao, W.-n., Lorentz, F. O., & Pechacova, Z. (1998). Perceived risk of crime in the Czech Republic. *Journal of Research in Crime and Delinquency*, *35*, 225–243.

Johnston, L. D., Bachman, J. G., & O'Malley, P. M. (1993). *Monitoring the future.* Ann Arbor, MI: Institute for Social Research.

Junger-Tas, J., Terlouw, Gert-Jan, & Klein, M. (Eds) (1994). *Delinquent behavior among young people in the western world.* Amsterdam: Kugler.

Katz, J. (1988). *Seductions of crime: Moral and sensual attractions in doing evil.* New York: Basic.

Kennedy, L. W., & Lum, C. M. (2003). *Developing a foundation for policy relevant terrorism research in criminology.* Unpublished manuscript, University of Maryland.

Koski, D. D. (Ed.) (2003). *The jury trial in criminal justice.* Durham, NC: Carolina Academic Press.

Krebs, C. P., Costelloe, M., & Jenks, D. (2003). Drug control policy and smuggling innovation: A game-theoretic analysis. *Journal of Drug Issues*, *33*, 133–160.

LaFree, G. (1998). *Losing legitimacy: Street crime and the decline of social institutions in America.* Boulder, CO: Westview.

LaFree, G. (1999). A summary and review of cross-national comparative studies of homicide. In: M. D. Smith & M. A. Zahn (Eds), *Homicide: A Sourcebook of Social Research* (pp. 124–148). Thousand Oaks, CA: Sage.

LaFree, G. (1989). *Rape and criminal justice: The social construction of sexual assault.* Belmont, CA: Wadsworth.

LaFree, G., & Drass, K. (2002). Counting crime booms among nations: Evidence for homicide victimization rates, 1956 to 1998. *Criminology*, *40*, 769–800.

LaFree, G., & Dugan, L. (2002). The Impact of Economic, Political, and Social Variables on the Incidence of World Terrorism, 1970 to 1997. Grant proposal to the National Institute of Justice.

Landes, W. M. (1978). An economic study of U.S. aircraft hijackings, 1961–1976. *Journal of Law and Economics, 21*, 1–31.

Laqueur, W. (1977). *Terrorism*. Boston: Little Brown.

Lawton, B. A., Taylor, R. B., & Perkins, D. D. (2003). Multilevel longitudinal impacts of incivilities: Fear of crime, expected safety, and block satisfaction. *Journal of Quantitative Criminology, 19*, 237–274.

Maguire, K., & Pastore, A. L. (1996). Bureau of Justice Statistics Sourcebook of Criminal Justice Statistics – 1995. Washington, DC: Department of Justice.

Maltz, M. (1994). Defining organized crime. In: R. J. Kelly, K. Chin & R. Schatzenberg (Eds), *Handboook of Organized Crime in the United States*. Westport, CT: Greenwood Press.

McCauley, C. (1991). Terrorism research and public policy: An overview. In: C. McCauley (Ed.), *Terrorism Research and Public Policy* (pp. 126–144). London: Frank Cass.

McCauley, C. (2003). Psychological issues in understanding terrorism and the response to terrorism. In: C. Stout (Ed.), *The Psychology of Terrorism*. Westport, CN: Praeger.

McCauley, C., & Segal, M. E. (1987). Social psychology of terrorist groups. In: C. Hendrick (Ed.), *Group Processes and Intergroup Relations* (pp. 231–256). Newbury Park: Sage.

McCleary, R., Nienstedt, B. C., & Erven, J. M. (1982). Uniform crime reports as organizational outcomes: Three time series experiments. *Social Problems, 29*, 361–372.

Merari, A. (1991). Academic research and government policy on terrorism. *Terrorism and Political Violence, 3*, 88–102.

Messner, S. F., Anselin, L., Baller, R. D., Hawkins, D. F., Deane, G., & Tolnay, S. T. (1999). The spatial patterning of county homicide rates: An application of exploratory spatial data analysis. *Journal of Quantitative Criminology, 15*, 423–450.

Mickolus, E. F. (1982). *International terrorism: Attributes of terrorist events, 1968–1977 (ITERATE 2)*. Ann Arbor, MI: Inter-University Consortium for Political and Social Research.

Mickolus, E. F., & Simmons, S. L. (1997). *Terrorism, 1992–1995: A chronology of events and a selectively annotated bibliography*. Westport, CT: Greenwood Press.

Moffitt, T. E. (1993). Adolescence-limited and life-course-persistent antisocial behavior: A developmental taxonomy. *Psychological Review, 100*, 674–701.

Nagin, D. S. (1999). Analyzing developmental trajectories: A semi-parametric, group-based approach. *Psychological Methods, 4*, 139–177.

Nagin, D. S., & Land, K. C. (1993). Age, criminal careers, and population heterogeneity: Specification and estimation of a nonparametric, mixed Poisson model. *Criminology, 31*, 327–362.

Pindyck, R. S., & Rubinfeld, D. L. (1998). *Econometric models and economic forecasts* (4th ed.). Boston: McGraw-Hill.

Pinkerton Global Intelligence Services (1998). *Annual intelligence summary, 1997*. Rosslyn, VA: Pinkerton Global Intelligence Services.

Pound, R. (1930). *Criminal justice in America*. New York: Henry Holt.

Prunkun, H. W. (1995). *Shadow of death: An analytical bibliography on political violence, terrorism, and low-intensity conflict*. Lanham, MD: Scarecrow Press.

Rosenfeld, R., Bray, T. M., & Egley, A. (1999). Facilitating violence: A comparison of gang-motivated, gang-affiliated, and nongang youth homicide. *Journal of Quantitative Criminology, 15*, 495–516.

Rosenfeld, R., White, N., & Phillips, C. (2003). The Effect of Network Ties on Criminal Victimization and Offending. Presentation at the American Sociological Association 2003 Annual Meeting. August 18, 2003.

Russell, C. A., & Miller, B. H. (1983). Profile of a terrorist. In: L. Z. Freedman & Y. Alexander (Eds), *Perspectives on Terrorism* (pp. 45–60). Wilmington, DE: Scholarly Resources.

Sampson, R. J., & Laub, J. H. (1995). *Crime in the making: Pathways and turning points through life.* Cambridge: Harvard University Press.

Schmid, A. P., & Jongman, A. J. (1988). *Political terrorism: A new guide to actors, authors, concepts, databases, theories and literature.* Amsterdam: North-Holland.

Senechal de la Roche, R. (1996). Collective violence as social control. *Sociological Forum, 11,* 97–128.

Sherman, L. W., Gottfredson, D., MacKenzie, D., Eck, J., Reuter, P., & Bushway, S. D. (Eds) (1997). *Preventing crime: What works, what doesn't, what's promising.* Available at www.preventcrime.org.

Short, J. F. Jr. (1997). *Poverty, ethnicity, and violent crime.* Boulder, CO: Westview Press.

Silke, A. (2001). The devil you know: Continuing problems with research on terrorism. *Terrorism and Political Violence, 13,* 1–14.

Skogan, W. G. (1990). *Disorder and decline: Crime and the spiral of decay in American neighborhoods.* New York: Free Press.

Smith, B. L., & Damphousse, K. R. (1996). Punishing political offenders: The effect of political motive on federal sentencing decisions. *Criminology, 34,* 289–321.

Smith, B. L., & Damphousse, K. R. (1998). Terrorism, politics, and punishment: A test of structural-contextual theory and the 'Liberation Hypothesis'. *Criminology, 36,* 67–92.

Smith, B. L., & Orvis, G. P. (1993). America's response to terrorism: An empirical analysis of federal intervention strategies during the 1980s. *Justice Quarterly, 10,* 661–681.

Stock, J. H., & Watson, M. W. (1988). Variable trends in economic time series. *Journal of Economic Perspectives, 2,* 147–174.

Sutherland, E. H., & Cressey, D. R. (1978). *Criminology* (10th ed.). Philadelphia: Lippincott.

Sutherland, E. H., Cressey, D. R., & Luckenbill, D. L. (1992). *Criminology* (11th ed.). Dix Hills, NY: General Hall.

Tauchen, H. V., Witte, A. D., & Long, S. K. (1991). Domestic violence: A nonrandom affair. *International Economic Review, 32,* 491–511.

Turk, A. T. (2002). *Policing International Terrorism: Options.* Unpublished manuscript, University of California, Riverside.

Uniform Crime Reports (2002). *Crime in the U.S. 2001.* Washington, DC: Federal Bureau of Investigation.

United Nations (2002) *Definitions of terrorism.* Retrieved from www.undcp.org/odccp/terrorism_definitions.html.

United States Department of State (2001). *Introduction: Patterns of global terrorism, 2000.* http://www.state.gov/s/ct/rls/pgtr.

Van Dijk, J., Mayhew, P., & Killias, M. (1989). *Experiences of crime across the world: Key findings of the 1989 international crime survey.* The Hague, The Netherlands: Ministry of Justice.

Weisburd, D., Bushway, S., Yang, S., & Lum, C. (2003). The Invariability of Crime at Place: Examining Crime Trajectories for Small Areas in Seattle. Working Paper.

TERRORISM AND EMPIRICAL TESTING: USING INDICTMENT DATA TO ASSESS CHANGES IN TERRORIST CONDUCT

Kelly R. Damphousse and Brent L. Smith

ABSTRACT

Terrorism research has been largely atheoretical and non-empirical. Efforts to examine changes in terrorist conduct, patterns of criminality, or organizational structure have been inhibited by the lack of available empirical data. This paper shows how a rare empirical data set (the American Terrorism Study) can be used to test and expand theories of terrorism. During the early 1990s, many terrorist group leaders, particularly those among the extreme right, began advocating a shift in tactics – to the use of "uncoordinated violence." If implemented, the use of tactics like "leaderless resistance" should be manifested in measurable ways. The current article uses data from the American Terrorism Study to assess whether empirical evidence exists to indicate the utilization of these tactics. The results suggest at least partial support for these expected manifestations. Specifically, terrorist groups became smaller and the number of counts per indictment increased after the advent of leaderless resistance. Other demographic and behavioral changes in the post-leaderless resistance era are noted as well.

Terrorism and Counter-Terrorism: Criminological Perspectives
Sociology of Crime, Law and Deviance, Volume 5, 75–90
© 2004 Published by Elsevier Ltd.
ISSN: 1521-6136/doi:10.1016/S1521-6136(03)05006-1

INTRODUCTION

Terrorism research has suffered from two fundamental shortcomings. First, an immature body of theoretical literature has inhibited the development of testable propositions and hypotheses (Wardlaw, 1989). Second, virtually no empirical data have existed from which to test those hypotheses or propositions that have emerged. Even efforts to examine atheoretical models that purport to assess changes in terrorist group characteristics, organizational structure, or behavioral dynamics have been precluded due to the lack of adequate empirical data (Blumstein, 1996; Crenshaw, 1988; Hoffman, 1992).

This failure comes at an extremely inopportune time. Significant changes in the tactics, organization, and characteristics of members of terrorist groups have reportedly taken place during the past decade (Barkun, 1997; Laqueur, 1999). Among domestic terrorists here in the United States, one of the most notable changes is the shift to what has been commonly called an "unstructured violence" strategy (Barkun, 1994). The strategy is thought to have emerged in the early 1990s among a variety of terrorist groups – from environmental to right-wing extremists and, to some extent, even among international terrorists. Newspaper accounts of "lone wolf" terrorists began to dominate the news, purportedly a byproduct of this new strategy.

Despite media and governmental accounts of the use of these new tactics, little empirical evidence has been available to assess whether the tactic has actually been implemented and to what extent its presence can be determined. Most of the accounts have been anecdotal and typically based more upon conjecture than confirmation.

Tactical changes in terrorist group behavior should be measurable. This should be particularly true of such substantial changes as the shift from a cellular or hierarchical organizational structure to a mandate advocating "unstructured" violence. The focus of this article is to identify hypotheses relative to this reported shift in tactical methods by terrorist groups to determine if these changes can be demonstrated from known sources of empirical data on American terrorism. Specifically, we use indictment data from the "American Terrorism Study" to address this issue.

THE EVOLUTION OF MODERN AMERICAN TERRORISM

The organizational structure of terrorist groups has been surprising consistent over time and region of the world. Contemporary terrorism since the 1960s has experienced only a couple of major strategic shifts in organizational management during this time. The most important of these would have to be: (1) the emergence of the use of terrorism as a tactic in rural revolution in the late 1950s; (2) the shift to urban cellular terrorism in the late 1960s and 1970s; and (3) most recently, the reported emergence of "leaderless resistance" and other forms of "unstructured violence." In the section that follows, we contend that the existence of these models should manifest themselves in verifiable ways. Differences in organizational structure should be evidenced in tactical decisions, target choices, size of conspiratorial groups, and the manner in which arrested terrorists behave at, and following, arrest and indictment.

The Rural Revolutionary Model: No discussion of modern terrorism can begin without acknowledging the contributions of Fidel Castro. The success of his "rural revolutionary model" in overthrowing the Batista regime in Cuba in 1959 shocked the world. Castro's strategy had two major characteristics: First, he used a military model of organizational structure, hierarchically organized in a pyramidal fashion with known leaders at each organizational rank. Second, his strategy followed traditional military tactics which focused upon the capture and holding of terrain. Castro's successful capture of the rural countryside in Cuba allowed him to recruit an increasing number of peasants into his growing army, while isolating and strangling Havana, Batista's seat of urban power. With Che Guevara at his side, he soon became the darling of the oppressed masses, exporting revolution through the "tri-continental conferences" and Soviet aid to remote corners of the world (Sterling, 1981).

Things changed, however, in 1967. Che Guevara left for Bolivia in an effort to export Cuban style revolution there. Guevara's camps and compounds in the Bolivian jungle were quickly identified, however, and the hierarchical structure of his army succumbed to desertion or capture following the identification of subordinate and group leaders. Guevara's failure and subsequent arrest in Bolivia caused shockwaves among the revolutionary left (Janke, 1983; Sterling, 1981).

The Urban Cellular Model: Following the failures of the rural revolutionary model, a new strategy emerged almost immediately. The extreme left had learned that fixed compounds and a hierarchical, military structure left revolutionary organizations open to infiltration and satellite surveillance technology. New theorists, like Abraham Guillen and Carlos Marighella, began advocating a complete shift in thinking – to an urban, cellular model. The goal was to avoid detection by blending in with the urban population, avoid liability for revolutionary leaders, and attack capitalism at its very base – urban centers. Capturing terrain was no longer as important as it had been under the rural revolutionary model. By the 1970s and 1980s, the United States was saturated by leftist groups carrying well-worn copies of Carlos Marighella's *Mini-Manual of the Urban Guerrilla*.[1]

The coalescence of these groups in the early 1980s led Congress and the Attorney General to create new guidelines for terrorism investigations in the United States (Office of the Attorney General, 1983). In 1983, the war on terrorism began in earnest here in the United States. By 1987, federal prosecutions of scores of American terrorists, both left- and right-wing, led terrorist groups to further refine the cellular model. Nowhere was this shift more apparent than among America's extreme right.

Leaderless Resistance and Unstructured Violence: The 1988 acquittal of the three primary leaders of the Identity movement – Louis Beam, Richard Butler, and Bob Miles – along with eleven other Order and Covenant, Sword, and Arm of the Lord (CSA) co-conspirators in federal court gave the extreme right a new lease on life.[2] They had finally learned the lessons that the leftists had learned back in 1967 – rural camps and compounds and a hierarchical structure left terrorist groups open to surveillance and infiltration.

During the next three years, Louis Beam devised a new model for terrorist action – one that he hoped would limit civil and criminal liability for group leaders. In 1992, following the siege at Ruby Ridge, Beam publicized the new strategy in a hastily called meeting of extreme right-wing leaders at Estes Park, Colorado (Beam, 1992). Beam seized the moment that summer to advocate the use of "leaderless resistance" – a strategy that emerged among not only the extreme right but also among Islamic radicals and single-issue terrorists as well.

CHARACTERISTICS OF "UNSTRUCTURED VIOLENCE" MODELS

The use of unstructured violence models was not unique to Beam's pronouncement. Islamic extremists, for example, exemplify the shift toward reliance on unstructured violence through the use of the "fatwa" – a religious proclamation advocating a specific "call to action." Uncoordinated violence strategists advocate strict separation between the terrorist theorists, theologians, and ideologues from the terrorist individuals or cells taking action. Although the ideologues continue to instill the motivation and, to some extent, the training (primarily through written manuals or internet directives), they no longer meet directly with operatives or provide definitive target selection.

Among domestic terrorists opposed to abortion, for example, "hit lists" of doctors and facilities engaging in abortion activities are publicized on websites for activists to view and, it is conjectured, to take further action. Ecological extremists in the United States adopted a similar strategy in 1992 creating lists of "deserving ecological rapists" to be targeted while publicly stating they will henceforth leave the "dirty work to the elves" (Arnold, 1997).

Nowhere has the model been more widely publicized than among the extreme right. Beam's paper on "leaderless resistance" has been widely publicized, read and studied, not only by extremists, but by academicians, students of terrorism, and law enforcement officials as well. Despite this interest, no empirical examination of the concept and its implementation has been conducted. If the model has been implemented, the ramifications for law enforcement and prosecutors are far-reaching.

What are some of the characteristics of leaderless resistance and in what ways might evidence of its use manifest itself? To answer this question, it is important to understand the motivation behind Beam's writing of the leaderless resistance essay. His overriding goal was to avoid a repeat of his indictment on seditious conspiracy charges stemming from the Order and CSA activities in 1984 and 1985. The new model must somehow clearly break the conspiratorial link between the person committing the terrorist act and those in planning or ideological positions within an organization. Beam was adamant about abandoning traditional pyramidal organization, calling it "not only useless, but extremely dangerous for the participants" (Beam, 1992, p. 3). Even traditional cellular models, he maintained, were "dependent upon central direction, which means impressive organization, funding from the top, and outside support" (Beam, 1992, p. 4) and therefore subject to possible infiltration. The only option left was an organizational structure or "non-organization" where "all individuals and groups operate independently of each other, and never report to a central headquarters or single leader for direction or instruction" (Beam, 1992, p. 5).

The most prominent feature of a shift to this model should manifest itself as a decrease in group size. Beam (p. 5) acknowledges this change: "It goes almost without saying that leaderless resistance leads to very small or even one-man cells of resistance." We therefore hypothesized that if right wing extremists have taken Beam's advice, federal criminal cases involving right-wing defendants after 1992 will be characterized by smaller numbers of defendants per case as well as a decline in the number of broad conspiracy cases.

Second, the self-selection process of leaderless resistance makes it necessary for the individual/isolated terrorist to engage in a wider range of criminal activities in preparation for a terrorist act. Unlike the winnowing experienced by the Weather Underground, Beam's faithful would have few others to rely on for psychological, moral, tactical, or materiel support. Those who survive the initial "weeding" process under the leaderless resistance concept find themselves truly alone. As Beam noted, "it becomes the responsibility of the individual to acquire the necessary skills and information as to what is to be done" (Beam, 1992, p. 5). This should manifest itself in an increase in the number of crimes committed by these individuals in preparation for a terrorist act. We therefore hypothesized that the adoption of leaderless resistance would lead to an increase in the average number of counts charged per person when this strategy was employed.

Third, Beam argued that this new strategy would call for a group of hard-core, highly dedicated, and ideologically committed individuals. When criminologists hear the term "commitment," they immediately think of Hirschi's (1969) discussion of commitment as a component of the social bond. It is not our intent here, however, to examine the concept in relation to social control or strain theories. In fact, Beam's use of the term is incongruous with Hirschi's assumptions regarding commitment to unconventional values. It is beyond the scope of this paper to debate the merits of whether a person can form commitments to unconventional or delinquent values. Instead, our purpose is to determine whether those who adopt the leaderless resistance model reflect an increased level of commitment, as defined and purported by Beam.

Beam contended that adopting leaderless resistance would have the effect of "weeding out" those lacking the psychological fortitude to "go it alone" (Beam, 1992, p. 5). The process is similar to that advocated by the Weathermen when they adopted a cellular structure and went underground in 1969 – the goal being to eliminate government informants and the marginally committed.[3] Thus, those who adopt leaderless resistance are much more likely to be committed ideologically to the "cause" than previous right-wing extremists. If so, we hypothesize that a change to leaderless resistance would manifest itself in a variety of ways: a decreased willingness to plead guilty so that the defendant might have an opportunity to voice his/her political position in court; a decrease in the number of defendants who turn "state's evidence;" and, finally, fewer demands by defendants to restrict prosecutor's use of terms that link the individual to a group or ideology (e.g. fewer motions *in limine*). The reasoning for each of these three consequences is depicted in Fig. 1.

A number of other hypotheses could be generated from such a model. Our intent in this paper, however, is not to test each of these hypotheses. Rather, our goal is to demonstrate that the types of hypotheses listed here can be quantified from court case data and empirically tested. To this end, we have selected three of these hypotheses for testing. Among extreme right wing cases, we will examine: (1) changes in the number of defendants per case; (2) changes in the average number of crimes for which each defendant is charged; and (3) the percentage of persons pleading guilty before and after Beam's introduction of leaderless resistance.

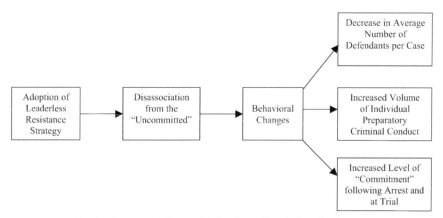

Fig. 1. Proposed Effects of Adoption of Leaderless Resistance.

METHOD

Efforts to study terrorism in America have been difficult at best. Little national level data has been available for analysis (Smith and Damphousse, 1996; Smith et al., 2002). Subsequently, scholars have been forced to collect data independently; using definitions of terrorism that frequently reflect the ideological persuasions of the researcher and employing empirical methods that are suspect at best. The data in the current paper are derived from the American Terrorism Study,[4] a project that began monitoring federal prosecutions of terrorists in 1988 (dating back to 1980) and continues to the current time.

The American Terrorism Study attempts to overcome some of these deficiencies by adhering strictly to the Federal Bureau of Investigation's definition of terrorism.[5] Despite criticism regarding the FBI's application of the definition (see Carlson, 1995, for example), FBI data on terrorism provides the greatest continuity over time. Furthermore, the study ensures adherence to the practical application of the definition by restricting itself to data collection only on cases that occurred as a result of an indictment stemming from a federal "domestic security/terrorism investigation." These investigations, conducted by the FBI in accordance with the *Attorney General Guidelines on General Crimes, Racketeering Enterprises, and Domestic Security/Terrorism Investigations*, "set forth the predication threshold and limits for investigations of crimes . . . in support of terrorist objectives"[6] (FBI, 1999, p. 2).

Once an indictment is issued these cases become a matter of public record, it is retained in the federal criminal case files at the federal district courts where the cases were tried. The FBI then releases information regarding the case number and place of indictment for further data collection by ATS staff.[7] Information on nearly 500 terrorists indicted in federal courts between 1980 and 2002 has been extracted from the dockets, court records, and trial transcripts of cases involving these defendants.

For this analysis, we looked only at right-wing cases, since we expected Beam's pronouncement to affect these groups more than left-wing or international terrorists. These right-wing cases were divided into those occurring prior to Beam's leaderless resistance speech in 1992 and those occurring after the speech. The pre-leaderless resistance (leaderless resistance) sample includes information on some 108 "indictees"[8] from 9 terrorist groups. They were charged with 390 federal counts. The post-leaderless resistance sample includes information on 73 indictees, representing 16 terrorist groups, who were indicted for over 301 violations of federal criminal law.[9] The comparisons rendered in this paper reflect analysis of 691 counts involving 181 federally indicted terrorists from 25 terrorist groups.[10] These sample represent approximately 80% of the population of persons indicted in federal court for "terrorism-related" activities from 1980 to 2002.

RESULTS

To test our hypotheses, we address three main research questions. First, among right-wing terrorists, has the number of defendants per case decreased since the adoption of leaderless resistance – reflecting a decrease in terrorist group size? Second, following the advent of leaderless resistance, have right wing terrorists been charged with a greater number of counts per case than before leaderless resistance – reflecting increased non-terrorism activity. Third, has leaderless resistance caused an increase in the percent of right-wing terrorists refusing to plead guilty – reflecting greater commitment to publicizing their cause? Before we address these issues, however, it is instructive to examine demographic and behavioral differences in terrorists during the two periods.

In Table 1, we present data comparing right-wing terrorists *before* the advent of leaderless resistance and the period *after* leaderless resistance was invoked (1992). First, we examined demographic differences. During the post-leaderless resistance period, the right-wing terrorists were slightly older (41 years of age compared to 39) and there were a higher percentage of right-wing female indictees (11% compared to 6%). The education level for right-wing terrorists in both eras was similar but the right-wing terrorists in the pre-leaderless resistance era earned less per month ($849) than those in the post-leaderless resistance era ($1,232). Due to the small sample size, none of these differences is statistically significant. Since

Table 1. Demographic, Behavioral, and Court-Related Differences for
Right-Wing Terrorist Indictees 1980–2002 (Sample Size in Parentheses).

	Pre-1992 (*N*)	Post-1992 (*N*)	|*t*| value (*p*)
Age at indictment	38.8 (96)	40.9 (71)	1.11 (0.269)
% Female	6% (108)	11% (73)	1.33 (0.184)
Education scale (1–9)	5.1% (88)	5.3% (59)	0.74 (0.468)
Income ($ per month)	$849.1 (90)	$1,232.4 (25)	1.43 (0.154)
Length of membership	42.6 months (54)	24.2 months (18)	2.17 (0.034)
% Leader	26.9% (108)	34.3% (73)	1.06 (0.289)
Average sentence length	221.3 months (71)	264.3 months (59)	0.44 (0.663)

we are examining a population (as opposed to a sample), however, the lack of
statistical significant is not pertinent.

Second, we examined behavioral differences in Table 1. The right-wing terrorists
in the post-leaderless resistance era were members of their terrorist groups for significantly shorter periods of time (24 months) than those in the pre-leaderless resistance era (43 months). Importantly, indicted right-wing terrorists were more likely
to be recognized as a leader in the post-leaderless resistance era (34%) than in the
pre-leaderless resistance era (27%), although this difference was not statistically
significant. While further examination is required, we believe that this increase in
the number of "leaders" is really reflective of the advent of leaderless resistance,
where "general" or "group" leaders have been replaced by "activity" leaders.[11]

Finally, we examined court-related results. Specifically, we show the differences
in sentencing outcomes for right-wing terrorists before and after the advent of
leaderless resistance. Right-wing terrorists in the post-leaderless resistance era
received sentences that were slightly longer (264 months) than those in the
pre-leaderless resistance era (221 months). It is just speculation, but this result
could represent a consequence of the advent of leaderless resistance. The goal of
the federal government in the 1980s was to decapitate the organization. One tactic
was to arrest the terrorists who conducted the act of terrorism and get them to
"turn state's evidence" against the group leaders in exchange for a more favorable
sentence. After leaderless resistance, however, there were no "group" leaders,
even though there were "activity" leaders. As a result, the people arrested for
terrorist acts following leaderless resistance had no one to testify against and were
thus given longer sentences. Of course, multivariate analyses beyond the scope of
this paper would be required to control for other important variables like severity
of offense.

Next, we examine our three research questions. First, we observe the extent to
which federal indicted right-wing terrorist groups became smaller following the

Table 2.   Average Number of Right-Wing Indictees Per Terrorism Trial
1980–2002.

	Pre-1992	Post-1992	Total
Number of cases	31	33	64
Mean no. defendants	3.32	2.21[a]	2.76

[a]$t = 1.30$ ($p = 0.19$).

advent of leaderless resistance in 1992. For this analysis, we examined the number
of right-wing defendants tried in federal trials over the two-decade period. The
results are shown in Table 2. The table shows that there was an almost even split
among the number of cases tried by the federal government before (31 cases)
and after (33 cases) leaderless resistance. The data suggest that there has, indeed,
been a slight decrease in the number of defendants per case following the advent
of leaderless resistance in 1993. Specifically, federal indictments of right-wing
terrorists before 1992 had, on average, 3.3 indictees per trial. In the years following
1992, the average number of defendants per case was 2.2. While the difference in
the average number of defendants during the two eras is in the expected direction
(a 33% decrease), the difference is not quite statistically significant ($p = 0.19$).
The lack of significance, however, is not problematic since we are examining a
population and not a sample. At any rate, the difference would likely be significant
if there was a larger population.

Our second research question examined the number of crimes attributed to
the indicted right-wing terrorists. If leaderless resistance became more prevalent
following 1992, then we would expect that terrorists who lack a centralized
support structure will have to engage in greater "preparatory" criminal acts before
the terrorist act takes place. That is, terrorists who are not part of a network
are more likely to participate in criminal acts like bank robbery to support
their independent terrorist organization. Unfortunately, our data only provide
an approximate way of measuring "preparatory" activity. The ATS data can
show the number of counts presented in an indictment and the number of counts
presented against an individual, but it does not currently present information that
distinguishes between a terrorism-specific offence and a preparatory offense. The
ATS staff began coding these distinctions in October of 2003.

In Table 3, we present data comparing the number of counts against right-wing
terrorists before and after the advent of leaderless resistance.[12] The table shows
that there were 108 right-wing terrorist indictees in the pre-leaderless resistance
era and 73 right-wing terrorist indictees in the post-leaderless resistance era. The
average number of counts listed per indictment was 3.61 before 1992 and 4.12 after
1992. This supports our hypothesis but the difference is not statistically significant

Table 3. Average Number of Counts Per Right-Wing Terrorism Indictee
1980–2002.

	Pre-1992	Post-1992	Total
Number of indictees	108	73	181
Mean no. counts	3.61	4.12[a]	3.82

[a] $t = 0.87$ ($p = 0.39$).

($p = 0.39$). Again, we are examining a population in these analyses, so testing for statistical significance is not essential.

Finally, we examine the extent to which the proportion of right-wing terrorists pleaded "not guilty" at a higher rate in the post-leaderless resistance era than before because of a heightened sense of commitment to the cause. When we examine the plea strategy among terrorists, it is important to observe only those indictees who were actually convicted. Otherwise, we could make the mistake of thinking that a not-guilty plea was a "strategy" instead of a real claim of "not guilty." Thus, in the tradition of the U.S. Sentencing Commission, we examine the "mode of conviction" for American terrorists before and after leaderless resistance (U.S. Sentencing Commission, 2003). In addition, it is important to note that there are many factors that determine the plea bargain process. The process is an exchange relationship that depends on the "capital" each party (defense and prosecution) has to expend. The negotiation also depends on the context in which the bargain is stuck. This "context" can include any limitations placed either side of the negotiation or on historical changes that occur over time. For example, plea bargaining by a prosecutor might be affected by the implementation of sentencing guidelines, changes in plea bargain guidelines, changes in political pressures during an election year, or the perception of a "crime wave."

Trial convictions for federal offenders have decreased steadily since the 1980s. From 1997 to 2001, for example, the proportion of convicted federal indictees who pleaded "not guilty" fell from 6.8% to 3.4% (US Sentencing Commission, 2003). This rate has fallen steadily since the 1980s when the proportion of convicted federal indictees who pleaded "not guilty" was about 15%. This decreased percentage of those pleading "not guilty" is problematic for our hypothesis. We have predicted that there would be a *increase* in the percentage of people pleading "not guilty" following leaderless resistance because the new terrorist actors would be more devoted to their cause (and thus more willing to take their cause public via a federal trial). But, since the proportion of federal convictions that have resulted from a trial has *decreased* over the same time period, any *increases* in the proportion of terrorists that plead "not guilty" might be masked.

Table 4.   Percent of Convicted Right-Wing Terrorists Whose Case was Resolved Via Trial Compared with Those Who Pleaded Guilty from 1980 to 2002.

	Pre-1992	Post-1992	Total
Did not go to trial pleaded guilty	44 (60.3%)	35[a] (60.3%)	79
Found guilty at trial	29 (39.7%)	23 (39.7%)	52
Total	73	58	131

[a] $\chi^2 = 0.0$ ($p = 0.99$).

Thus, if the proportion of convicted *terrorists* who pleaded "not guilty" decreased at about the same rate as it has for the convicted *nonterrorists*, then it would appear that there has not been a change in the post-leaderless resistance era. If the proportion pleading "not guilty" does *not* change at the same rate (it either stays the same or increases), then we can conclude that there *has* been a change in the proportion pleading "not guilty" in the post-leaderless resistance era. This is an example of a condition called *regression discontinuity* (Rossi, Freeman & Lipsey, 2003).

Our data concerning mode of conviction are shown in Table 4. The results suggest that, *before* the advent of leaderless resistance, 60% of convicted terrorists pleaded "guilty" while 40% of convicted terrorists pleaded "not guilty." This finding supports our notion that terrorists are more likely to plead "not guilty" than non-terrorists (i.e. terrorists are more willing than non-terrorists to be convicted at trial in order to gain publicity). Recognize, of course, that prosecutors might also be less willing to "negotiate" with a *terrorist* for political reasons.

According to our hypothesis, we expected to find that an even higher proportion of the post-leaderless resistance terrorists would be convicted via a trial (by pleading "not guilty") because of an increased adherence to their cause. In Table 4, however, we observe that *after* the advent of leaderless resistance, there was no change in the proportion of convicted terrorists who pleaded guilty – 40% pleaded not guilty.

The consistency is remarkable, given the changes that have taken place among modes of conviction for non-terrorist federal offenders. Indeed, the finding suggests that there *has* been some change in the likelihood of a terrorist pleading "not guilty." That is, the proportion of non-terrorists that pleaded "not guilty" decreased for some systematic reason over the past two decades. This unknown reason might be the result of the new federal sentencing guidelines or changes in prosecutorial strategy. At any rate, we would have expected the proportion of terrorists who pleaded "not guilty" to *decrease* for that same systematic reason. That the proportion stayed exactly the same over time suggests an increased willingness to plead "not guilty" (thereby overcoming the increasing tendency to plead guilty among convicted federal offenders).

DISCUSSION

In this paper, we discussed how the lack of empirical data has limited the expansion of terrorism theory testing. To remedy this problem, we proposed using empirical data collected in the American Terrorism Study to examine the effect of Louis Beam's call for leaderless resistance among American right-wing terrorists. Our findings suggest that there have been some changes in American terrorism following the advent of leaderless resistance. For example, right-wing American terrorists have become more demographically diverse than before 1992. Following the introduction of leaderless resistance, right-wing terrorists were more likely to include females, those with higher education, those with higher income, and slightly older individuals.

In addition to these demographic changes, we also showed that some behavioral changes took place as well. For example, more right-wing terrorists appeared to take on the mantel of "leader" than before leaderless resistance was introduced. In fact, this might be considered a small irony, in that the advent of leaderless resistance actually created many leaders, although these new leaders were most certainly leading small packs of terrorists. The call for leaderless resistance also seemed to attract new active followers, since the terrorists indicted *after* 1992 had been members of their terrorist groups for much shorter periods of time (about two years) compared to the terrorists indicted *before* 1992 (three and a half years). Terrorists who were indicted before leaderless resistance also shorter sentences than those sentenced after leaderless resistance. This, however, almost certainly has to do the coincidental beginning of the federal sentencing guidelines that were incorporated during the late 1980s (see Smith & Damphousse, 1998).

Based on our review of leaderless resistance, we attempted to answer three research questions. First, we found that group size (measured by number of defendants in a criminal case) decreased by about one-third following the call for leaderless resistance. This suggests that right-wing terrorists actually began to adopt the leaderless resistance strategy following 1992. There is, however, another possible explanation. It has been alleged that the federal government actively tried to avoid the appearance of on-going conspiracies in the decade before the 9/11 attacks (Posner, 2003). If this was really the case, then we could be observing the manifestation of government activity (in combination with terrorist activity) in the courtroom. The extent to which this is the case is, of course, unknown and perhaps unknowable.

Second, we found support for our hypothesis that terrorists who engage in leaderless resistance will commit more crimes to support their cause because they cannot rely on a network to support their needs. This finding is tenuous, however, because our measure (number of counts per indictee) is not precise.

Third, we addressed our hypothesis that states that right-wing terrorists would be more likely to plead "not guilty" following 1992 because of an increased commitment to their causes. The findings are subtle because of the systematic changes that have been occurring in the federal sentencing system over the past several years, but our findings suggest that the post-leaderless resistance terrorists were convicted via trial at a higher rate than pre-leaderless resistance terrorists, given the underlying decreases in federal trial convictions over the same time period. Thus, we conclude that after 1992, right-wing terrorists appeared to be more willing to go to trial than the right-wing terrorists before 1992. Again, the role that the prosecution plays in the plea bargain process may have impacted this finding (i.e. prosecutors may have been less willing to offer acceptable plea bargain "deals"). In addition, the lack of organizational "leaders" in the post-leaderless resistance era might have resulted in terrorist defendants having less to offer the prosecution during the plea bargain negotiation – there was no one else on whom to turn state's evidence.

The goal of this paper was to illustrate how the use of empirical data can be used to strengthen and extend theories about terrorism. The example used in the paper was the effects of a proposed new strategy by right-wing terrorists. We found support for each of our three hypotheses. The study also points to some weaknesses in the data that will need to be addressed in the future, including a better measure of commitment and the capacity to distinguish between preparatory and terrorism-specific acts. Further expansion and specification of the American Terrorism Study can only enhance its capacity to inform theories about terrorism. Until other terrorism databases become available, the ATS data provides one of the best examples of the kind of empirical data that are needed to test theory.

NOTES

1. The *Mini-Manual* was first published in June 1969 as an underground publication. It can readily be found on numerous websites and in other works. It was reprinted in Jay Mallin (1971).

2. Jury's Verdict in United States v. Robert E. Miles et al. (CR-87-20008), United States District Court, Western District of Arkansas, Fort Smith Division.

3. Taken from *Weather Underground Organization (Weather Underground)*, a 420-page summary of the group's activities prepared by the FBI's Chicago Field Office in 1976. The report is available on the FBI's Freedom of Information Act website at http://foia.fbi.gov/weather.htm.

4. The American Terrorism Study was conducted with the cooperation of the Federal Bureau of Investigation's Terrorist Research and Analytical Center and was sponsored by the U. S. House of Representatives Judiciary Subcommittee on Crime.

5. The FBI defines terrorism as "the unlawful use of force or violence against persons or property to intimidate or coerce a government, the civilian population, or any segment thereof, in furtherance of political or social objectives." *Terrorism in the United States: 1997*, Washington, DC: U.S. Government Printing Office.

6. In response to the September 11, 2001 attack, new AG Guidelines were implemented by Attorney General John Ashcroft in May 2002. None of the cases in the current analysis were investigated under the Ashcroft Guidelines.

7. The procedure for release of the data was evaluated and approved by the Office of General Counsel at both FBI Headquarters and the U. S. House of Representatives.

8. An "indictee" is distinguished from a "person" since a few of our terrorists were indicted more than one time. When providing demographic characteristics, we use the "person" as the unit of analysis; when describing case outcomes, such as whether someone pleaded guilty or went to trial, we use the "indictee" as the unit of analysis.

9. The case involving the Montana Freeman standoff was eliminated from these analyses because the situation did not reflect an act of terrorism and the number of defendants is an anomaly which really had its start prior to leaderless resistance.

10. New cases are being added continuously to the database. By the middle of 2003, information was available on over 430 terrorists. For this analysis, we will restrict discussion to the 344 right-wing indictees for which more complete information is available and "quality control" checks for accuracy have been conducted.

11. The distinction is that "general" or "group" leaders give commands to followers who then conduct the activity. "Activity" leaders lead the small group that performs the activity. The military analogy is the distinction between commanding generals and squad leaders.

12. It would seem appropriate to examine also the number of counts per *case* as well, but those data are not available yet for the pre-leaderless resistance data. As of this writing, ATS staff is currently working to code these data.

REFERENCES

Arnold, R. (1997). *Ecoterror: The violent agenda to save nature*. Bellevue, WA: Free Enterprise Press.

Barkun, M. (1994). *Religion and the racist right: The origins of the christian identity movement*. Chapel Hill, NC: University of North Carolina Press.

Barkun, M. (1997). Changing U.S. domestic threats. Presentation to the International Conference on Aviation Safety and Security, January 13, Washington, DC.

Beam, L. (1992). Leaderless Resistance. Presentation made to leaders of the extreme right, October 23, 1992, Estes Park, Colorado. First published in *The Seditionist*, Number 12, in February 1992; it has been reprinted by scores of websites.

Blumstein, A. (1996). Comments before the Committee on Law and Justice, National Research Council, Planning Meeting on Terrorism, Hate Crime, and Anti-Governmental Violence, 20 March, Washington, DC.

Crenshaw, M. (1988). Theories of terrorism: Instrumental and organizational approaches. In: D. Rapoport (Ed.), *Inside Terrorist Organizations* (pp. 13–31). New York: Columbia University Press.

Hirshi, T. (1969). *Causes of delinquency.* Berkeley, CA: University of California Press.

Hoffman, B. (1992). Current research on terrorism and low-intensity conflict. *Studies in Conflict and Terrorism, 15*(1), 25–37.

Janke, P. (1983). *Guerrilla and terrorist organizations: A world directory and bibliography.* New York: Macmillan.

Laqueur, W. (1999). *The new terrorism.* New York: Oxford.

Mallin, J. (1971). *Terror and urban Guerrillas: A study of tactics and documents.* Coral Gables, FL: University of Miami Press.

Office of the Attorney General (1983). *The Attorney General's guidelines on general crimes, racketeering enterprise and domestic security/terrorism investigations.* Washington, DC: U.S. Government Printing Office.

Posner, G. (2003). *Why America slept: The failure to prevent 9/11.* New York: Random House.

Rossi, P., Freeman, H., & Lipsey, M. (2003). *Evaluation: A systematic approach* (7th ed.). Newbury Park: Sage.

Smith, B. L., & Damphousse, K. R. (1996). Punishing political offenders: The effect of political motive on federal sentencing decisions. *Criminology, 34*(3), 289–321.

Smith, B. L., & Damphousse, K. R. (1998). Terrorism, politics, and punishment: A test of structural contextual theory and the liberation hypothesis. *Criminology, 36*(1), 67–92.

Smith, B. L., Damphousse, K. R., Jackson, F., & Sellers, A. (2002). The prosecution and punishment of international terrorists in federal courts: 1980–1998. *Criminology & Public Policy, 1*(3), 311–338.

Sterling, C. (1981). *The terror network.* New York: Holt, Rinehart & Winston.

U.S. Sentencing Commission (2003). *Sourcebook of Federal Sentencing Statistics.* Washington, DC.

Wardlaw, G. (1989). *Political terrorism* (2nd ed.). New York: Cambridge University Press.

COUNTERACTING TERROR: GROUP DESIGN AND RESPONSE MODALITIES

Michael J. Thomas

ABSTRACT

Through the use of qualitative analysis, this study seeks to analyze the manner by which the United States government categorizes, classifies and responds to terrorist groups. Little or no research has been performed appraising the methods governments utilize in classifying or categorizing terrorist groups, or the modality governments might employ when responding to incidents of transnational terrorism. The underlying assumption is that the current systems employed by the United States government both fail to comprehensively categorize terrorist groups, or sufficiently address the motivating factors behind transnational terrorism. These systems are inadequate for classifying terrorist groups or responding to incidents of transnational terrorism; therefore, new models will be presented.

The purpose of this chapter is to analyze the manner by which the United States government categorizes terrorist groups, and has responded to previous incidents of transnational terrorism. As will be presented and discussed, little or no prior research has evaluated the methodologies used by governmental entities when classifying or categorizing terrorist organizations, or the manner by which governments respond to incidents of transnational terrorism. Through content and conceptual analysis of models currently employed by the United States government, inadequacies will be revealed concerning governmental identification,

Terrorism and Counter-Terrorism: Criminological Perspectives
Sociology of Crime, Law and Deviance, Volume 5, 91–110
Copyright © 2004 by Elsevier Ltd.
All rights of reproduction in any form reserved
ISSN: 1521-6136/doi:10.1016/S1521-6136(03)05007-3

classification and response to transnational terrorism. In hopes of resolving these governmental inadequacies and oversights, proactive methodologies have been developed categorizing terrorist groups, and addressing the underlying motivations for transnational terrorist attacks.

REVIEW OF CURRENT LITERATURE

A review of the literature dealing with transnational terrorism revealed a significant wealth of information; however, very little was applicable to the critical analysis of governmental response or terrorist classification. It is difficult to pinpoint an exact or commonly accepted definition of terrorism, and it is even more difficult to arrive at a commonly accepted definition of transnational terrorism. However, scholars have suggested the following definitions:

- Terrorism is the use or threatened use of force to bring about political change – Brian Jenkins
- Terrorism constitutes the illegitimate use of force to achieve a political objective when [targeting] innocent people – Walter Laqueur
- Terrorism is the premeditated, deliberate, systematic murder, mayhem, and threatening of the innocent to create fear and intimidation in order to gain a political or tactical advantage, usually to influence an audience – James M. Poland (Simonsen & Spindlove, 2000, p. 19)

Just as scholars have difficulty agreeing on a common definition of terrorism, so too does the United States government as many of her agencies employ a wide variety of terminology and definitions concerning terrorism. The FBI uses one definition of terrorism, the Department of State utilizes another far more reaching definition, and still the Department of Defense employs its own organic definition of terrorism. As a result of this variance and for the purposes of this research, the following definitions will apply:

- A terrorist group or organization will be defined as individuals grouped or orga-nized for the intent of participation in unlawful activities designed to intimidate a civilian population or coerce a government, or any segment thereof, in further-ance of political or social objectives.
- In addition, a transnational terrorist incident or attack will be defined as actions perpetrated by a terrorist group or organization against the civilian population or government of a nation other than their own, in furtherance of political or social objectives.

These definitions have been selected based upon other commonly accepted and similar terms put forth by scholars such as Brian Jenkins, Walter Laqueur, James M. Poland and Jonathan White (Ibid.). In addition, these terms were also garnered from terminology utilized by the U.S. Departments of Defense and State, the FBI, and applicable United States federal statutes.

With regards to governmental response to terrorism, a limited number of research studies were uncovered during a review of the available academic literature. These studies made the following contributions.

Bryan Brophy-Baermann and John Conybaere (1994) applied rational expectations theory to Israeli retaliatory policies against transnational terrorism. The authors concluded that only unexpected retaliations bear any deterrent effect towards transnational terrorist organizations. Furthermore, the authors also suggested that transnational terrorists expect a certain or specific level of retaliatory action in response to each attack; therefore, no long term deterrent effect results from a retaliatory based policy (Ibid.).

An earlier study conducted by Walter Enders, Todd Sandler and Jon Cauley (1990), performed a statistical analysis on the impact of the U.S. retaliatory aerial bombardment of Libya in April 1986. The authors concluded that transnational terrorist attacks actually increased in response to the U.S. retaliatory strike, but that the increase was only temporary as the terrorists simply altered the timetable for previously planned attacks (Ibid.).

Todd Sandler, John Tschirhart and Jon Cauley collaborated on a 1983 study of various transnational terrorist hostage situations in which the terrorists appeared open to negotiations with government forces. The authors applied several "rational-actor" models in conjunction with variable constraints, and concluded that a "no-negotiation" strategy is not the best response policy (Sandler et al., 1987). The authors further concluded the efficacy of such policies are dependent upon the levels of risk terrorists are willing to face in order to achieve their objectives (Ibid.).

In 1993, Walter Enders and Todd Sandler co-authored an article in which they applied vector autoregression and intervention analysis in evaluating six intervention policies. The six intervention policies examined were the installation of metal detectors in U.S. airports, resource allocations for the "target hardening" of U.S. embassies, implementation of the Reagan "get tough" policy based upon passage of two Federal statutes, and the 1986 U.S. retaliatory raid on Libya (Enders & Sandler, 1993). The authors concluded that the implementation of these policies did not deter future attacks; rather, it resulted in transnational terrorists simply modifying their attack styles in order to compensate for any imposed countermeasures (Ibid.).

Bruce Jentleson authored a 1991 article in which he suggested the United States has employed three basic foreign policy strategies of deterrence, coercive diplomacy and decisive military strategy. Jentleson defined deterrence as the threat of force, or the show of force "to dissuade an opponent from doing something he has not yet started to do" (Jentleson, 1991). The author explained coercive diplomacy as the use of threats and limited shows of force in order to get an adversary "to stop short of his goal . . . [or] undo his action" (Ibid.). Jentleson further defined coercive diplomacy as a political strategy involving a limited and measured use of force inflicting just enough casualties on one's adversary so as to influence and dissuade him from whatever offensive or egregious action he has undertaken.

Jentleson differentiated coercive diplomacy from decisive military strategy in that the military strategy should employ quick definite military action dispensing with any "threats, diplomacy or subtle modes of persuasion" (Ibid.). The military action should speak for itself, free from any political constraints so that it may accomplish pre-determined objectives and a clearly defined mission. Jentleson also suggested that while any use of a military strategy may entail deterrent or coercive diplomacy characteristics, it is vital that the distinctions be pointed out for analytical purposes (Ibid.). Though Jentleson's article was not entirely on point with regards to this current research, his article was included because it characterized strategies likely to be employed by the United States government when responding to incidents of transnational terrorism.

Aside from specific military actions in Lebanon during 1983 and 1984, the 1986 retaliatory strike against Libya, and the Reagan Administration's "get tough" policies, the articles reviewed do not offer any analysis or examination of governmental activity employed by the United States government in response to incidents of transnational terrorism.

CLASSIFICATION AND DESIGNATION OF TERRORIST GROUPS

As threadbare as the academic literature is regarding the analysis of governmental responses to transnational terrorism, the body of knowledge is even more threadbare when dealing with the categorical classification of terrorist groups. No academic articles were located during a review of the literature on this subject. As a result, the review was shifted to include any government publications or documents concerning a terrorist classification system. As anticipated, very few government documents were located regarding the classification or designation of terrorist groups, and a brief review of those documents revealed the following contributions.

The FBI is the only governmental entity offering any methods or typologies for the categorical classification of terrorist groups or organizations. According to Director Louis Freeh in testimony before the U.S. Senate in May 2001, the FBI only differentiates between domestic terrorism, incidents occurring within the United States, and international terrorism, or incidents occurring outside the United States. Director Freeh expanded further on international terrorism when advising that this transnational terrorist threat can be divided into three categories of "loosely affiliated extremists," "formal terrorist organizations" and "state-sponsors of terrorism" (Freeh, 2001).

Director Freeh testified that the "loosely affiliated extremists" category included groups or organizations motivated by political or religious beliefs, and that the single common element among these groups was their commitment to the "radical international jihad movement" (Ibid.). In his testimony, the FBI Director characterized this movement as embracing a "radicalized" Islamic ideology. This ideology promotes an agenda endorsing the use of violence against the "enemies of Islam" in order to overthrow all governments not ruled by Sharia, or conservative Islamic law (Ibid.). Continuing with his testimony, Director Freeh also advised that a primary tactical objective of terrorist groups in this category was the planning and carrying out of large-scale, high-profile, high-casualty terrorist attacks against U.S. interests and citizens (Ibid.).

Discussing the category of "formal terrorist organization," FBI Director Freeh testified that the category was comprised of transnational organizations having their own infrastructures, personnel, financial arrangements, and training facilities (Ibid.). Director Freeh further commented on how these organizations are capable implementing transnational terrorist attacks on an international basis, and then added that several groups from the "loosely affiliated extremists" category can also be categorized as "formal terrorist organizations" (Ibid.).

FBI Director Freeh further testified that the category of "state-sponsored terrorism" included countries utilizing transnational terrorism as an instrument of foreign policy (Ibid.). In conclusion, Director Freeh advised that the Department of State listed the seven countries of Iran, Iraq, Sudan, Libya, Syria, Cuba and North Korea as state-sponsors of terrorism (Ibid.).

As evidenced above, the only agency within the federal government to offer any categorical approach to transnational terrorism is the FBI. While the State Department may not categorize or classify transnational terrorist groups, the State Department is responsible for the official designation of foreign terrorist organizations (U.S. Department of State, 1999, 2001a, b). Pursuant to the Antiterrorism and Effective Death Penalty Act of 1996, the office of the Secretary of State is the responsible Federal entity for determining what groups and organizations shall be designated foreign terrorist organizations, hereafter referred to as FTO (Ibid.). Any group so designated by the Secretary of State will remain on the Foreign Terrorist Organization list for two years, at the end of which the group must be re-designated as an FTO or they will be automatically removed from the list (Ibid.). A re-designation by the Secretary of State is a determination that the organization is continuing to engage in and remains supportive of terrorist activity (Ibid.).

Criteria for designation as an FTO include that the entity must indeed be a foreign organization, engaging in terrorist activity as defined by appropriate Federal statute, and its activities must threaten the security of United States nationals, or threaten the national security of the United States (Ibid.). In accordance with applicable Federal statutes, an FTO designation makes it unlawful for a person in the United States, or a person subject to the jurisdiction of the United States, to provide funds or other material support to designated organizations (Ibid.). Also, representatives of FTO's are unable to gain entry to the United States, and financial institutions in the United States must block all FTO funds and report the blockage of funds to the appropriate Federal agency (Ibid.). Other contributory effects of a designation include a heightened sense of public awareness and scrutiny concerning terrorist organizations, deterring international donations or support for such organizations, and the designation stigmatizes and isolates FTO's in the international community (Ibid.).

As of October 5, 2001, twenty-eight groups have been designated as foreign terrorist organizations (Ibid.). The most recent addition to the list was that of al-Qa'ida in 1998 following their bombings of two U.S. embassies in Africa, and the Islamic Movement of Uzbekistan in 2000 primarily due to their strong ties and connections to Usama Bin Laden (Ibid.).

PROPOSED MODEL OF GOVERNMENTAL RESPONSE

For over twenty years and without any change, alteration or otherwise meaningful adaptation, the United States has utilized the same decision-making model in response to transnational terrorism. This system has been identified as the Incident Driven Response model, or IDR model, and it fails to suggest any course of action adequately suited for deterring transnational terrorism, or resolving its underlying causes. The IDR model is a reactionary-based system of responses correlating to each individual transnational terrorist attack. That is, for each transnational terrorist attack the government employs a response corresponding to the terrorist action undertaken. A low-level terrorist action calls for a low-level governmental response, and vice versa, a high-level terrorist action calls for the supposedly appropriate high-level governmental response.

The response model proposed in this article, entitled Comprehensive Analysis and Reactionary System (CARS), seeks to resolve the aforementioned inadequacies present in the IDR model. Furthermore, CARS is based upon techniques, principles and practices utilized in problem-solving systems or models. More specifically, CARS is based on the force-field analysis technique proposed by Stephen Covey in his 1989 book, *The 7 Habits of Highly Effective People*. Covey describes this technique as beneficial for the identification of forces both impeding and enhancing goal achievement when using problem-solving techniques in the resolution of deep-seated problems or situations.

The crux of the problem-solving approach is an understanding that any deep-seated problem has underlying causes and issues that first must be elucidated prior to the enactment of any worthwhile or comprehensive solution. This methodology offers a proactive approach rather than a reactive approach (as evident in the current IDR model) in the resolution of problems or other outstanding issues. As such, CARS will not only suggest an adequate retaliatory response to incidents of transnational terrorism; but in addition, it seeks to address any underlying or fundamental issues motivating transnational terrorists.

Reducing both CARS and the force-field analysis approach to their lowest common denominators, a comparison of both systems is presented. The basic steps in CARS are listed, followed by the associated force-field analysis steps:

(1) The overall situation or transnational terrorist incident is reviewed and analyzed to determine the most-likely perpetrator. This initial review of the situation is similar to Covey's statement of the problem as an undesirable situation in a state of equilibrium (Covey, 1989, p. 279).

(2) Then the likely causes or motivations for the perpetrator's actions are determined, and a course of action is suggested in order to seek their resolution. This step resembles Covey's identification of restraining and driving forces, and the devising of a plan to change the equilibrium (Ibid.).

(3) Next, the suggested course of action is implemented or employed. This step refers to Covey's final step of implementing the devised plan (Ibid.).

(4) The now implemented course of action is evaluated for adequacy and successfulness, and a determination is made whether to continue the course of action or implement a secondary course of action. No associated step exists for Covey's force-field analysis (Ibid.).

(5) Finally, the crisis is successfully resolved or a new course of action is required beginning the process anew. No associated step exists for Covey's force-field analysis (Ibid.).

For further explanatory purposes, practical applications of CARS will be presented. However prior to this, a discussion will be presented detailing some common motivations or underlying reasons why the United States has so often become victimized by transnational terrorists. It should be noted the authors have interpreted the aforementioned motivations and underlying reasons for the United States' victimization through transnational terrorism.

The fundamental basis of these motivations is the presupposition that the ultimate objective of any transnational terrorist attack is the downfall of the United States government. In other words, perpetrators of transnational terrorism seek to negate or otherwise hinder the ability of the United States government to affect change, seek resolution or influence crises and other significant issues confronting the international community.

An example of such an occurrence took place in Beirut, Lebanon in the early 1980s. The United States had deployed military forces to Beirut with the expressed mission of supporting the Lebanese Army in their reclamation and pacification of Beirut. Initially it appeared as though the United States was accomplishing their stated objectives, until several transnational terrorist organizations began offensive operations against the United States military and other personnel. Through the implementation of several attacks, these transnational terrorists successfully negated and removed the United States from a position of power and influence over the region. The United States government was taken aback by the high death tolls resulting from these attacks, and subsequently withdrew all military forces from the region and abandoned all support of the Lebanese Army.

In this particular instance, the transnational terrorists accomplished the removal of any influence the United States held over the events occurring in Beirut. Had CARS been employed during this crisis, it might have led the United States government to pursue not only a different military strategy, but different political and humanitarian strategies as well. Below are several different military, political or humanitarian strategies the United States might have employed had CARS been utilized regarding the United States involvement in Lebanon in 1983.

- When reviewing the situation and realizing the warring factions in Beirut were largely being supplied with arms from sympathetic neighboring countries, the United States could have chosen to interdict these international shipments of arms through brute military force or diplomatic efforts.
- Furthermore, realizing these warring factions lacked the military manpower and strength required for sustained military operations, the United States might have called for much more aggressive offensive actions against any warring faction opposing the United States' intervention.
- Another proposed strategy might have dealt with obtaining increased levels of allied Lebanese or Israel forces needed to effectuate a large occupying force. Once assembled, this large occupying force could not only begin offensive

operations against the warring factions, but it would also possess the needed strength and ability to successfully overcome any likely counter-offensive from the warring factions.

- The proposed political strategy might have attempted to broker peace accords amongst the warring factions in Beirut. Levying increased economic and other international sanctions against countries supporting the warring factions might have enhanced this strategy.
- The proposed humanitarian strategy might have consisted of supplying covert or overt aid to any warring faction voluntarily willing to lay down their arms in exchange for a brokered peace agreement.

It is noted by the authors that after nearly twenty years these proposed strategies may appear rather simplistic or easily derived at solutions. However, the authors would counter this supposition by suggesting that the strength of CARS lay in its ability to suggest such logical, rational and seemingly simple solutions to difficult situations.

CARS' ability to quickly suggest comprehensive and legitimate courses of action is its most attractive and powerful attribute when compared to the IDR model. Where the IDR model fails to adequately consider any primary, secondary or even tertiary underlying causes of any given incident of transnational terrorism, CARS easily incorporates such factors into any suggested strategy or response mechanism. Also, while CARS was designed primarily to serve as a problem-solving model for issues related to transnational terrorism, the versatility of CARS enables it to be utilized as a problem-solving model for any crisis, situation or difficult problem.

With regards to a much more relevant transnational terrorist attack, namely the attacks of September 11, 2001, it appears CARS can be applied and effectively implemented. Pursuant to CARS' protocol, a review of the likely perpetrators' motivations is in order. Many underlying issues exist with reference to Usama Bin Laden's disapproval of the United States government and its policies. It has been reported that Bin Laden has been opposed to the presence of all U.S. military forces in the Kingdom of Saudi Arabia and the surrounding region. In addition, it has also been reported that Bin Laden holds views critical of the unparalleled support the United States government provides for the state of Israel. Finally, Bin Laden has been known to hold extremely critical views of any influence the western world, but in particular the United States, may hold within the popular culture of Muslim populations and countries.

It can be argued Bin Laden has mainly addressed his grievances against the United States through the incidents of transnational terrorism that he has financed, supported and perpetrated against United States targets. With this in mind, it is probable that Bin Laden's transnational terrorist campaign has been designed with two main underlying goals and objectives.

The first objective or goal has been the obvious and immediate physical destruction, emotional outcry and psychological anguish resulting from each incident of transnational terrorism. It is believed by Bin Laden that the cumulative results of his sustained transnational terror campaign will negatively affect public opinion and support for the deployment of U.S. military forces in Saudi Arabia and the Persian Gulf region. Furthermore, it is deduced that such a shift in public opinion and support would compel the United States government to remove those forces from the above-stated locales.

The second main goal and objective of Bin Laden's has been to significantly reduce or completely destroy the ability of the United States to continually support the state of Israel with foreign trade, commerce, military and economic aid. The United States has maintained this ability to provide such support to Israel primarily because of a strong and robust economy.

With this in mind, some have argued the transnational terrorist attacks of September 11, 2001, were specifically designed to have an overwhelmingly adverse impact on the economy of the United States. In addition, some claim the same attacks were also aimed at reducing the public's support and confidence in their government's ability to adequately protect the country.

The World Trade Center was a lucrative target for Bin Laden primarily because it housed the headquarters of many high profit and influential commodities, trading and investment firms. It is possible that Bin Laden believed the destruction of these firms would adversely affect the New York Stock Exchange, which would in turn adversely affect the national economy of the United States.

It could be speculated that Bin Laden further assumed the method of attack, namely the hijacking and forced downing of four civilian aircraft within minutes of each other, would absolutely bring consumer confidence in air travel to an all-time low if it were not stopped altogether. This in turn would also severely affect the national economy, which is largely dependent on consumer spending through high volumes of air travel and the shipment of goods by air. The resulting effects on the airline industry would only stand to exacerbate the above stated problems for the United States government. With a weakened economy and a public unsupportive of its policies, some may claim the United States government would be compelled to withdraw its military forces from the Persian Gulf region and also withdraw its support for Israel.

Through the application of CARS, several of these underlying motivations of Bin Laden's support for transnational terror attacks against the Unite States may be addressed. Regarding his attempted impact on the national economy, it becomes vital for the Federal government to ensure that no long-term damage to the economy has occurred.

This can be accomplished through a wide variety of ways including but not limited to:

- Providing for an economic stimulus designed to encourage consumer spending.
- Providing low interest business loans specifically designed to encourage the retention of employees so as to avert mass layoffs, or designed to encourage business expansion so as to create new jobs.
- Providing for sale-tax "holidays" designed to encourage consumer spending, or the issuance of tax-rebates to encourage consumer spending.
- Government provided financial aid to citizens and or industries adversely affected by the attacks.

In reference to addressing citizen fears resulting from the transnational terrorist attacks having occurred within the United States, the Federal government should have a significant display of governmental response capability. In other words, the Federal government should reassure the public that the government has the capabilities to appropriately and adequately respond to this particular incident of transnational terrorism. This could include the issuance of a presidential statement condemning such transnational terrorist attacks and vowing a forceful retaliatory response. It might also include expediting all Federal assistance to any attack site.

At this juncture, it is vital the Federal government respond not only in statements and rhetoric, but also in strong and reassuring actions. The Federal government needs to reassure its citizens that their governmental agencies are fully able to carry on with the business of government, and that their lives will be impacted as minimally as possible. These types of governmental actions will only stand to reassure the public that despite the circumstances, the Federal government is strong, capable and able to carry on.

Finally, regarding what method of retaliatory action to employ, the Federal government should ensure a hybrid combination of criminal justice responses, military responses and diplomatic responses, where applicable. Direct military action must be thought of has only one of many components to any governmental retaliatory action. Military force must be utilized in conjunction with other appropriate strategies and response mechanisms, such as law enforcement and diplomatic efforts. Military action when needed, should be overwhelming; however, it should be never be used as the sole response mechanism to incidents of transnational terrorism.

PROPOSED MODEL OF ORGANIZATIONAL STRUCTURE

As previously stated in this chapter, the current body of knowledge is lacking not only in research examining governmental responses to transnational terrorism, but it is also lacking in research regarding any categorical classification system for terrorist groups or organizations. As a result, a system titled the Terrorist Group Design (TGD) has been designed to offer three general categories of terrorist groups, subdivided by common traits or characteristics shared by categorical members.

Please refer to Appendices A and B for a graphical representation and summary of the TGD. The graphical representation of TGD in Appendix A consists of two parts, the TGD triangle and the Governmental Concerns arrow. The TGD triangle provides a visual adaptation of the three general terrorist categories of Disgruntled, Revolutionary and Dominant. In addition, the triangle represents the total population of terrorist organizations, of which the Dominant category accounts for the highest percentage.

The Governmental Concerns arrow provides an alphabetized list of fundamental issues governments should consider when responding to or initiating any retaliatory actions against terrorist groups. The arrow indicates that the higher a terrorist group progresses up the design and the closer they come to the Dominant category, the more affected governments should consider the ramifications and consequences of any terrorist activity or governmental retaliatory response. In other words, the higher a terrorist group progresses up the TGD triangle and Governmental Concerns arrow, the more likely they are to incorporate significant levels of violence, and they become more of a significant and legitimate threat to public safety.

As mentioned earlier, the TGD encompasses three general categories of Disgruntled, Revolutionary and Dominant. These categories are exhaustive, mutually exclusive and rank ordered. In addition, TGD's categories have been designed as building blocks in order to facilitate any possible progression upward or downward through the categories. That is to say, one individual or group may conceivably enter the paradigm at any of the three categories, and progress or regress their way through another category or categories.

The Disgruntled category consists of lone individuals or very small groups of individuals having a common affinity for a single issue, or point of contention. These single-issue groups are typically enraged over a single governmental action, policy, or initiative to societal change. These small groups very often serve as nothing more than a sounding board for disgruntled citizens; however, amongst their ranks certain individuals exist willing to cross the line from political speech into acts of terrorism. Individuals from this category often act alone or with very few accomplices in their terrorist activities, such as the Oklahoma City bombers Timothy McVeigh and Terry Nichols, or the accused abortion clinic bomber Eric Robert Randolph.

Typically, this category of terrorist is not very successful in their attacks, if they attack at all. These terrorists will often attempt to use explosives, arson or some other viable method of property damage. Usually any type of target hardening, such as the use bulletproof windows or shatter-resistant glass, the installation of vehicle barriers or metal detectors can successfully defend against most assaults.

This category of terrorist is also very susceptible to law enforcement investigations, and it is very likely that any level of investigation will yield successful apprehensions and prosecutions. Military responses or retaliations are not recommended in response to this category of terrorists. These terrorists are largely citizens of the nations in which they reside, and civilized jurisprudence dictates a criminal justice response rather than a military retaliation.

The next category of terrorists is termed Revolutionary, and is comprised primarily of individuals having surpassed the initial Disgruntled stage. Typically, these individuals are prepared and sufficiently motivated to join forces with similarly like-minded individuals, thus enabling the advancement and promotion of their individualized group ideology, philosophy or agenda.

This category will primarily consist of domestic terrorist groups such as hate groups like the Ku Klux Klan, separatist groups like the Republic of Texas or Puerto Rican separatist group Los Macheteros, or radical animal or eco-terror groups such as the Earth Liberation Front. These groups are typically very cohesive in structure, often paying homage to an overriding or ultimate goal or group agenda. The group identity often supercedes the member's, removing any individuality, and replacing it with the group's mantra, ideology or philosophy.

Unlike the Disgruntled category, these groups are often successful in their attacks, usually causing property damage or minor injuries. These groups will rarely cause serious injuries or large-scale death because such collateral damage will likely erode any potential bases of public support for their cause. Their group proficiency and modus operandi of their attacks can be described as novice to advanced.

This is the most divergent category because of the varying levels of group sophistication, training, tactical proficiency and funding featured among category members. This occurs because the category often serves as a "go between" for groups just progressing from Disgruntled, and groups progressing into Dominant. Logically speaking, former Disgruntled groups will not have the group sophistication, training, tactical proficiency and funding of groups progressing into Dominant. Those groups elevating into Dominant are typically well versed in the use of explosives, weapons and group tactics. These groups typically commit various felonies from white-collar crime to armed robbery in order to finance the group's day-to-day activities.

Target hardening of potential targets will not likely dissuade these groups' attacks; however, it can successfully serve to limit any damage or possible injury. Law enforcement investigations will likely prove successful; however, most groups are typically unknown to authorities until the first few attacks occur and responsibility is claimed. Once discovered however, most groups are successfully investigated, apprehended and prosecuted for their illegal activities. Again as with the Disgruntled category, military retaliation is not recommended as most groups will also be citizens of the nation in which they reside, and civilized jurisprudence dictates a criminal justice response.

The final category of terrorist groups is termed Dominant, and these groups pose a significant risk to not only public safety but to national security as well. These groups often perpetrate terrorist activities in their own countries, but they also commit transnational acts of terrorism. These groups seek the total destruction and annihilation of any group enemies; this often includes seeking the downfall of any opposed governmental body or institution.

This category consists of international and transnational terrorist organizations such as Islamic Jihad, Hizballah, Hamas, al-Qa'ida, Palestinian Liberation Front, Revolutionary Armed Forces of Columbia (FARC), and Basque Fatherland and Liberty (ETA). These groups are characterized as being extremely well financed, equipped, trained, indoctrinated and highly organized. This category of terrorist groups poses the most significant risk of any category in the TGD, primarily due to overwhelming group sophistication featured in this category.

These groups are extremely successful in their attacks primarily as a result of meticulous planning, preparation and training. Modalities of attack from this category include but are not limited to hijackings, suicide bombings, hostile takeovers, assassinations, kidnappings, mass shootings, forced downing of aircraft and other such significant terroristic activities.

These groups are extremely proficient in their method of attack resulting from their well-organized and financed training operations. These training operations offer solid periods of indoctrination into group philosophy and ideology for new recruits. Recruits are instructed on a wide variety of tactics from basic to advanced techniques of bomb making, marksmanship, close quarters battle, hostage taking, kidnapping other such useful activities.

The effects of target hardening against this category are largely negated due to the high levels of sophistication, destructive nature and violence employed when these groups strike. These groups typically take into consideration the philosophy of target hardening in the planning phase of their offensive operation. As a result, their battle techniques typically circumvent most defensive measures employed at the attack site, and usually are designed to capitalize on unperceived or unknown weaknesses in the target's security structures or mechanisms.

Law enforcement investigations of this category are somewhat successful; however, most investigations are only conducted in a post-attack environment and often serve only to appease the public's outcry against attack. Pre-attack investigations are extremely difficult because these groups tend to stay underground until they attack. Investigations against this category are typically prolonged, exhaustive, extremely expensive, time consuming and enormously complicated. The end result is typically an investigation yielding such a dichotomy of complicated dealings and sophisticated organizational structure that most juries would be hard pressed to comprehend the vast majority of evidence presented in any potential criminal trial.

The suggested governmental response to groups in this category is a combination of criminal investigations and decisive military action. This hybrid governmental response can be justified because of the significant risk to national security these groups pose to any government they oppose. These groups will typically stop at nothing in order to further their organizational philosophy and mandate. Attacks from these groups may be considered acts of war because they are often financed with foreign funds, supported by foreign governments and/or perpetrated by citizens of foreign hostile nations. Attacks from these groups often target large public gatherings of civilians, governmental offices or facilities or other governmental entity.

Such attacks are clear violations of commonly accepted international treaties designating lawful combatant activities. Victimized governments are able to designate these terrorist actions as overt acts of war. This designation further enables victimized governments to respond accordingly with decisive military action such as aerial bombings, commando raids or other such appropriate military action.

The proposed models discussed by the authors are not intended to fill the void in the current literature concerning governmental response to transnational terrorism and terrorist classification. Rather, it is hoped these recommended methodologies will offer a basis of intellectual thought initiating future research or scientific inquiries into these areas.

CONCLUSIONS

This research inquiry has uncovered a significant lapse in the current body of knowledge regarding the categorical classification of terrorist groups, and the analysis or examination of governmental responses to transnational terrorism. As a result, this article advocates two researcher-developed models intended to minimize the aforementioned lapse in knowledge.

The first model, Comprehensive Analysis and Reactionary System or CARS, is an approach to decision-making similar in design to problem-solving techniques and principles. CARS does not simply propose or suggest appropriate retaliatory actions in response transnational terrorism; rather, it also seeks the resolution of any deep-seated or fundamental issues motivating transnational terrorists.

The second model, Terrorist Group Design or TGD, serves to assign categories or classifications to terrorist groups on the basis of their organizational structure and commonly held characteristics. Under this model, a terrorist group's organizational structure is the primary source of information used in determining the appropriate category to assign. However, the commonly held traits or the support mechanisms of groups in each category can be used to further delineate the appropriate category.

The three categories in this model are exhaustive, mutually exclusive and rank ordered. As such, it is conceivable for a terrorist group to enter the model initially in one category, and progress or regress to different categories resulting from an evolution or devolution in group structure, philosophy, attack methodology or other group characteristics. The Terrorist Group Design can be used in profiling any terrorist group, regardless of previous characterization as a domestic, international, transnational or state-supported terrorist group, organization or entity.

This scientific inquiry proposes a model of governmental response to transnational terrorism that is relevant, appropriate and adequately addresses concerns not presently resolved under the currently utilized retaliatory system. First of all, the IDR model now in use by the United States government has failed time and again at identifying, detecting, negating or adequately responding to the underlying motivations or causations of transnational terrorism. Furthermore, the IDR model is reactive in nature, and as such, forces the United States to remain idle while transnational terrorist organizations train, fund, plan, organize, and eventually carry out any pre-planned or future attacks.

Because of the reactive nature of the IDR model, the United States government, rather than proactively pursuing other courses of action appropriately suited for countering the transnational terroristic threat, must expend significant sums of taxpayer money responding to transnational terrorist incidents on a case by case basis. By replacing this flawed system with the proposed CARS model of retaliatory actions, the United States government can not simply save untold millions of dollars. The implementation of CARS will hopefully enable the United States government to mitigate or even negate the causations of transnational terrorism before such attacks can even occur.

Aside from that, implementation of the suggested CARS model will not simply put transnational terrorists on notice that the United States has successfully adapted and modified its retaliatory actions and policies. The selection of the proposed model will also serve to reassure the people of the United States that their government has not lost touch with the inherent values of self-reliance, economy of choice and autonomy.

As the true costs of the transnational terrorist attacks of September 11, 2001 are still being calculated and adjusted, the United States government stands to misappropriate vast sums of money by maintaining an outdated, unresponsive and costly system of retaliatory actions to transnational terrorism.

With the adoption and implementation of the proposed model of governmental response set forth in this research, the United States government will stand to gain more than just budgetary windfalls. The government will also be calling for adequate, responsive and proactive measures specifically designed to not only respond to incidents of transnational terrorism, but to negate and counter the underlying cases of such terrorism.

The proposed models presented in this chapter are not intended to remedy or comprehensively address the above stated lapse in the body of knowledge. Rather, these models are intended to serve as a basis or foundation upon which future researchers may ultimately manipulate, improve upon or utilize in attempts to further an academic discourse regarding governmental response to transnational terrorism, or the classification of terrorist groups and organizations.

REFERENCES

Brophy-Baermann, B., & Conybaere, J. A. C. (1994). Retaliating against terrorism: Rational expectations and the optimality of rules vs. discretion. *American Journal of Political Science, 38,* 196–210.

Covey, S. R. (1989). *The 7 habits of highly effective people.* New York: Simon & Schuster.

Enders, W., & Sandler, T. (1993). The effectiveness of antiterrorism policies: A vector-autoregression-intervention analysis. *The American Political Science Review, 87,* 829–844.

Enders, W., Sandler, T., & Cauley, J. (1990). UN Conventions, technology, and retaliation in the fight against terrorism. *Terrorism and Political Violence, 77,* 84–105.

Freeh, L., Director Federal Bureau of Investigations (2001). *Threat of terrorism to the United States.* Washington, DC.

Jentleson, B. W. (1991). The Reagan administration and coercive diplomacy: Restraining more than remaking governments. *Political Science Quarterly, 106,* 57–82.

Sandler, T., Tschirhart, J. T., & Cauley, J. (1987). A theoretical analysis of transnational terrorism. *The American Political Science Review, 77,* 36–54.

Simonsen, C. E., & Spindlove, J. R. (2000). *Terrorism today: The past, the players and the future.* Upper Saddle River, NJ: Prentice-Hall.

U.S. Department of State. Office of the Coordinator for Counterterrorism (1999). *Designations by Secretary of State Madeline K. Albright.* Washington, DC.

U.S. Department of State. Office of the Historian (2001a). *Significant Terrorist Incidents, 1961–2001.* Washington, DC.

U.S. Department of State. Office of the Coordinator for Counterterrorism (2001b). *2001 Report on Foreign Terrorist Organizations.* Washington, DC.

APPENDIX A

Terrorist Group Design

Terrorist Group
Design

Governmental
Concerns

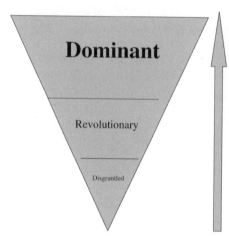

Collateral Damage
Consequence Management
Crisis Management
Incident Response
Investigative Costs
National Security Risk
Public Outcry
Retaliatory Action
Risk to Citizenry
Risk to Infrastructure
Security Countermeasures
Terrorist Effectiveness
Terrorist Fanaticism
Terrorist Funding
Terrorist Lethality
Terrorist Networking
Terrorist Proficiency
Terrorist Violence

APPENDIX B

Summary of Terrorist Group Design

Disgruntled

1. Examples: Timothy McVeigh, Theodore Kaczynski, Eric Robert Rudolph. . .
2. Motivation: Reaction to single issue, typically as a result of single government action, policy or initiative, or to societal change.
3. Success Prospect: Minimal, likely to cause property damage and injury, but seldom causing death (with the obvious exception of McVeigh's Oklahoma City attack).
4. Proficiency: Novice to Advanced, particularly with explosives.
5. Counter Efforts: Extremely successful, very likely that target hardening procedures can defend against most attacks.

6. Investigations:	Extremely successful, very likely that pre and post attack investigations can result in successful apprehension and prosecution.
7. Military Response:	Not recommended, almost assuredly terrorist will be American citizen and criminal justice response is most effective and acceptable to citizenry.

Revolutionary

1. Examples:	Hate groups like the Ku Klux Klan, The New Order, and domestic terror groups like Earth First!, ALF, FALN, FARC...
2. Motivation:	Ultimate goal, one overriding ultimate goal or objective is typically sought by such groups.
3. Success Prospect:	Moderate, likely to cause property damage, and injury, but seldom death because unnecessary death and collateral damage will likely erode current and future bases of public and open support.
4. Proficiency:	Novice to Advanced, particularly with explosives and felonious activities such as armed robbery (such felonious acts often serving to finance groups activities).
5. Counter Efforts:	Successful, however target hardening will not likely dissuade attacks but only serve to limit damage and injury.
6. Investigations:	Extremely successful, however most groups typically unknown to authorities until first attack occurs. Once discovered, most are successfully apprehended and prosecuted.
7. Military Response:	Not recommended, almost assuredly terrorist will be American citizens and criminal justice response is most effective and acceptable to citizenry.

Dominant

1. Examples:	Islamic Jihad, Hizballah, Hamas, al-Qa'ida.
2. Motivation:	Total government downfall, most groups seek total destruction and annihilation of a people or downfall of governmental body or institution.
3. Success Prospect:	Extremely successful, most attacks extremely successful as a result of meticulous planning, preparation and training.

4. Proficiency:	Highly advanced and proficient, groups are extremely well financed offering solid indoctrination and training of basic to advanced skills such as hijacking, hostage taking, close quarters battle skills, and bomb making.
5. Counter Efforts:	Successful, however target hardening will not likely dissuade attacks but only serve to limit damage, injury and death toll. Most attacks occur with innovative assault plans that overcome hardened targets, or attacks made at points exposing and taking advantage of weaknesses in security.
6. Investigations:	Somewhat successful, however most investigations are post-attack and serve only to appease the public's outcry against terrorist attack. Pre-attack investigations of such groups are extremely difficult because these groups often stay "underground" until attacking. Investigations are typically prolonged, exhaustive, extremely expensive and enormously complicated.
7. Military Response:	Acceptable, attacks from these groups may be considered acts of war because they are often financed with foreign funds, supported by foreign governments, or perpetrated by foreigners. These attacks often target large public gatherings of innocent civilians, or government personnel; as a result, appropriate responses include criminal justice and military responses, such as criminal investigations and prosecutions and/or military bombings, raids and assaults.

TERRORISM AND THE FEDERAL SOCIAL SCIENCE RESEARCH AGENDA

Margaret A. Zahn and Kevin J. Strom

ABSTRACT

The understanding of terrorism, strategies to counter it, and an improved comprehension of its consequences requires the work of a diverse range of researchers including social scientists. There has been substantial investment in terrorism-related research since 9/11, yet the extent to which federal funds have been allocated to the social sciences has been less clear. Out review shows that while federal funding for social science research on terrorism has increased since the 9/11 attacks, it remains a small proportion of the federal research agenda. Emphasis in the social sciences has shifted from research in FY2002 on the consequences of the 9/11 attacks to the improved prediction and understanding of terrorism organization and events in FY2003.

BACKGROUND

The nation's ability to prevent and if necessary respond to terrorism concerns many different areas of research. The understanding of terrorism, development of strategies to counter it, and an improved comprehension of the consequences of terrorism requires the work of engineering and computer specialists as well as those in the physical, biological, and social sciences. Since the terrorist attacks of 9/11, the United States has invested increasingly larger sums of money in terrorism-related activities. A total of nearly $49 billion was funded for combating terrorism in FY2003 and nearly $53 billion has been requested for FY2004

Terrorism and Counter-Terrorism: Criminological Perspectives
Sociology of Crime, Law and Deviance, Volume 5, 111–128
© 2004 Published by Elsevier Ltd.
ISSN: 1521-6136/doi:10.1016/S1521-6136(03)05008-5

(OMB, 2003). The FY2004 budget request is 83% higher than the amount funded prior to 9/11, as $29 billion was enacted for terrorism in FY2002. In addition to spending more money on terrorism-related activities since 9/11, budget increases reflect a broadening scope that now includes previously excluded areas such as aviation and transportation security (OMB, 2002).

The sharp rise in overall federal terrorism funding since 9/11 has included a sizable increase in terrorism-related research and development (R&D) activities, generally defined as activities related to scientific discovery or technological innovation (OMB, 2002; AAAS, 2002). About $2.6 billion was enacted for terrorism-related R&D in FY2003 and $3.2 billion was requested in FY2004 (OMB, 2003). The FY2003 budget represents more than double the amount spent on terrorism-related R&D prior to 9/11 in FY2002 (including the FY2002 supplemental funds enacted in September 2001). Overwhelmingly, the majority of R&D funds related to terrorism have been allocated to bioterrorism research, biological preparedness, and technology development. In FY2003, nearly 90% of the R&D terrorism-related funds went to either the Department of Health and Human Services (DHHS) (31%), the Department of Homeland Security (25%), or the Department of Defense (DOD) (23%) (Table 1). The FY2004 budget request shifts funding even more heavily towards DHHS (OMB, 2003). According to the FY2004 budget request, DHSS would receive 51% of R&D funding and DHS 26% of requested funds.

While we know that the federal government has invested substantially in terrorism-related activities, including R&D, the extent to which funds have been allocated to social science research is less clear. There has been much discussion of the need for social science research on terrorism, as an improved understanding of behavior can help predict terrorist events, help governments and communities prepare for and respond to terrorist attacks, and guide the longer-term political, economic, and cultural processes of recovery. Groups that include the National Academy of Sciences (NAS) and the Consortium of Social Science Associations (COSSA) have strongly recommended that the social and behavioral sciences play a more prominent role in terrorism research (COSSA, 2003; NRC, 2002a–c). In addition, shortly following the 9/11 attacks, the White House's Office of Science and Technology Policy (OSTP) established an Antiterrorism Task Force comprised of four working groups, one of which was dedicated to social science issues (OMB, 2002). The Social, Behavioral, and Educational Working Group included representatives from all major federal agencies with social science research capabilities; the group developed an entire agenda of social science research related to terrorism.

A number of federal agencies' missions include the support of social science research. The subject areas supported vary depending on the primary mission

Table 1.　Research and Development Funding to Combat Terrorism, by Agency (FY2002–FY2004).

Agency	FY2002 (Enacted)	FY2002 (Supplemental)	FY2003 (Enacted)	FY2003 (Percent by Agency)	FY2004 (Requested)	FY2004 (Percent by Agency)
Department of Agriculture	$28.0	$52.2	$30.4	1.1	$42.1	1.3
Department of Commerce	$11.7	$7.0	$16.4	0.6	$19.4	0.6
Department of Defense	$259.0	$2.0	$597.0	22.5	$157.0	4.9
Department of Energy	–	–	$19.0	0.7	–	0.0
Department of Health and Human Services	$117.2	$85.0	$831.2	31.4	$1,648.2	51.4
Department of Homeland Security	$110.0	$93.4	$658.2	24.8	$844.0	26.3
Department of Justice	$13.1	$76.1	$173.5	6.5	$174.7	5.4
Department of State	$1.8	–	$1.8	0.1	$1.8	0.1
Department of Transportation	$54.7	$54.0	$3.7	0.1	$3.9	0.1
Corps of Engineers-Civil Works	–	$3.0	–	0.0	–	0.0
Environmental Protection Agency	$2.8	$1.5	$49.7	1.9	$29.0	0.9
National Science Foundation	$228.8	–	$268.5	10.1	$285.7	8.9
Postal Service	–	$9.5	–	0.0	–	0.0
Total	$827.0	$383.6	$2,649.4	100.0	$3,205.7	100.0

Note: The FY2002 supplemental fund ($383.6 million) was enacted in September 2001.
Source: OMB's *Annual Report to Congress on Combating Terrorism, 2003.*

of the agency, with, for example, the National Institute of Justice (NIJ) dealing with law enforcement and justice issues, while the National Science Foundation (NSF) has a broader mission to promote general science that furthers the health, prosperity, and defense of the nation. This chapter discusses sources of social science funding devoted to terrorism and the impact that the 9/11 attacks has had on the social science research agenda. We discuss the funding streams related to terrorism at the agency-level both prior to and after 9/11. Recommendations for future research are also discussed.

TRACKING FEDERAL FUNDING RELATED TO TERRORISM

Thoroughly tracking terrorism funding across federal agencies is not a straightforward task. Many of the difficulties that we faced when attempting to isolate federal spending related to terrorism are summarized in the 2002 U.S. General Accounting Office (GAO) report "Combating Terrorism: Funding Data Reported to Congress Should Be Improved." One obvious issue is that federal agencies cannot always themselves distinguish between terrorism spending and non-terrorism spending. Agency-level funds can be difficult to track in part because activities related to combating terrorism are often funded through budget accounts that also fund other activities. In addition, while terrorism funding for R&D in general is consistently reported in federal budget summaries, there is no systematic distinction for social science-related terrorism allocations.

The information for this chapter was compiled during two different time periods. The post-9/11 portion of this chapter builds on an earlier study that sought to determine the extent to which federal research funding supported violence research, of which terrorism was considered a subset. This earlier analysis was completed as part of a strategic planning process for NIJ's Violence and Victimization Division (Zahn, 2001). For our study, violence was defined as "the use or threatened use of physical force by one or more persons that results in physical injury or nonphysical harm" (Weiner et al., 1997). Terrorism was defined as a form of violence that may be distinguished from other forms in that its aims are political or social change. Despite the numerous discourses on the definition of terrorism, most agree that terrorism is a genre of violent behavior, and that is how it is defined for our purposes. Finally, we define social science-related projects as those that seek to provide a better understanding of the causes, responses and reactions to, and the social consequences of terrorism (e.g. impact on the economy).

In collecting the pre-9/11 data, a search was conducted of existing web databases on federal agency funding for studies of violence from 1997 to June 2001. Websites of different agencies varied in thoroughness of presentation, an issue that should be taken into account, as this could result in projects being omitted from our review. Abstracts from the NIJ, the NSF, CRISP,[1] the National Institutes of Mental Health (NIMH), the National Institute on Alcohol Abuse and Alcoholism (NIAAA), the National Institute of Drug Abuse (NIDA), the National Institute of Child Health and Human Development (NICHD), CDC, and the National Consortium on Violence Research (NCOVR) were used. Information on the focus of each project was coded from the abstracts or titles and became the basis for the data analyses. Because not all of the websites provided information on funding, the number of studies funded is used as a proxy for the level of federal support for specific topics.

For the updated post-9/11 review we conducted a search of web databases for agencies associated with social science funding, including NSF, NIJ, CDC, DHS, and CRISP, and searched project titles and abstracts on the keyword "terrorism" for FY2002 and FY2003. We then reviewed the contents of the abstracts to establish whether these projects represented social science-related research. Several agencies did not disclose project funding information.

We fully acknowledge that our review of social science funding of terrorism has a number of limitations. Several agencies did not provide the amount of money involved in either the general solicitation or the specific funded projects. In addition, solicitations could support a range of research topics, some of which were terrorism-related and some of which were not. Even for those agencies that provided funding information, we cannot guarantee that our accounting of terrorism funding is exhaustive. Many of the problems faced with tracking funding related to terrorism are due to the issues that we previously discussed. This includes that fact that there is no detailed breakout of terrorism funding by federal agencies, much less a systematic breakout of terrorism funding in the social sciences (GAO, 2002). Furthermore, the definitions we apply both for terrorism and social science research could impact our findings. With these limitations considered, we recommend that readers view our summary of terrorism research in the social science as an approximation and not a comprehensive account of all funds spent on these activities. Nonetheless, we believe that the contextual findings we present can illustrate how federal funding has changed since 9/11, as well as help define areas of need for social science researchers.

SOCIAL SCIENCE FUNDING OF TERRORISM PRIOR TO 9/11

Findings from the pre-9/11 analysis showed that there were 603 studies of violence funded by federal agencies between 1997 and 2001 (Zahn, 2001). NIJ

Table 2.   Number of Violence Related Projects Funded by Federal Sources, 1997 to June, 2001.

Type of Violence		Funding Source								Grand Total
		CDC	NCOVR	NIAAA	NICHD	NIDA	NIJ	NIMH	NSF	
General	N	4	30	18	3	27	39	40	20	181
Family, domestic, & child abuse	N	23	1	12	6	12	82	31	9	176
Violence against women/sex crimes	N	9	0	2	2	5	29	12	1	61
Gun	N	8	2	0	0	0	14	0	1	25
School	N	0	0	0	0	0	2	1	1	4
Youth/gang	N	24	10	6	16	21	21	16	2	117
Police	N	0	0	0	0	0	7	0	0	7
Workplace	N	1	0	0	0	0	2	0	0	3
Hate	N	0	0	0	0	0	1	0	0	1
Political	N	0	0	0	0	0	0	4	11	15
Terrorism	N	0	0	0	0	0	0	0	0	0
Other	N	0	5	0	0	1	2	3	2	3
Total	N	69	48	38	27	66	199	107	47	603

Source: Adapted from NIJ Strategic Plan, Contract No. 535300.

funded the largest number ($n = 199$), followed by the NIMH and the CDC (Table 2). The majority of the research funded was basic, as opposed to evaluation or policy research. Victims were studied more often than offenders, and studies of interpersonal violence far outweighed those of collective violence. Studies of U.S. cities, rather than other geographic entities, predominated, and most studies were nationally based, with few including international dimensions. The topic areas were dominated by general studies, domestic violence, and family violence, followed by studies of youth violence. There were relatively few studies of hate crimes. *And, there were no studies of terrorism.* In summary, past federal funding has not focused on terrorism, and, while relevant work certainly exists in the social sciences, terrorism was not a focus of social science research funding entities from 1997 through June 2001.[2]

FEDERAL FUNDING OF RESEARCH ON TERRORISM POST-9/11

This section discusses, through profiles of federal agencies that historically fund social science research, how terrorism funding has changed in the social sciences since 9/11. These agencies include NSF, NIJ, CDC, NIH, and the newly created Department of Homeland Security (DHS).

National Science Foundation (NSF)

As the nation's primary basic research funding agency, NSF shares a broad mission that seeks to "to promote the progress of science; to advance the national health, prosperity, and welfare; and to secure the national defense." Since 9/11, NSF has expanded the scope in a number of program areas to include terrorism-related research initiatives. For example, one research solicitation in NSF's Social, Behavioral and Economic Sciences (SBE) Directorate that has looked at the effects of extreme events and shocks to social systems now includes terrorism within its purview. The vast majority of the $268.5 million funded for NSF terrorism-related R&D in FY2003 was not in the area of social science research (OMB, 2003). Rather, these funds were allocated to combating bioterrorism in the areas of infectious diseases and microbial genome sequencing, as well as to R&D or critical infrastructure protection.

Based on our review of the NSF Awards Database, we found that NSF awarded approximately $21 million to terrorism-related social science research in FY2002 and FY2003 ($14 million in FY2002 and $7 million in FY2003). Interestingly, there was a shift from projects investigating the consequences of the 9/11 attacks in FY2002 (i.e. social, behavior, psychological impacts) to projects seeking to improve our basic understanding of terrorist behavior as well as our ability to predict and/or detect terrorist events. These prediction and detection projects typically utilized technological tools and other statistical modeling procedures.

NSF has been creative in using grants from numerous research directorates to fund a diverse range of terrorism research (NSF, 2002). Using Small Grants for Exploratory Research (SGER), they were one of the first federal agencies to generate social science research immediately following the 9/11 attacks. While SGER's are small in size (none exceed $100,000), they are custom-made for the kind of quick response required in situations of urgency, when data must be collected quickly. NSF's SBE Directorate awarded 10 SGERs to social scientists in either late 2001 or early 2002, including grants for social science researchers to conduct post-disaster assessments at the attack sites (COSSA, 2002). Other funded research included studies in law and social science, political science, sociology, science and technology, risk management, social psychology, geography and regional sciences, and human cognition and perception. For example, one SGER study in geography found that the 9/11 tragedy prompted people to have second thoughts about where they want to live, even if that residence is not in New York

City or Washington, DC. These researchers found that the terrorist events led people to become more interested in living in low-density suburbs or other communities away from a central city. Another study focused on the psychological impact of the U.S. anthrax attacks and found that the exhaustive media coverage of the incidents made Americans feel substantially more vulnerable to contracting the disease than they actually were. The result was extreme overuse of Cipro and other antibiotic prescriptions, which in turn depleted drug supplies.

In FY2003, NSF's SBE Directorate budget request included $3 million for research on extreme events and shocks to social systems, including research into their causes and aftermaths and their implications for risk analysis and decision-making. Terrorism – including its economic and social consequences on markets and organizations – and the formulation of beliefs, trusts, and decision-making is included within the scope of this research. NSF has also provided a number of terrorism grants that, while not solely social science-focused, have direct implications for social science research. NSF's Directorate for Computer, Information Science, and Engineering funded several projects that employed advanced computer modeling as a platform for studying complex problems such as the relationship between state stability and terrorism. Researchers at the University of Pennsylvania received a $300,000 NSF grant to employ a new simulation technology in order to identify patterns of variability and similarity associated with specific types of countries, situations, and threats. This research attempts to increase the usability of complex computer applications by non-computer programmers, including social scientists. In addition, NSF technology research included $6 million to support data mining techniques related to homeland security and several projects that study techniques for identifying sparse events in high-speed stream data, useful in both network security and the monitoring of terrorist activity.

National Institute of Justice (NIJ)

NIJ is the research arm of the U.S. Department of Justice (DOJ) and the primary funding agency for criminal justice research. Prior to 9/11, NIJ's funding of terrorism-related projects was mainly related to the establishment of terrorism research centers following the Oklahoma City attacks of 2000. This included the Institute for Security Technology Studies (ISTS) at Dartmouth College and the Oklahoma City National Memorial Institute for the Prevention of Terrorism (MIPT), which both opened in 2000 with support from NIJ. ISTS serves as a national center for cyber security and counterterrorism research, development, and analysis. The institute focuses heavily on developing technologies that protect computer networks, the Internet, and other information infrastructures, including research on predicting cyber attacks. MIPT supported initiatives have included projects to construct domestic and international terrorism incident databases, as well as investigations on the psychological effects of terrorism and the identification of useful technologies for first responders.

Similar to NSF, NIJ has used a variety of different types of solicitations to fund social science research on terrorism. In FY2002, NIJ made four awards to social science research on terrorism for slightly under $1 million, including the support of a National Academy of Sciences (NAS) Roundtable on terrorism and the social and behavior sciences. The three funded research studies included a project by Gary LaFree and Laura Dugan of the University of Maryland, to analyze and code data from the Pinkerton Global Intelligence Service, an Interpol database of 74,000 terrorist incidents from 1970 to 1997. The goal of this study is to better understand the impact of economic, political, and social variables on detailed terrorist events. Also funded were a study of local law enforcement and their response to terrorism and a study of the link between terrorism and money laundering, with the first study investigating the responses of the New York and Arlington police departments following the 9/11 attacks. The latter study investigated the role money laundering plays in terrorist organizations, including the role the Informal Value Transfer Systems (IVTS) had in funding groups such as Al Qaeda. This study recently reported that terrorist groups use additional mechanisms, such as trade diversion, to ensure the funding of their operations.

In FY2003, NIJ funded nearly $5 million in social science research related to terrorism. This was highlighted by NIJ's first solicitation dedicated solely to the study of terrorism, which requested proposals in two general research areas. The first area called for investigations of the similarities/differences between transnational organized crime and international terrorists. The second area sought to produce findings with immediate impact on public safety and public policy, including issues impacting law enforcement and the criminal justice system in responding to terrorism, links between terrorism and other forms of crime, and the use of nonclassified information to inform the criminal justice system about terrorist groups. Overall, 14 grants were funded using FY2003 funds totally over $4.3 million (see "2003 Awards" at http://www.ojp.usdoj.gov/nij/funding.htm).

The FY2003 grants were almost evenly divided between projects that aid understanding and prediction of terrorism and those geared to facilitate system preparedness to counter future attacks. One group of funded projects was related to the improved understanding of the motives, activities, and predictive indicators of terrorism incidents. These included research on the links between international crime and terrorism, including financial ties; the relationship between white collar crime and terrorism; tactical and operational learning of terrorist groups; and pre-incident indicators of terrorist events. The second set of projects was concerned with criminal justice systems. These included investigations of the response of local prosecutors to terrorism, the impact of terrorism on state law enforcement and criminal justice systems, the coordination between law enforcement and public health agencies, the role of private security in protecting against terrorism, and the protection of critical infrastructures, such as ports of entry and the American agricultural system.

Centers for Disease Control and Prevention (CDC)

CDC is more heavily geared toward evaluation than basic research. One of CDC's primary roles has historically been to recognize and respond to epidemiological health outbreaks, including infectious diseases. CDC has invested increasingly larger proportions of funding to bioterrorism-related activities (CDC, 2003). Since 9/11, CDC's research funds have been largely dedicated to boost CDC's laboratory security against bioterrorism and to fund CDC research on bioter-rorism threats. These include cooperative agreements to upgrade state and local public health jurisdictions' preparedness for and response to bioterrorism, other outbreaks of infectious disease, and other public health threats and emergencies. In addition, CDC's Center for Injury Prevention and Control, which has funded numerous projects on violence-related injuries, provides information and tools for mass trauma events, which includes large-scale natural disasters and terrorist attacks. If a mass trauma were to occur, CDC would assist state and local health departments in responding. CDC also provides information and tools to help the public, public health professionals, and clinicians prepare for and respond to mass trauma.

CDC also funds several large surveillance system projects that seek to use information systems in hospitals, laboratories, and other public health entities to identify events such as infectious disease outbreaks and bioterrorism events (CDC, 2003). A major goal of these public health surveillance efforts is to develop dual-use systems that can monitor both bioterrorism and other public health-related emergencies (e.g. SARS). CDC is working with state and local health departments as well as information systems contractors in developing real-time surveillance and analytic methods. These include systems that attempt to monitor special events, such as the CDC Enhanced Surveillance Project (ESP), which monitors hospital emergency department data to establish syndrome baseline and threshold levels. Statistical models have been developed that can identify deviations in emergency department visits for specific types of symptoms. These models have been tested at major events that include the World Trade Organization meeting in Seattle, the Republican and Democratic National Conventions in Philadelphia and Los Angeles, and the Super Bowl in Tampa, Florida.

Finally, CDC is a partner in the recently implemented World Trade Center Health Registry, an unparalleled collaborative effort that involves the New York City Department of Health and Mental Hygiene and CDC's Agency for Toxic Substances and Disease Registry (ATSDR). The Health Registry coordinates activities with other entities including the New York School System, the New Jersey Department of Health, and numerous medical centers and universities. The goal of the project is to better understand the health effects of exposure to smoke, dust, and debris from the collapse of the World Trade Center. By focusing on the people most heavily exposed, it will help identify patterns of illness and recovery that, in turn, will help all exposed individuals and their doctors. When completed, it will be the largest registry of its kind, with between 100,000 and 200,000 people enrolled. RTI International received $15 million in funding to collect the data and compile it into forms that are useful for the public, health care providers, and health researchers.

National Institutes of Health (NIH)

NIH has traditionally not funded social science research on terrorism. But through a FY2002 grant program NIH funded several studies that assessed the psychological impact of both the 9/11 terrorist attacks and the U.S.-based anthrax attacks. The goal was to better understand the nature of problems people experienced after the attacks, the types of service assistance they sought, and the readiness of health and human services delivery systems. Specifically, CRISP identified 3 NIH studies that involved social science research, all funded in FY2002. These included an assessment of the behavioral and psychological effects of the 2001 anthrax attacks, an evaluation of the preparedness of health services among New York City residents, and the identification and development of useful training protocols for first-responders.

In addition, NIH's National Institute on Alcohol Abuse and Alcoholism (NI-AAA) has encouraged funded investigators as well as future applicants to expand existing or new research projects to include challenges presented as the result of terrorism and bioterrorism events (NIH, 2003). These challenges could include changes in alcohol or drug use among certain populations, changes in chemical dependence and rates of relapse, and investigations of potential interactions between alcohol and antibiotic agents commonly used to combat bioterrorism. NIAAA has indicated that grant supplements with a maximum of $100,000 will be considered for terrorism-related investigations or meaningful extensions to existing grants.

Department of Homeland Security (DHS)

While the established agencies are addressing social science issues, we would be remiss if we failed to discuss the new Department of Homeland Security (DHS) and the potential impact this agency could have on social science funding. It is clear that DHS will have a wide range of responsibilities related to homeland defense and terrorism. Yet the extent to which science and technology will be funded under DHS, specifically social science research, remains unclear.

The Science and Technology (S&T) Directorate will become the primary research and development arm of DHS, seeking to organize scientific and technological U.S. resources related to the prevention or mitigation of terrorist events. Major areas of emphasis in the S&T Directorate will include the examination of the nation's vulnerabilities, continued testing of U.S. security systems, and a comprehensive evaluation of threats and weaknesses. The S&T Directorate, which will have an FY2004 budget of $874 million up from $521 million in FY2003, will fund several social science-related initiatives including the establishment of university-based research centers across a range of R&D areas (AAAS, 2003; OMB, 2003). These initiatives include risk-based economic modeling of the impact and consequences of terrorism, behavioral research on terrorism and counterterrorism measures, public safety technology, agro-terrorism countermeasures, and R&D of response technologies and operations (DHS, 2003). The first Homeland Security grant is expected to be awarded in November 2003, with funding estimated at $12 million (3 years at between $2 million and $4 million a year) for purposes that include risk-based modeling, with a heavy emphasis on economic aspects (DHS, 2003). The goal is to guide policy makers by providing tools for modeling and simulation that can support risk analysis and the development of responses to attacks on the nation's critical infrastructure.

CONCLUSIONS

The survey of information on federal funding for social science research on terrorism and counterterrorism shows, first, that support for such research has increased substantially since the 9/11 attacks. However, since there was no funding for such work in the 2 years immediately preceding the attacks, any increase is substantial. Second, while some of the increase stems from new funding, much of the work results from reallocation of existing funds to meet this new purpose. Further, it is difficult to track the exact allocations to social science research, especially given the current sources of public information.

While the federal research agenda on terrorism is still, in a sense, being developed, at present it is fair to conclude that the vast majority of federal funding for research on terrorism is not social science-related. Specifically, based on our post-9/11 review of agency-level funding related to terrorism, we have found that that a very small percentage of federal terrorism R&D funding was directed to the social sciences. Of the approximately $2.6 billion allocated to terrorism-related R&D in FY2003, we estimate that less than $40 million was used to fund research in the social sciences, including projects supported by NIJ, NSF, DHS, and CDC. Approximately $14 million of these FY2003 funds were allocated to the university-based Homeland Security Centers of Excellence, to be funded by DHS's Science & Technology division. NIJ and NSF were the largest contributors to general research in terrorism. NIJ funded 14 projects in FY2003 for approximately $4.6 million, highlighted by its first terrorism-only solicitation in September 2003. NSF, in part because of its organizational structure and larger budget, has funded the most diverse array of social science terrorism research, beginning with a series of small grants immediately following the 9/11 attacks. Overall, NSF funded about $14 million in social science terrorism research in FY2002 and approximately $7.2 million in FY2003. DHS possesses the budget and clout to have a potentially significant impact on social science research in this area, although the level of that impact remains uncertain.

Interestingly, in addition to NIJ, NSF, and DHS, another major source for terrorism-related social science funding is the MacArthur Foundation (MacArthur Foundation, 2002). In January 2002, the MacArthur Foundation awarded 29 grants totaling more than $5 million to address issues related to the 9/11 attacks and their aftermath. The grants were awarded in three categories: (1) information and analysis; (2) strengthening the U.S. and the world's response to terrorism and understanding its underlying causes; and (3) civil liberties, constitutional guarantees, and adherence to international law. In addition, the MacArthur Foundation announced in August 2003 that it will commit over $50 million over the next 6 years to U.S. and international scientists and researchers to help reduce the threat of weapons of mass destruction (MacArthur Foundation, 2003).

Opportunities for terrorism research in the social sciences, then did increase after 9/11, although these increases are miniscule compared to other terrorism research funding. With the emergence of DHS, these opportunities may continue to grow, opening up more research opportunities in fields such as criminology, sociology, and political science. The White House's OSTP The Social, Behavior, and Educational Working developed three major areas of emphasis for future social science research on terrorism – (1) prediction and detection, which can include investigations into the root causes of behavior, as well as research on the development and assessment of technologies for improved prediction and detection of events; (2) consequences; this may involve studies dealing with effective response strategies to attacks as well as studies that provide a better understanding of the costs of terrorism (e.g. psychological, social, economic) as well as effective interventions to mitigate against negative consequences; and (3) prevention and preparedness, which includes first-responder activities as well as the development of a solid infrastructure that provides (and improves) the tools and data essential to social science research. We have found that emphasis in the social sciences has shifted from research on the consequences of the 9/11 and anthrax attacks in FY2002 to an increasing emphasis on the improved prediction and understanding of terrorist organizations and events. Studies related to coordination and preparedness of first-responder agencies also appear to be on the rise.

There is obviously much work for criminologists and other social scientists within (and across) these general research areas (see Rosenfeld, 2002). Criminologists are well positioned to handle research on the links between terrorism and transnational organized crime, the modus operandi of terrorist groups, and the various federal, state, and local criminal justice system responses to terrorist groups. Opportunities abound here, including new roles in working with state and local law enforcement and criminal justice systems. Researchers are also needed to assess how specific policies and agency restructuring impacts the different segments of the public, including measures of trust and confidence of the general public. Increased attention on terrorism may also force justice systems to collaborate on an international scale. In this respect, terrorism may in fact help globalize criminology, reducing its nationalistic focus.

For research on terrorism to improve, a number of issues and obstacles must be overcome. Obviously one of the first things that needs to improve is the quality and quantity of data on terrorist-related incidents and terrorist groups, as well as on the reactions of people (and agencies) to terrorist actions. To this point, social science, and criminology in particular, has relied heavily on data sources such as Census data, the Uniform Crime Reports (UCR), the Supplementary Homicide Reports (SHR), and the National Crime Victimization Survey (NCVS). The research partners of criminologists and other social scientists have typically not been the State Department, DOD, or DHS. These departments associated with national security have typically used different databases and impose special requirements on researchers. We should seek to develop new databases for research on terrorism such as those of private security agencies (now being investigated for the first time by Gary LaFree and Laura Dugan). Another researcher, Robert Pape from the University of Chicago, constructed an events database of every suicide bombing and attack from 1980 to 2001 (Pape, 2003). There are certainly other databases that are still unknown to us (or that could be constructed) but are potentially highly useful. Toward this end, NIJ has commissioned a study at the Library of Congress to assess the databases worldwide that social scientists, especially criminologists, can access for studies on terrorism. That report, or compilations like it, could be of great assistance to the entire research community.

Second, the size of the social science researcher pool needs to increase in the area of terrorism. This should include individuals with expertise that augments traditional criminology, from fields such as geography, information technology, history, foreign languages, and accounting. At the very least, criminologists need be willing to assemble and work in teams that include individuals with expertise not usually associated with criminological work. Our methodological and statistical approaches will also have to be augmented by skills and creative approaches if we want to address one of the most salient issues faced by our society today. It is imperative that criminologists and other social scientists evolve as the field of study does. One potential area for collaboration is the integration between social scientists and information technology research; many studies are likely to focus increasingly on technological detection and surveillance devices. Despite the fact that human intelligence is perhaps the most important defense against terrorism, research dollars are being heavily invested in technology development. For example, some of the projects funded under NSF utilize cutting-edge technologies in order to better predict, and ultimately better understand, the factors that contribute to ethnic conflict, terrorism, and related events. Just as geographic information system (GIS) technology has emerged as a vital tool for criminologists, technologies can emerge that help social scientists better explain, model, prepare for, and respond to terrorism events. An example of this is statistical modeling, which allows for better prediction of events and situations. Another example is simulation models that attempt to predict the responses of populations (down to the individual level), which can be used to model likely behavior during terrorism incidents (e.g. EpiSims, developed at Los Alamos Laboratory). Applications such as these can have multiple uses including training for first responders and planning for state and local policy makers.

Third, we need to increase the use of comparative studies in terrorism research. Comparative studies are excellent sources for improving our knowledge of both the characteristics and dynamics of terrorism. They are also highly useful in identifying which strategies and procedures have been successful and which have been unsuccessful in countries with lengthy experience with terrorism (e.g. Israel). In regard to structure, comparative studies could provide structural typologies of terrorist organizations. Estimates of organizational effectiveness and/or vulnerability according to type could also be generated. In addition, comparative research could be used to identify best practices for improving cross-agency coordination at multiple levels of government. For many of these purposes, comparative studies are ideal for learning from other countries' experiences and identifying procedures that have worked and those that have not worked. Naturally, one would have to take into account the differing organizational structure of other countries and the likelihood that specific procedures could work in the U.S. However, while the U.S. has dealt with imminent terrorist threats in recent years only, other countries, such as Israel and the UK, have had to handle these types of events and develop reaction/response protocols for many years.

There is no denying that terrorism research is an important area of study for social science research. Violence has never been off the federal research agenda, although international and domestic terrorism, as a form of violence, will now capture some of the federal research budget. We have attempted to describe how terrorism research has been supported by federal agencies, yet the course of future social science funding remains uncertain, especially with the creation and yet to be defined role of DHS in relation to the social sciences. It does appear that the vast majority of future funding on terrorism research will not be social science focused. Rather, funding will continue to focus on technological development and counter-terrorism features, especially bio-terrorism. Whatever the outcome of departmental reorganization and science advisors' budgetary recommendations, it is clear there will continue to be a federal research agenda on terrorism. It remains for us to grasp the important opportunities and challenges presented.

NOTES

1. The Computer Retrieval of Information on Scientific Projects (CRISP) is a searchable database of federally funded biomedical research projects. The database, maintained by the National Institutes of Health (NIH), includes projects funded by the NIH, Substance Abuse and Mental Health Services (SAMHSA), Health Resources and Services Administration (HRSA), Food and Drug Administration (FDA), Centers for Disease Control and Prevention (CDC), Agency for Health Care Research and Quality (AHRQ), and Office of Assistant Secretary of Health (OASH).

2. The only exceptions to this were studies associated with the Institute for Security Technology Studies (ISTS) at Dartmouth College and the Oklahoma City National

Memorial Institute for the Prevention of Terrorism (MIPT), which both received funding following the Oklahoma City bombing as a special appropriation.

REFERENCES

American Association for the Advancement of Science (AAAS). R&D Budget and Policy Program (2002, August 22). Bush Administration Seeks $2.9 Billion for Counter-Terrorism R&D in FY 2003. Washington, DC. Retrieved August 12, 2003, from http://www.aaas.org/spp/rd/terr03p.htm.

American Association for the Advancement of Science (AAAS). R&D Funding Update (2003, September 24). New DHS Receives Final Portfolio of $1.05 Billion. Washington, DC. Retrieved October 2, 2003, from http://www.aaas.org/spp/rd.

Centers for Disease Control and Prevention (2003). Emergency Preparedness & Response. Retrieved August 15, 2003, from http://www.bt.cdc.gov/.

Consortium of Social Science Associations (COSSA) (2002, June 24). *COSSA Washington Update, 21*(12). Retrieved August 26, 2003, from http://www.cossa.org/volume%2021/21.12.html.

Consortium of Social Science Associations (COSSA) (2003). *COSSA Washington Update, 22*(15). Retrieved August 26, 2003, from http://www.cossa.org/volume%2022/22.15.pdf.

Department of Homeland Security (DHS) (2003). Research and Technology: Cutting Edge Technology to Protect America. Retrieved August 5, 2003, from http://www.dhs.gov/dhspublic/theme_home5.jsp.

MacArthur Foundation (2002). MacArthur Foundation Completes Grantmaking Through Special Fund Related to Terrorist Attacks and Their Aftermath Announces $5.1 Million in Support." Retrieved from http://www.macfound.org/announce/press_releases/1_18_2002.htm, on August 24, 2003.

MacArthur Foundation (2003). John D. and Catherine T. MacArthur Foundation Announces $50 Million in Program of Grants Designed to Help Reduce Threat Posted by Weapons of Mass Destruction." Retrieved from http://www.macfound.org/announce/press_releases/8_18_2003.htm, on August 24, 2003.

National Institutes of Health (2003). Terrorism and Bioterrorism-related Research Opportunities. Retrieved from http://www.niaaa.nih.gov/extramural/terrorism.htm, on August 1, 2003.

National Research Council (NRC) (2002a). *Discouraging Terrorism: Some Implications of 9/11.* Panel on Understanding Terrorists in Order to Deter Terrorism. Neil J. Smelser and Faith Mitchell, editors. Division of Behavioral and Social Sciences and Education. Washington, DC: National Academies Press.

National Research Council (NRC) (2002b). *Making the Nation Safer: The Role of Science and Technology in Countering Terrorism.* Committee on Science and Technology for Countering Terrorism. Neil J. Smelser and Faith Mitchell, editors. Division of Behavioral and Social Sciences and Education. Washington, DC: National Academies Press.

National Research Council (NRC) (2002c). *Terrorism: Perspectives from the Behavioral and Social Sciences.* Panel on Behavioral, Social, and Institutional Issues, Committee on Science and Technology for Countering Terrorism. Neil J. Smelser and Faith Mitchell, editors. Division of Behavioral and Social Sciences and Education. Washington, DC: National Academies Press.

National Science Foundation (2002). *SES Responds to September 11th.* SBE Science Nuggets. Retrieved August 12, 2003, from http://www.nsf.gov/sbe/nuggets/032/nugget.htm.

Office of Management and Budget (OMB) (2002). *Annual Report to Congress on Combating Terrorism, 2002.*

Office of Management and Budget (OMB) (2003). *Annual Report to Congress on Combating Terrorism, 2003.*

Pape, R. A. (2003, September 22). Dying to kill us. *The New York Times.*

Rosenfeld, R. (2002). Why criminologists should study terrorism. *The Criminologist, 27,* 1–4.

U.S. General Accounting Office (GAO) (2002). Report to Congressional Requesters. *Combating Terrorism: Funding Data Reported to Congress Should Be Improved.* (GAO-03–170).

Weiner, N. A., Zahn, M. A., & Sagi, R. J. (Eds) (1997). *Violence: Patterns, Causes, Public Policy.* New York: Harcourt Brace Jovanovich Publishers.

Zahn, M. (2001). *Strategic Plan for the Violence and Victimization Division of the National Institute of Justice.* National Institute of Justice, Submitted as the final report on Contract No. 535300.

PART III:
COUNTER-TERRORISM, IDEOLOGY, AND SECURITY

NEOCONSERVATIVISM AND AMERICAN COUNTER-TERRORISM: ENDARKENED POLICY?

Willem de Lint

ABSTRACT

This chapter highlights the role of public relations, secrecy and executive power in a re-articulation of autocratic rule that might be called endarkened governance. It proceeds by assessing the case of Guantánamo Bay "unlawful combatants" as an outpost of reason and justice. In understanding how this phenomenon came into existence, the "signal crime" of 9/11 and the political ideology of neoconservativism are assessed. Elements of neoconservatism include elitism, secrecy and dissemblement, strategies helpful to America's short-term imperial ambitions but ultimately, it is argued, unhelpful to sound counterterrorism policy.

INTRODUCTION: GUANTÁNAMO BAY

In September, 2003 at Guantánamo Bay, Cuba there were approximately 680 "detainees" from 43 countries kept as "unlawful combatants." Guantánamo is 45 square mile territory leased from Cuba since 1903 and used as a Naval Base. For 20 years, the U.S. has used the land to hold refugees, but now it holds persons captured in the so-called "war on terrorism."

Terrorism and Counter-Terrorism: Criminological Perspectives
Sociology of Crime, Law and Deviance, Volume 5, 131–153
Copyright © 2004 by Elsevier Ltd.
All rights of reproduction in any form reserved
ISSN: 1521-6136/doi:10.1016/S1521-6136(03)05009-7

The detainees began arriving at Camp X-Ray, hooded and shackled, in January 2002, but moved to a new facility, Camp Delta in April 2002, where they have been held in cells measuring eight by six and lit 24 hours. Detainees include children and the very old. The military confirmed that three are 16 and younger, with one news report (CNN, April 23) pegging the ages from 13 to 15. The children, according to Lt Col. Barry Johnson, chief spokesperson for the Guantánamo mission, were all "captured as active combatants against U.S. forces." They are being kept because they "have the potential to provide important information in the ongoing war on terrorism." As of January 1, 2004, none of the detainees had been charged with an offence.

In addition to Camp Delta, the U.S. holds "unlawful combatants" at Bagram air base in Afghanistan and perhaps at its base in Diego Garcia. A report from the Washington Post (December 26, 2002, A1) on conditions at Bagram noted that:

> Those who refuse to cooperate inside this secret CIA interrogation center are sometimes kept standing or kneeling for hours, in black hoods or spray-painted goggles, according to intelligence specialists familiar with CIA interrogation methods. At times, they are held in awkward, painful positions and deprived of sleep with a 24-hour bombardment of lights – subject to what are known as 'stress and duress' techniques.

Human Rights Watch said on December 27, 2002, that the CIA's method of inter-rogating al Qaeda detainees could constitute torture and result in the prosecution of U.S. officials by courts around the world. It sent a letter to President Bush calling for an investigation of the "stress and duress" techniques allegedly used by the CIA on some captives at Bagram and other facilities. An A. P. report of March 13, 2003, subsequently presented similar findings from interviewing released prisoners.

But Guantánamo is an avoidance of national and international jurisdiction. The Bush administration cites precedents in which U.S. courts have declined to find jurisdiction to consider the claims of foreigners held outside the U.S.[1] On July 31, 2002, a District of Colombia court reaffirmed that U.S. courts lack jurisdiction over the prisoners. In April, 2002, the Bush Administration also rejected a claim by the Inter-American Commission on Human Rights of the Organization of American States, saying that it "plainly does not have the competence to interpret or apply the laws and customs of war to this case" (in Davies, 2002).

Although the term "unlawful combatant" has been used in military texts and case law since the beginning of the last century (Doemann, 2003), international law governing hostilities has been clear that a detainee must be either civilian or combatant and protected by established law in either case. As Doemann (2003, p. 73) summarizes,

> the guarantees contained in Article 75 of PI [Protocol I] constitute the minimum protections that apply to all persons, including unlawful combatants, in the hands of a Party to an

international armed conflict, irrespective of whether they are covered by GC IV [Geneva Convention, Protection of Civilian Persons in Time of War] or not.

Article 4 of the Fourth Geneva Convention states: "Every person in enemy hands must have some status under international law; he is either a prisoner of war – covered by the Third Convention, a civilian covered by the Fourth Convention, or – a member of the medical personnel of the armed forces covered by the First Convention. There is no intermediate status; nobody in enemy hands can be outside the law." As Fitzpatrick (2002, p. 345) argues "the Geneva Conventions contemplate internment during hostilities of prisoners of war (POWs), civilians in occupied territory, and enemy aliens in the territory of warring states, [but] they do not provide a legal framework for indefinite detention of suspected criminals in a global and indefinite campaign against non-state actors." Moreover, the U.S. has signed the International Covenant on Civil and Political Rights which stipulates treatment of peoples in accordance with due process guarantees.

The most familiar picture of Camp X-Ray was released by the military and depicts detainees in orange jump suits kneeling with heads bowed and arms tied behind their backs inside the perimeter of an iron cage while heavily armed guards stand behind. The reception of the release was less than positive and media control by Joint Task Force 170 (JTF 170), which has command over the base, is now tight. Photographers are allowed to shoot Camp Delta from a single observation post 180 metres away using nothing stronger than a 200-millimetre lens. The shot offers no aerial perspective and consists of guard towers, razor wire and the fine-meshed green plastic screening that shields the concrete cell blocks. As for spontaneous interviews, even U.S. soldiers and civilians working at the base are off-limits. "Public affairs" personnel sit in on all encounters and censor all staff communications (Knox, 2002).

The orange jump suits sprung to life with the term "unlawful combatants" belongs in a frame and to a narrative. The frame includes a way of thinking about foreign and domestic affairs. The narrative unfolds with the outrageous "flashpoint" event of 9/11. The consequence appears to be extraordinary adjustments to longstanding divisions, restrictions and exceptions in governance. But this only begs the question: are these brightly coloured men better comprehended as subjects of law or power?

THE FRAME

The good have to crucify him who devises his own virtue! . . .They hate the creator most: him who breaks the law-tables and the old values, the breaker – they call him the law-breaker. . .They [the good] crucify the whole human future! The good – have always been the beginning of the end.

– Nietzsche (1961, p. 229).

The Project for the New American Century is a non-profit educational organization dedicated to a few fundamental propositions: that American leadership is good both for America and for the world; that such leadership requires military strength, diplomatic energy and commitment to moral principle; and that too few political leaders today are making the case for global leadership.

– Project for the New American Century Website

Ideological Consolidation

Over the past 20 years American politics has seen the rise of a neo-conservative movement. Spearheaded in large part by disillusioned liberal intellectual pundits circa 1970, it has converted a selective sampling of political philosophy into a geopolitical storyline. Its genesis is most commonly located among those who sought, among other things, to forge a new relation between more powerful and unilateralist instruments in American foreign policy and deregulated and privatized delivery systems. In short form, it is a political credo which favours a singular view of American empire, one which links American cultural and political precedence to military strength in a *moral* affirmation. Irving Kristol (2003) sums up the elements of its foreign policy by saying simply that patriotism is good, world government is not, and "statesmen" (sic) should be capable of distinguishing friends from enemies. And while neoconservatives may reject Kissingerian realism and its expectation of billiard ball counterforces, reactions and détentes, they are not so far estranged from Hobbes that they cannot see the solitary leviathan as a (fresh) requirement of global relations.[2] Similarly, son William Kristol together with Robert Kagan (1996), argue that "benevolent hegemony" characterised by "military supremacy and moral confidence" (based on "the understanding that [America's] moral goals and its fundamental national interests are almost in harmony") needs to form its basis. While they agree with free market elements of the liberalism of Hayek with regard to services delivery, their "moral" commitments take from conservativism a hostility toward "relativistic multiculturalism." They also follow a Troskyist line in the conviction that executive power ought to be consolidated and its means more forthrightly engaged. For them, a rejection of moral relativism leads to ideological consolidation around leadership and intrepidity to produce rather than follow the norm. Thus the moral agenda includes not only revivifying patriotism but an attitude of moral certitude. As a procedural agenda it breaks, particularly, from liberal consent politics and notions of balance, fairness, and accountability. Put another way, neoconservatives wish to substitute the priority of the rule of law for the rule of power.

There are, then, at least three features of American neoconservative praxis. The first is a newfound affirmation of political elitism. The neoconservative movement differs from religious and political conservatism in that it rejuvenates an ideological consolidation around leadership as a good in itself. Neoconservatives agree with the teachings of German ex-patriot political philosopher Leo Strauss that "some are fit to lead, and others to be led" and that leadership requires the moral attitude and practice of the innovator and risk taker – a charging toward a future rather than present order. The neoconservative credo is also inspired by the political philosophy of Karl Schmitt, who argued that exceptionalism as a policy originating in national security crises will and perhaps must lead to permanent consolidation of executive power. Leadership also dramatically bifurcates roles into loyal following and bold direction.[3] The priority of leadership may be upheld only where policy affords leaders ample room and few restrictions, especially those of a procedural nature. Those who lead cannot be expected always to explain their actions. In the meantime, those who follow must acquiesce to the exceptional authority of the leader and the ubiquitous scrutiny that is deployed to maintain asymmetries of power.[4] Finally, whereas leadership must resist the bonds of morality, the subordinate is, with Nietzsche (and Foucault) and under this power-restorative view, diminished as a standpoint for both knowledge and virtue.[5] Leadership is an individual value that is also a national creed, because it is America that must lead the world, and those that would lead America cannot shirk from the duty.

A second feature closely tied to leadership elitism is an affirmation of the necessity of governmental dissembling and secrecy. In democracies, political action depends upon some quotient of public approval. This presents a problem where only leaders are believed fit to make leadership decisions or where the truth, in the words of Leo Strauss, may not be suitable for public consumption. Leaders must therefore become skilled in communicating using "code": an "esoteric message" for those in the know, and an "exoteric message" to pacify or agitate ignorant masses. Such duplicity is said to be necessary to avoid ratcheting down policy to mere populism, but it also fits nicely with extant national (in)security practice. Some of the comments on the washing of intelligence on Iraq suggest that the message for the masses and the message for elites was sometimes confounded. Paul Wolfowitz: "For bureaucratic reasons we settled on weapons of mass destruction because it was the one issue everyone could agree on" (in Cook, 2003).[6]

This second quality is tied closely to the oldest justification for power consolidation: enemies at the gate. While empires lose their way without enemies, the call to arms awakens the leader. Strauss, like Machiavelli, also links a stable political order "to the necessity of an external threat." Here, there is also borrowing from a Troskyist version of Marxist millenarianism which has it that destruction will inspire the forces of freedom and democracy. In order to meet the unrighteous enemy, power must be free, not crippled or vulnerable: a Leviathan can do no good blinded or over-exposed. After the consolidation afforded by a forty year cold war, the terrorist has emerged as the most versatile foil for a new hyperpower: he appears within and without boundaries (allowing selective breaches) and is *revealed* by authoritative state proclamations (leaders who can distinguish friend from foe) using tools of exceptional (secret state) politics. Building more from a twist of the "repressive hypothesis" of Foucault than regard for the tradition of Burke, neoconservatives argue that *destruction* (of terrorists, terrorist networks, and supporting environments) will release suppressed *freedom*.

Neoconservative political thought represents a bold new consolidation of American foreign policy founded on a rejection both of much of Enlightenment thought and postmodern cultural relativism. With concepts such as "preventative war," and situating "just response" in a space between criminal and martial norms, it asserts an "exceptional" politics beyond longstanding principles of international law. In citing leadership in itself as a value, it also discards the means of social democracy as (law tables and old values) weak and destructive to the reality of power generally and the ends of American interests in particular. With slogans such as "benevolent hegemony," it celebrates the chance and necessity of protecting American dominance in cultural, economic, and military globalisation.

Neoconservativism has in this way been a re-politicization of governmental knowledge for the rule of power. It should not be forgotten that it is made possible in the aftermath of thinking on power and knowledge by Foucault, and on post-Holocaust modernity by thinkers like Bauman. Where postmodern thought weakens the separation between power and truth, reflections on modernity severs the relation between liberty and knowledge. Into this step the neoconservatives: If knowledge is already political, then the deliberate advancement of selective knowledges according to power-political affirmations is inevitable, simply a matter of choosing sides. If the modern state is not linked to the advancement of respect for human liberty but to a scandalous rationality in which genocide can be meticulously recorded by students trained in classical philosophy, then it is clear that the convergence of the good and the right is perilous. Finally, if as realists insist, international relations are naturally chaotic where there is no center, then it would appear that domination is the duty of those who can.

A Storyline (A Signal Crime/Villains and Victims)

Donald Black improved criminological understanding of the reflexive relationship between victims and offenders with the concept "self-help" (Black, 1983).

Offenders are often caught in the act of retribution for a previous victimization and it is often timely chance which divides official victims from offenders. Since then, social reaction is better understood in the long cycle of tit-for-tat retributions. But the spotlight of official reaction continues to strip or sanitize the contingency and dependency of the criminal event from its history and frame in order to make the selection of response appear more just. The complexity of the event is cleansed so that law's truth (Green, 1997), with the right of prosecution by the executive arm of government, may appear unambiguous and imperative. Put another way, we prefer to see the rule of law instead of the rule of power.

At the same time, we understand with Innes (2002) that a signal crime is profoundly mobilizing. An act of predatory violence against an innocent party in the context of primed public anticipation (the streets are getting unsafe, violators are laughing at our rules) may be enough to justify exceptional social control measures (cf. Hall et al., 1978). The murder of Polly Klaas was seized upon by Republican politicians, victims' rights organizations, correctional and police lobbies and others, to relate a new political term for the incumbent to governmental action on crime – in "three strikes" legislation. Calls to ratchet down the age of criminal responsibility typically follow in the wake of particularly horrific wrongdoing by a juvenile offender.

In the arena of foreign policy we have seen the importance of signal crimes as well. As in criminal law, in international relations an aggressive action may be justified where one perceives a threat or where one is the victim of a provocation (Walzer, 1977). The international relations convention is a normative requirement. The U.S. Constitution stipulates that Congress and not the president must be the decision-maker in declaring war. This has underscored the value of ongoing opinion preparation for the military engagement. The "Vietnam syndrome" is identified with public reticence for aggressions involving "friendly" casualties. However, support may be expected where a threat to security is demonstrated and this, in turn, may be anticipated where evidence is presented of an adversary's provocation. The Vietcong attack on the *USS Maddox* and the *Turner Joy* and the Japanese attack on Pearl Harbour were symbolic attacks on the United States that *demanded* response.

In crime aetiology (and construction) we know that contexts (social, cultural, structural) are important to judicious response. In foreign policy and diplomatic relations the interdependency and historical contexts of actions and reactions are likewise important. However, in the time-space compression of information age smoke and fog, the distinction between a predatory and defensive war effort may be increasingly difficult for distant observers to make. In the meantime, in moves already well-rehearsed, a predatory war effort can get legislative approval if an acceptable rationale is given, even where a lie is needed to gain it.[7] The Vietcong and Japanese attacks took place against a backdrop of open questions about American military engagement. We now know, at least, that there was no attack on the *Maddox* and *Turner Joy* (Ellsberg, 2002).

The most recent proclamation of the "war on terrorism" has also depended on a signal crime and a storyline. After 9/11, the right to retribution of a worthy victim afforded ample room for bold new foreign and domestic policy initiatives – like the doctrine of preventative war. The eruption of terrorism provided an opportunity for the world's leviathan to rise up and demonstrate its capacity to secure order through its power. It also offered a spotlight behind which accords of international agreements (on weapons, the environment and war crimes prosecution) could be rejected with the putative weakness of multilateralism and international law. When the smoke cleared after 9/11 the victims and villains were starkly distinguished in a snapshot of destruction and consequences. Is excising the complication of history from the frame all too convenient?

The men in orange jump suits suddenly look like they fit. They belong as symbols of the relocation of right in might, the long arm of hyperpower retribution, and the strategies and exceptions that attend the administration of governance. In rolling out a "colder war" against terrorism, a signal crime and the case for global leadership advance one another in an "elective affinity." The offence is already contextualized and political ambiguity is suspended just long enough for extraordinary initiatives to be undertaken. There is no shirking from the disreputable tools of power: secrecy, dissembling, and executive consolidation.

A POWER TOOLKIT

Expanded Executive Authority

At a news conference on July 19, 2003 with British Prime Minister Tony Blair at his side, President Bush said of detainees at Camp Delta that "the only thing I know for certain is that these are bad people." At the same time, American officials stated that the United States would not seek the death penalty against the two British detainees facing military trials, a promise they also extended to the Australian government in reference to its detained citizens. British representatives were also assured that the pair would be exempt from other norms of the Delta detainees: their conversations with defense lawyers would not be monitored, their trials would be open to reporters, and they would be allowed to consult British lawyers. Two years earlier in a joint press conference with President Chirac of France on November 5, 2001, Bush said "Over time it's going to be important for nations to know they will be held accountable for inactivity. You're either with us or against us in the fight against terror." Britain and Australia were two staunch supporters of the American action in Iraq.

This, then, is the esoteric message for "those in the know" which Leo Strauss speaks of: the rule of law is available for those who accede to the rule of power or the exception of the leader. Here, it is not important that the Bush administration will actually deliver a substantive improvement in legal rights. What is being communicated is the message that the president has authority to do so. The president, like the monarch, may dole out mercy or majesty (cf. Hay, 1975). The President knows who is "bad" and who must face death. That the legitimacy and the internal security of liberal democracies requires attentiveness to normative principles of non-aggression and other tenets of civility and justice does not dislodge this privilege and priority of might. Instead, the craft of leadership becomes the ability to augment power advantages despite or through such constraints, when necessary.

The Bush administration is seeking through a "legal black hole" to establish new precedents for international law. The status of Guantánamo detainees and the military commissions ordered to prosecute them are a gambit of American executive authority intended to dodge juridical review in the short term and pay off as precedent in the long term. That gambit seeks to perpetrate a number of jurisdictional exclusions in favour of a broadened executive authority. Indeed, the November 13 authorization order of the President, establishing military commissions and "war on terror" protocols, included the following: "(2) the individual shall not be privileged to seek any remedy or maintain any proceeding, directly or indirectly, or to have any such remedy or proceeding sought on the individual's behalf, in: (i) any court of the United States, or any State thereof, (ii) any court of any foreign nation, or (iii) any international tribunal." In using the term "unlawful combatants" and arguing that the war prosecuted in Afghanistan against the Taliban and Al Qaeda is novel in not being limited to geographical or national boundaries, the Bush administration is seeking to usurp international criminal and martial law and also American and extra-American jurisdictional claims.

As according to established practice, the executive orders establishing unique or exceptional circumstances cite threats to the national security. Thus, since September 14, 2001, the United States has been in a state of emergency. Coupled with the wide congressional Authorization for Use of Military Force passed within days of the 9/11 attack (Hj. Res. 64/Sj. Res. 23 2001), the president has a legal foundation to claim expansive powers under both the "take care" and "commander in chief" clauses of Article II of the Constitution (Baker, 2002). In addition to using executive orders as above to authorize military tribunals for trials of suspected terrorists (Military Order of November 13, 2001), the President has signed them to freeze assets of terrorist groups (Executive Order 13224, September 25, 2001), redefine the scope of airline security, establish the Office of Homeland Security within the Executive Office of the President (Executive Order 13228, October 10, 2001), revise Justice Department regulations concerning the treatment of attorney-client conversations by certain federal detainees (Department of Justice/Bureau of Prisons regulation of October 31, 2001), and prosecute military action against the Taliban in Afghanistan and Iraqi forces in Iraq. While some of these actions were also clearly authorized by Congress, significant steps were taken unilaterally (Mayer & Price, 2002, p. 2).

As for the commissions, to the extent that no successful claims against the President under international law will succeed, they will have served their most martial function, which is to facilitate interrogations according to Pentagon criteria. In the meantime, they further an arrogation of executive authority. To set the trials in motion, President Bush will sign an executive order finding a "reason to believe" the recommendations of the Pentagon's Office of Military Commissions. Judges will be chosen and removed at any time without reason by the Pentagon's "Appointing Authority." The final appeal for amnesty in death cases will also go to the President. Quite obviously, commissions fail the separation of powers test; they blend the executive and judicial in one branch of government (Koh, 2002).

Indeed, the Bush administration has moved quickly to usurp the separation of power doctrine. Limitations on domestic law enforcement and restrictions on military aid to law enforcement (as in the U.S. 1878 *Posse Comitatus Act*), already long eroded as with federal drug exceptions, are even less robust. Not only is the White House reviewing *Posse Comitatus*, the Defense Department has a military command and control structure for operations in the continental United States, called Northern Command. The Northern Command will be responsible for homeland defense and homeland security, the latter referring to the "prevention, pre-emption, and deterrence of, and defense against aggression targeted at U.S. territory, sovereignty, domestic population and infrastructure as well as management of the consequences of such aggression and other domestic emergencies" (in Peters, 2003).

Perhaps this development may be interpreted as a form of "grey control" (cf. Hoogenboom, 1991), according to which there is seamlessness or fluidity between military and police action across state and region, public and private domains, and intelligence and law enforcement institutions.[8] Recent resurgence of executive authority in the United States can be tied to the ebb and flow of divisions within the executive as well as to resistances from without. Without, the collapse of the Soviet Union called for a refocusing of intelligence and military capacity on international narcotics trafficking, alien smuggling, terrorism, and proliferation of weapons of mass destruction. Time-space compression under globalization, information age technologies capable of crippling critical infrastructure from anywhere, and collapse between foreign and domestic jurisdictions all suggested to policymakers the opportunity if not the necessity of reconfiguring domestic boundaries and dissolving some of the distinction between military and police, domestic and foreign.

In the meantime, defence policy in the 1990s asserted that the United States must be pre-eminent. After 9/11, the logic of pre-eminence displaced hesitant steps towards multilateralism by Clinton. Michael Glennon, a well-known specialist on international law, could then write in the leading foreign policy journal *Foreign Affairs* (2003) that Americans should recognise that international law and international institutions are "hot air." They have proven their inapplicability by the fact that the United States disregards them, and is right to do so. It must maintain the right to use force as it chooses, independent of these institutions, which must be dismissed and disregarded. This follows what others have similarly argued: that normativity in foreign policy is what the actors involved accept as reasonable options given the context of power distributions.

In sum, Camp Delta may be seen as an expedient consistent with shifts towards executive authority within liberal democracies. If so, this is a tilting of the ship of state dangerously towards autocratic (and totalitarian) practices. Historically, such shifts do not occur without correction. The dynamic capacity that attracts governments to the use of national security agencies works both ways. While these may offer a policy quick fix for an overripe executive, their officials and resources are reversible and can be directed for *or against* the leader. Within security intelligence bureaucracies it is well known that rampant politicization will ultimately weaken or destroy institutional grounding, lending interest to resistances against such use. In addition, policy solidarity may be a victim of internal conflicts and turf wars between national security agencies.

Expanded Public Relations

A number of hours after the Word Trade Centre was hit, Secretary of Defence Donald Rumsfeld called for another attack on Iraq: "Judge whether good enough to hit S. H. at same time. Not only UBL [Usama bin Laden]. Go massive. Sweep it all up. Things related and not" (CBS, 2002). During the 18 months before the United States acted, an extensive propaganda effort was unleashed to make the case for this action. One prong of this effort was the decision to use WMD as the main argument for a preventative war, a sortie now widely recognized as dependent on governmental lies and deceptions and falsely interpreted intelligence. By the time the United States invaded, a *New York Times*/CBS News survey estimated that 42%

of the American public believed that Saddam Hussein was directly responsible for the September 11 attacks on the World Trade Center and the Pentagon. An ABC news poll found that 55% of Americans believed that Saddam Hussein directly supported Al-Qaeda.

On June 13, 2002, Colonel Donald Woolfolk, Deputy Commander of JTF 170, as acting commander of Guantánamo Bay, wrote that

> we are now living in an age where our nation is engaged in international armed conflict against terrorism. Unlike and previous conflict, we face a foe that knows no borders and perceives all Americans, wherever they may be, as targets of opportunity. Under such circumstances the need to maintain the tightly controlled environment, which has been established to create dependency and trust by the detainee with his interrogator, is of paramount importance. Disruption of the interrogation environment, such as through access to a detainee by counsel, undermines this interrogation dynamic. Should this occur, a critical instrument may be lost, resulting in a direct threat to national security (Woolfolk, 2003).

Intelligence needs, including control of access to information and informants, is often inconsistent with rule of law observance. Even Supreme Court judges have agreed that constitutional liberties must yield somewhat to national security exceptions under the stewardship of executive authority. Here we have two expressions of information age governance practice: the manipulation of whole populations and of selected individuals through strategic management of information access.

Long seen by modern nation-state liberals to belong only with totalitarian government practice, state knowledge of population in the maintenance of government is now well-established as concomitant to the development of modern liberal democracies. The discovery and manipulation of popular opinion in the service of governmental objectives may, with Holquist (1997) be understood as *the* modern form of government. Beneath the perceived distinction between liberal and totalitarian states lies the more telling difference between national security states, governmental states, and territorial states. Whereas the latter is concerned with the protection of territorial sovereignty the former are concerned with the control of populations and power through the management of information. As Holquist demonstrates, beginning during WWI with the "massive, routinized, perlustration of the internal mail between 1915 and 1917, France, England, Germany and Russia actively managed populations through the instrument of surveillance" (Holquist, 1997). Additionally, all political movements passed through the experience of the First World War and emerged from it thinking of surveillance "as indispensable to governing." Holquist reports that by 1915, Russian officials took the view that they could no longer rely on commands "but must instead seek to harness the country's 'vital forces'" (5). For this, regular monthly reports on the country's "mood" were needed. These began to quantify and categorize the political attitudes and turned into "political summaries" (6). During the war, the British did likewise, and by 1918 they employed a staff of 1,453 postal censorship workers. Also by 1918, the British Ministry of Information was embarking on active home propaganda.

Both White and Red Russians described their information collection networks and dissemination tasks not as propaganda but as "enlightenment." The Izba-chital'nia or reading hut, a cabin in some small out of the way community stocked with newspapers and political pamphlets is quaintly emblematic of government's discovery of the persuasive arts.[9] As Holquist notes, war was the context in which a "type of modern governmental politics in the form of the national security state" could be rolled out in a "large scale and in a state form." These features of the national security states did not disappear between wars, but were upheld at a lower register in preparation for future wars. It may be added that relation between the institution of large scale national security state initiatives and war has since been exploited to the point that war has been viewed by many as a periodic necessity in the expansion of this form of governmental politics. Thus, rather than seeing national security mobilizations as a consequence of new military and security initiatives, it may be better to perceive new military and security initiatives as the by-product of the continuous unfurling of modern governmental politics.

That public opinion matters has been a singular lesson for liberal democracies. By 2001, the ten major public relations firms made revenue of about $2.5 billion, much of it through government contracts (Miller, 2003). Rendon Group and Hill and Knowlton have been paid millions to spin politics, particularly the politics of war. This development is a result of false steps in cold war hostilities. The British concluded in an internal government report in 1957 on the Suez campaign that the "over-riding lesson" was that "world opinion is now the absolute principal of war" (in Miller, 2002). By the time of the Falklands War, this learning was practiced in what has now been called "embedding." That intervention featured close control of the 29 journalists allowed to accompany the military to the South Atlantic and allowed no independent facilities for reporting. All news-copy was censored on naval vessels in the South Atlantic and then again at the Ministry of Defence in London (Miller, 2002).

The United States was a self-conscious student of the British effort. Lt Commander Arthur Humphries of the U.S. Navy said following the Falklands War: "In spite of a perception of choice in a democratic society, the Falklands War shows us how to make certain that government policy is not undermined by the way a war is reported" (in Miller, 2002).[10] Humphries argued that if there was one deficiency in the Falklands policy, it was in failing to fill the resulting void with pictures. "In the Falklands the British failed to appreciate that news management is more than just information security censorship. It also means providing pictures" (in Miller, 2002). Meanwhile, Pentagon post-mortems on the U.S. Vietnam campaign routinely made the argument that failure to assure domestic public opinion was a large factor in the US's reluctant withdrawal. American military strategy with the invasion of Grenada and Panama included more comprehensive information security censorship and propaganda. What was learnt by the time of both attacks on Iraq is that access to the fighting must be controlled, full censorship practiced, and a clear, positive message delivered. Of the subsequent control of the press in the Gulf War, NY Times correspondent Malcolm Brown said

> I've never seen anything that can compare to it, in the degree of surveillance and control the military has over the correspondents. When the entire environment is controlled, a journalist ceases to be a reporter in the American or Anglo-Saxon tradition. He works a lot like the PK (Propagandakompanien)' (in Miller, 2002).

It is often assumed that the rise of institutions of civil society has made this type of governmental politics risky or illegal for its advocates and practitioners. Legal institutions, including constitutional provisions and guarantees, governmental and non-governmental watchdog agencies, and non-establishment media, are a fourth estate check on the expansion and "truths" of governmental knowledge and expose some of the practices of the national security state. However, media corporatization and the dependency of news corporations on regular sources (Ericson et al., 1989; Herman & Chomsky, 1988) have limited the exposure of critical views. Secrecy legislation and freedom of information exceptions have compounded this lack. This has allowed the coterminous proliferation of massive monitoring and disruption programs alongside the development of an independent (but dependent) press. But government press offices as regular sources have helped to fill the resultant void with the sound bytes.

It has been often said that in a society that institutionalizes open politics and the free flow of information, governments can practice less visible control over public opinion. We can see that this is possible because the unlimited constituting discourses "citizens" have theoretical access to is in practice delimited by co-dependency between free press and free government on public relations shortcuts which do not offend dominant ideologies and interests. Elite interests and ideology connects government, media, economic and military echelons (Mills, 1956) while leaving liberal institutional principles explicitly in place. Ideological dissent is permitted, but it wallows in the troughs or valleys, too "hot" for prime time media. In the meantime, confidentiality agreements and need to know protocols of public relations insiders and national security supports paints black much important information. In this way, plutocratic actions can be taken in plain sight attended by a full chorus of liberal institutional representatives: judiciary, media, NGOs. How do we then know that the "enlightenment" we discover is *not* the blowback from public relations firms?

Expanded Secrecy

Criminologists are familiar with the term "dark figure of crime," which refers to that quantity of "actual" criminality missing from the official statistics. Similarly, political scientists are aware that there is a dark figure of politics, which refers to that quantity of political "action" which is taken and removed from public view. The history of American national security governance and of important signal events is in large measures unknown and unknowable. The extent of this "absent totality" (cf. Giddens, 1986) may be gleaned from the extent of government non-disclosure and classification. Already in 1971, William Florence, a retired Air Force security classification official, estimated that the Defence Department had at least 20 million classified documents (in Moynihan, 1998). Other testimony in 1971 estimated that the Department of Defence had one million cubic feet, the State Department about 35 million documents, and the National Archives another 470 million pages, all marked classified (Ibid.). Twenty-five agencies were authorized to classify documents. By 1997, there were 1.5 billion classified pages of government records over 25 years old in government vaults. Moynihan (1998) notes that 17,000 documents were stamped "classified" every day or between 6 and 7 million every year, with 400,000 getting the Top Secret stamp. Only 3% of government records are preserved for posterity and agencies can unilaterally make records disappear permanently with little fear of punishment.

Where the ideal of democracy is personal privacy and open government, Friedrich (1957), defined totalitarianism as that by which private information about individuals is made open, and that which should be open – government information – is kept secret. Open government is manifest in public access to government bureaucracies. Indeed, bureaus displaced the princely courts and parliaments, and rulemaking became the dominant mode of government, in the 19th century. But Weber (Gerth & Mills, 1946) argued that secrecy is the normal mode by which bureaucracies in modern societies conduct business. Moreover, the capacity to store and code information, providing a resource to populations, is a requirement of the modern state, without which it could not exist (Giddens, 1985). More distressing, the secrecy operation in bureaucracies has spawned a deviation from the regulation of citizens by *promulgated rules*, as per the bureaucratic mode. Because control over how, when and if information is released is indispensable to the proper and efficient functioning of the organization and its leaders (Lowry,

1980, p. 299), bureaucracies have learned to collect and disseminate stores of information according to non-transparent non-disclosure principles. Since as Lowry (1980) also argues, "secrecy maximizes the power potential of the knowledge" (p. 299) and because "what one knows and does not know determines who has power and how that power can be utilized," "exotic knowledge" has become a new source of power (pp. 298–299). As Birkinshaw (1988, p. 20), notes "take away a government's preserve of information, and its preserve of when and what to release, then take away a fundamental bulwark of its power."

In 2002, more federal records were officially classified than ever before (according to the Information Security Oversight Office, Washington, DC) and the G. W. Bush administration is regarded as the most secretive government of the past 40 years. Various federal and state governments and agencies have finessed 9/11 and the new presidential culture to empower themselves accordingly. Provisions in the Patriot Act gave law-enforcement agencies "the authority to search homes and businesses without a warrant (a practice known as 'sneak and peek') and to secretly track an individual's Internet surfing, library records, and book purchases" (Franklin, 2003). The House Judiciary Committee was told by the Justice Department in June 2003 that information as to how many times the FBI had used each of the new powers was classified. Under a policy restricting access to "sensitive but unclassified" information, "agencies have also made it harder for the public to see records that are often used by health and safety advocates that industry has long sought to keep secret" (Ibid). In just one of several new initiatives, Attorney General John Ashcroft directed federal agency heads to "search for and use any legal authority for denying access to records under the FOIA" (EPIC, 9.05: 2).

> The EPA, for instance, now limits access to the "risk management plans" that companies must file to inform communities what is being done to prevent toxic chemical accidents. The Federal Energy Regulatory Commission has withdrawn information on hazardous materials stored at power plants (Franklin, 2003).

Taking a cue from intelligence agencies, "officials are withholding information that could embarrass government agencies or businesses" (Ibid). In the summer of 2002, the Department of Agriculture "tried to suppress a National Academy of Sciences study that revealed no government secrets but warned that terrorism using foreign pests or pathogens could 'pose a major threat to U.S. agriculture' " (Ibid). The Agency for Toxic Substances and Disease Registry no longer allows online access to a report that characterizes security at chemical plants as "fair to very poor." As Franklin (2003) reports, "the Nuclear Regulatory Commission has restricted access to two reports – one of which had been available for 20 years – that suggest that nuclear power plants are not adequately protected against airplane crashes." Environmental Protection Agency officials similarly finessed the secrecy culture in arguing that disclosing information about new appointees would constitute a security risk: they washed résumés of information on education levels and job experience (Franklin, 2003). State officials are following the federal government's lead in closing off public records.

Pennsylvania has dismantled a database with environmental information about mines and soil conditions. Iowa has classified architectural information on school buildings. And several states, including Louisiana, have passed anti-terrorism laws that allow local police to keep secret any information gathered in connection with terrorism investigations (Ibid).

The harnessing of secrecy for state power is matched by private enterprises. Private companies are aided in sealing information from public exposure by various provisions of intellectual property law, other proprietary rights, freedom of information legislation and secrecy acts, and by governments afraid of the free circulation of the substance of their contractual relationships with various corporations. For instance, Attorney General John Ashcroft has "singled out 'sensitive business information' as one of the categories federal officials should shield from Freedom of Information Act requests" (Ibid). Companies can also finesse the government's secrecy culture and protect information they don't want disclosed by sending it to the federal government.

And under legislation creating the Department of Homeland Security, most information provided by business – on anything from software security problems to toxic spills – will be exempted from public-access laws. For example, if an improperly stored load of hazardous material were to explode at a chemical plant, information on the substances involved – and even evidence of negligent storage – could be off-limits to firefighters, local investigators, and the victims themselves (Ibid).

"Notes Natural Resources Defense Council attorney Jon Devine, the only thing the government can use the information for is to determine whether they need more security. But they can't force the company to do anything about it" (in Franklin, 2003). In the area of public contracts, there is also a culture of non-disclosure. The Defence Policy Board members do not need to disclose who their clients are and this is why Kissinger accepted membership while declining to lead to the 9/11 investigation, according to Charles Lewis of the Centre for Public Integrity (Lewis, 2003).

As noted above, this tool of modern governmental states is consistent with an intelligence protocol: sources and methods are cultivated and protected and information released for policy or political expedience as disclosures, leaks and (more problematically) prosecutions. This has well-known consequences where an open society attempts to hold the intelligence and executive institutions to account. But it also means that public policy is grounded on a limited, selective, and majoritarian presentation of information. How can public policy – especially where policy concerning national security straddles, informs or colours other initiatives – reflect republican values when knowledge of the relevant facts is disallowed except to the very few?

Expanded secrecy, together with active production of disinformation stewarded through national security executives are features of a modality of governance which might be called endarkened. Endarkened or sneaky governance finesses a secrecy bureaucracy, information age security protocols and standards, and national emergency exceptionalism. It is a variation of governmentalized politics in which the power of information is stewarded so that ambiguity (or politics) (cf. Hänninen, 2000) may be squeezed from policy deliberations. Expanded executive authority, secrecy, and public relations are also instruments of a newfound messianic political philosophy (neoconservatism) which has produced a context where it is reasonable to expect the inverse of what John Dean of Watergate infamy suggests (ought to happen to Bush): the impossibility of an impeachable offence.

CONSEQUENCES OF GOVERNMENTALIZED POLITICS: ENDARKENED POLICY?

This chapter has highlighted the role of public relations, secrecy and executive power in a re-articulation of autocratic rule that might be called endarkened governance. Endarkened governance is the manipulation of national security protocols in the service of an opaque autocracy. This modality of governance is perceived in America today. Whereas globalization points logically to the necessity of a truly supranational authority and counter-terrorism policy – one embedded within international law and organization – the unique power of the United States after the collapse of the Soviet Union has instead set the stage for global counter-terrorism initiatives consistent with the exclusive national ambitions of American empire, a cause taken up in neoconservative foreign policy. Rule of power for the privileged leader, not rule of law and its dependencies and contingencies of knowable truths, is the narrative that we see being unfurled in the politics of America today. Neo-conservative political opinion and endarkened governance is a one-two punch against constructive enemies. The war on terrorism, with its incessant reloading of top 20 FBI head shots or Guantánamo Bay body counts is launched one perpetual target at a time.

Such policy fails internally and externally. First, it fails the Hobbes test that demands that the Leviathan must produce domestic security: the end result must still be greater long-term security no matter the authorized means, be it preventative war or curbs on liberties. However, since the United States invaded Iraq, the Al Qaeda network has experienced a spike in recruitment. A senior counterterrorism official based in Europe added that there is an increase in radical fundamentalism all over the world. The CIA predicted as much. This can only result in more insecurity for Americans abroad and at home.

Second, endarkened counter-terrorism policy fails the freedom test. In modern societies the procedural republic grounded on liberal freedom has displaced politics based on the republican theory that liberty "depends on sharing in self-government." As Sandel (1996, p. 330) citing Aristotle notes, any polis striving after the good cannot be sustained where inequality undermines the knowledge – and the social and economic security – needed to make meaningful exercise of choices. Aristotle and Rousseau both argued that severe inequality undermines freedom. The war against communism while putting curbs on labour and political expression and feeding American expansionist interests, also delivered to the American poor after both world wars. The deficiency of the (colder, perpetual) war on terrorism argument is that it provides no promise of compensation for those whose support (tacit or otherwise) is needed. It is widely expected that the poor will get poorer (or prison), and counter-terrorism actions abroad and domestically appear only to be exacerbating this as they stream public monies into interdiction rather than redistribution. Indeed, the equation seems to be: *not* more bounty *and* less freedom.

Third, it fails the legitimacy test. The neoconservative symmetry with intelligence protocols is a fearful one and unworthy of twenty-first century politics. Despite vigorous spin doctoring, public opinion polls in the U.S. in August of 2003 found that between 40 and 45% of Americans thought that Bush was lying or exaggerating in making the case for war against Iraq.[11] Three Foreign Service officials resigned in the lead-up to the Iraqi invasion, publicly chastising the Bush administration for endangering American legitimacy built up over 50 years. And at a time of perplexing fascination with forensics, the most significant crime of our time is excused from due analysis. In just one illustration of this, the amount of funds the 9/11 Independent Commission originally received to explore the causes of the attacks was $3 million. This compares to $50 million given to a 2003 commission to look into the Shuttle crash and $5 million a 1996 commission was given to study legalized gambling (Pelisek, July 4–10, 2003). A paltry sum to contextualize a signal crime which has precipitated historical reversals in democracy and its freedoms. As Lustgarten and Leigh (1996) have noted, where the means of liberal democracy are not honoured for national security policy the ends also cannot be reconciled with that form of government.

Lastly, this policy is weak according to its own terms of reference. Although power consolidation through secrecy and public relations may serve executive authority in the short term, dynamic capabilities within national security agencies are likely to produce profound reversals. Craft allegiances and inter-agency conflicts will inevitably detract from policy preferences. Even where the logic of the argument for consolidation around both counter-terrorism and American exceptionalism lends credence to an American leviathan, the intelligence foundation is weak and dangerous where politicization is likely to result in resistances, destabilizing leaks and cover-ups. The weak foundation of the national security state is exacerbated where neo-conservatives already embrace duplicity as a governing principle. Exceptions to judicial and even governmental scrutiny afford the intrusion of the rationality of intelligence into the very heart of some of the most essential decisions over public policy. The sacrosanct role of sources and methods and the privileged place of national security in the governmentalization of politics produce a condition explicitly hostile to democratic institutions, but also to executive direction. Counter-intelligence/terror networks are a sub-rosa source of power that will subvert the health of the root and branch on which executive direction depends.

As Scheuerman (1994) has shown, the security problem of liberal democracies is more a question of what lies between the norm and the exception than what lies at the extremes of normative and realist thought. The stark insights of Nietzsche in any case cannot ground a political philosophy which is not already slavish. As Walzer (1977) argues, even warriors must sell their intentions through the normativity of civil discourse. Consequently, it is more sensible to revitalize Enlightenment values and classical liberal means, including human rights and political institutions crafting balance of powers and open government. After all, this laid the groundwork for the republican ideal practiced in early American constitutionalism. In the context of globalization today, that enforcement authority must belong increasingly to a suitably empowered United Nations or equivalent. Only a properly constituted global authority observant and committed to human and ecological preservation could have legitimacy to "combat" those who violate human rights where a national government is unwilling to do so. Susceptible as the rule of law already is to the rule of power, a policy merely affirming the latter is, as a matter of historical record and perhaps ironically, too weakly grounded. Counter-terrorism in this way must strive beyond the limited politics of "national security" to the more broadly conceived "human security" (Bajpai, 2000). It must reject Guantánamo Bay detention as an instance of aberrant, abhorrent, and dangerous power politics.

NOTES

1. Eisentrager v Forrestal (1949) 174 F.2d 961.
2. Reference is made to American Albert Wohlstetter, a RAND corporation researcher and military strategist. Wohlstetter criticized the joint nuclear weapons control policy with

Moscow because it bridled US technological creativity in order to maintain an artificial balance with the USSR. In the 1970s, he proposed accepting limited wars that would eventually use tactical nuclear weapons with high-precision "smart" bombs capable of striking at the enemy's military apparatus. Ronald Reagan launched the Strategic Defense Initiative (SDI) on Wohlstetter's thinking.

3. With respect to loyalty, Kristol and Kagan (1996) argue that American exceptionalism must harness "elevated patriotism" from Americans "proud of their country's leading role in world affairs." Consistent with this insistence on strong bifurcation between leaders and followers, the Bush administration is known to place a very high premium on staff loyalty.

4. In the book, *Bush at War*, Bob Woodward quotes G. W. Bush as saying, "that's the interesting thing about being the President. Maybe somebody needs to explain to me why they say something, but I don't feel like I owe anybody an explanation." Accountability, as transparency to the norm, marks the termination or end of leadership or its lack (of resolve, authority, might).

5. Nietzsche calls the slave's so-called autarchy a position akin to the manner of false stoics who are simply in denial about the influence of culture and its humiliations. The standpoint of the slave is more distorted than that of the master because while it may be that the superior height of the superordinate "falsifies the image of that which it despises" this is "far less serious a falsification" than that produced by "the submerged hatred, the vengefulness of the impotent" (Nietzsche, 1989, p. 39). In criticizing the mobilization of executive authority, this perspective has it, critics are taken with resentment. Similarly, Foucault dismissed the Freudian and vulgar Marxist view that disinherited truth and knowledge from power.

6. When the ideology includes a dim view of social democracy (not a good in itself rather but a "mythical" endpoint) it is not surprising that there should be confusion and perhaps even surprise when the exposure of duplicity raises eyebrows.

7. There is still lively debate regarding the failure of intelligence to reach the Navy base in time at Pearl Harbour in 1941, not to mention the failure to pick up Japanese intentions sooner, given the success against Japanese ciphers since 1919 (Bamford, 1982, p. 19). There is suggestion by Richard Nixon and others that the attack was foreknown and not interceded because it was just what was needed to mobilize public opinion behind the war. On January 19, 1961, the Joint Chiefs of Staff under Gen. Lyman Lemnitzer, knowing that an armed invasion of Cuba would be condemned domestically and internationally, developed and approved a plan to "trick the American public" into believing that the United States had to respond to an unprovoked Cuban attack (Bamford, 2001, p. 73). The Gulf of Tonkin incident is also well known as a classic illustration of duplicity intended to win congressional approval and domestic public support for war escalation. The US saw the importance of orchestrating events to make itself appear to be a worthy victim goaded into aggressive self-defence, or self-help, by the prior actions of "enemies." Israel, as shown in Bamford's *Body of Secrets*, was also a good student of the strategy. In 1967, Israeli Foreign Minister Abba Eban told US Ambassodor Walworth Balbon that Israel "is the victim of [Egyptian President] Nassar's aggression" and launched a brutal strike and land occupation as a result. But as Bamford (2001, p. 203) found with evidence from the NSA ship *USS Liberty*, which had intercepted Israeli military communications:

> from the very beginning the Israeli battle plan seemed to have been to hide much of the war behind a carefully constructed curtain of lies. Lies about the Egyptian threat, lies about who started the war, lies to the American president, lies to the UN Security Council, lies to the press, lies to the public.

Indeed, this practice is beginning to have several twists: on July 3, 1979, six months before the Soviet invasion and on the advice of his national security advisor, Zbigniew Brzezinski, President Carter signed a finding authorizing CIA covert operations in Afghanistan, in order to provoke a Russian incursion and give the USSR' its own Vietnam.

8. The FBI still has formal authority over domestic intelligence operations. If the CIA or the Military wants a "national security letter" opened to get access to financial and electronic records, it must go through the FBI to do so. However, the Bush administration has been trying to change this requirement so that the CIA and Military can themselves ask for such letters without the intermediation of the FBI. In the meantime, civil liberties groups warn that the FBI has this power because as a law enforcement agency, it has accountabilities not in place with the CIA and the Military. Patriot II wants to expand CIA influence over domestic intelligence by authorizing the agency to request individual surveillance.

9. In Germany, too, "enlightenment activity" was the term used by officials to designate the nurturing "of spiritual resources of one's own soldiers and civilians in order to transform them from subjects occupying a given role in an established order into better, more conscientious agents" (Holquist, 1997, p. 10).

10. Humphries also noted that if there was one deficiency in the policy, it was in failing to fill the resulting information void with pictures. "In the Falklands the British failed to appreciate that news management is more than just information security censorship. It also means providing pictures" (in Miller, 2002).

11. Newsweek poll conducted by Princeton Survey Research Associates. August 21–22, 2003; the Harris Poll, August 12–17, 2003.

REFERENCES

Bajpai, K. (2000). *Human security: Concept and measurement.* Kroc Institute Occasional Paper No. 19: OP: 1. Notre Dame, IN: University of Notre Dame.

Baker, R. (2002). What are they hiding? *The Nation, 274*(7), 11–16 F 25.

Bamford, J. (1982). *The Puzzle palace.* Houghton Mifflin.

Bamford, J. (2001). *Body of secrets.* New York: Doubleday.

Birkinshaw, P. (1988). *Freedom of information: The law, the practice and the ideal.* London: Weidenfeld & Nicolson.

Black, D. (1983). Crime as social control. In: D. Black (Ed.), *American Sociological Review* (Vol. 48, pp. 34–45).

CBS (2002). Plan for Iraq attack began on 9/11. *CBS,* Washington (September 4).

Cook, R. (2003). Britain must not be suckered a second time by White House. *Guardian* (May 30).

Davies, F. (2002). U.S. rejects call to weigh detainees' status. *The Miami Herald* (April 18).

Doemann, K. (2003). The legal situation of 'unlawful/unprivileged combatants'. *IRRC, 849*(85), 45–74.

Ellsberg, D. (2002). *Secrets: A memoir of Vietnam and the Pentagon papers.* New York: Doubleday.

Ericson, R., Baranek, P., & Chan, J. (1989). *Negotiating control: A study of news sources.* Toronto: University of Toronto Press.

Fitzpatrick, J. (2002). Jurisdiction of military commissions and the ambiguous war on terrorism. *American Journal of International Law, 96*(2), 345–354.

Franklin, D. (2003). Official secrets. *Mother Jones* (January/February).

Friedrich, C. (1957). *Constitutional reasons of state.* Providence: Brown University Press.

Gerth, H. H., & Mills, C. W. (1946). *From Max Weber: Essays in sociology*. New York: Oxford University Press.

Giddens, A. (1985). *The nation state and violence*. Cambridge: Polity Press.

Giddens, A. (1986). Action, subjectivity and the constitution of meaning. *Social Research, 53*, 529–545.

Green, A. (1997). How the criminal justice system knows. *Social and Legal Studies, 6*(1), 5–22.

Hall, S. et al. (1978). *Policing the crisis: Mugging, law and order and the state*. London: Macmillan.

Hänninen, S. (2000). The ghost of politics in the soft machine. In: Hänninen & Vähämäki (Eds), *Displacement of Politics*. SoPhi: University of Jyväskylä.

Hay, D. (1975). Property, authority and the criminal law. In: D. Hay et al. (Eds), *Albion's Fatal Tree: Crime and Society in Eighteenth Century England* (pp. 17–64). London: Allen Lane.

Herman, E., & Chomsky, N. (1988). *Manufacturing consent: The political economy of the mass media*. New York: Pantheon.

Holquist, P. (1997). Information is the alpha and omega of our work': Bolshevik surveillance in its pan-European context. *Journal of Modern History, 69*(3).

Hoogenboom, B. (1991). Grey policing: A theoretical framework. *Policing and Society, 2*(1), 17–30.

Innes, M. (2002). Control creep. *Sociological Research, 6*(3). http://www.socresonline.org.uk/6/3innes.html.

Koh, H. (2002). The case against military commissions. *IRRC, 849: Knox, Globe and Mail* (August 23).

Kristol, I. (2003). *The Neoconservative Persuasion, 8*(47) (August 25).

Kristol, W., & Kagan, R. (1996). Toward a neoconservative foreign policy. *Foreign Affairs* (July/August).

Lewis, C. (2003). All things considered. *National Public Radio* (June 13).

Lustgarten, L., & Leigh, I. (1996). *In from the cold: National security and parliamentary democracy*. London: Oxford.

Mayer, K., & Price, K. (2002). Unilateral presidential powers: Significant executive orders, 1949–1999. *Presidential Studies Quarterly, 32*, 367–386.

Moynihan, D. P. (1998). *Secrecy*. New Haven: Yale University Press.

Miller, D. (2002). Eliminating truth: The development of war propaganda. Mediawatch.org?

Miller, D. (2003). Unspinning the globe. *Znet* (May 31).

Mills, C. W. (1956). *The power elite*. New York: Oxford University Press.

Nietzsche, F. (1961). *Thus spoke Zarathustra*. Penguin.

Nietzsche, F. (1989). *On the genealogy of morals and ecce homo*. New York: Vintage.

Pelisek, C. (2003). The list. *LA Weekly* (July 4–10).

Peters, K. (2003). Troops on the beat. *Government Executive* (May 1, 2003). http://www.govexec.com/features/0503/HSs6.htm.

Sandel, M. (1996). *Democracy's discontent: America in search of a public philosophy*. Cambridge: Harvard.

Scheuerman, W. (1994). *Between the norm and the exception*. Cambridge: MIT Press.

Walzer, M. (1977). *Just and unjust wars: A moral argument with historical illustrations*. Basic Books.

Woolfolk, D. (2003). Declaration of Donald D. Woolfolk. Findlaw.com.

RIGHT-WING IDEOLOGY, TERRORISM, AND THE FALSE PROMISE OF SECURITY

Bonnie Berry

ABSTRACT

Relying on news sources and terrorism literature, this analysis draws parallels between far right terrorist groups and the U.S. right-wing political establishment. The false promise of security refers to the U.S. White House avowal to protect a frightened post-9/11 public without real, effective measures to ensure public safety. This absence of security speaks to a seeming lack of interest in national vulnerability and to a desire to control the public through fear. In addition, the harsh rhetoric threatening anyone who is "against us," as put forward by the Bush administration, has fueled anti-US hatred of a terrorist variety, thus increasing the likelihood of more violence.

INTRODUCTION

Long after September 11, 2001, the United States remains highly vulnerable to terrorist attack; indeed, it can be and has been argued that we are at greater risk. Our airports, airplanes, shipping ports, nuclear facilities, and other likely targets are open to terrorist violence, as is the population as a whole through germ and chemical attack. Beyond questionably-legal detentions of the non-US-born,

Terrorism and Counter-Terrorism: Criminological Perspectives
Sociology of Crime, Law and Deviance, Volume 5, 155–172
ISSN: 1521-6136/doi:10.1016/S1521-6136(03)05010-3

reduced civil liberties for all, and other constitutional infringements, another endangering response to 9/11 has been a preemptive war against Iraq (a country with no known connection to 9/11) and, more generally, to declare other nations to be members of an "axis of evil." Such belligerent behavior by the right-wing political segment of the U.S. aggravates an already frightening situation, heightening the likelihood of additional terrorist attacks in the U.S. and abroad, as has become evident by repeated carnage on all sides and as evidenced by the impressive growth of those determined to carry out anti-US attacks (Stern, 2003). A proposition has been advanced, and I will discuss it here, that the Bush administration promotes terrorism.

While the current presidential administration has promised to protect the U.S. citizenry, the nation has become overextended financially by giving the wealthiest 1% enormous tax breaks, disallowing economic and other attention to safeguarding the public against terrorist attack as, for instance, we have found in reduced funds for first responders. Moreover, the administration is sidetracked from terrorism control by re-building a country it destroyed (Iraq), and not incidentally, rewarding corporate donors and oil companies in that re-building effort. The false promise of security is grounded partly in corporate greed, partly in a political power grab by the right, and partly in intentional public distraction from the destructive domestic policies of the neo-conservatives, including the erosion of human rights, the environment, and the economy.

Controlling the public through fear and threatening socially-constructed enemies is behavior shared by the current administration and less legitimate far right organizations. Both formalized far-right government organizations and less-formalized far-right hate organizations hope to deny human rights and to narrow the arena of power to a limited, privileged number. As will be shown, both forms of the far right use religion, racism, violence, and moral absolutisms to achieve their purposes.

THE NEGLECT OF TERROR CONTROL

Neglect of public safety against terrorist attack since 9/11/01 includes insufficient funding of the "Homeland Security" agency and, more grandly, to window-dressing pretenses for actual, effective security measures (Berry, forthcoming). In essence, the U.S. public is told two messages: The administration will protect us from terrorism while actually doing little in that direction and while, simultaneously, riling up Al Qaeda and other enemy groups, thus ensuring that anti-US hatred and violence will be kept at a high boil.

There is evidence, from abundant news sources, that the Bush administration was likely pre-warned about the 9/11 attack. For brevity, I will point the reader to Douglas Kellner's (2003) academic work and Gore Vidal's (2002) more popular, journalistic treatment. These, among other sources, raise questions that have yet to be answered, or even properly posed, on the failure of the administration to respond to evidence that we were to be attacked, the manner in which we were to be attacked, and the probable date for the attack.

But now that the disaster has occurred, the risks remain. To give some examples, it was 16 months after 9/11/01 that the U.S. authorities at airports nationwide finally had the capacity to check all bags loaded onto commercial airliners for explosives (Wolf, 2003). In the wake of 9/11, the newly-created Transportation Security Administration (TSA) hired more screeners to screen passengers and luggage through airport security checks, an important move since these screeners comprise the first line of defense for commercial airliners. Yet in April 2003, we learn that the U.S. will reduce the screener ranks by 6,000 screeners or 11%, due to our ailing budget. According to the TSA director, "While we still live in a dangerous world, it also is time to assess our workplace requirements in relation to budget realities" (*Reuters*, 2003a). The icing on the threats-to-airliners cake was the decision to cut the federal air marshal program despite renewed hijacking threats (Meeks, 2003a; Miller, 2003). The federal air marshal program places highly-skilled, well-trained, armed federal marshals on board flights to manage hijacking situations. In a story line that has become commonplace, the Bush administration decided to cut the funding for this program because it costs too much for the air marshals' overnight hotel stays. Given that "airliners remain the most alluring terrorist target," such a decision is "inexcusable" (*New York Times*, 2003a, p. 20). Because of shock and anger registered by the public at this decision, the TSA decided against this cut-back. However, the federal marshals who told the media about the proposed cut-back have been threatened with prosecution under the Patriot Act (Meeks, 2003b).

The Democratic party leveled its criticisms directly at the U.S. president who, they say, "is failing the first responders in the war on terrorism by not adequately funding police, fire, and health personnel" (*Reuters*, 2003b). The first responders still do not have the necessary equipment, training and communication systems necessary for homeland defense according to a report issued over 500 days after the 9/11 attacks. The Bush administration's neglect of homeland defense funding has relegated the task of funding homeland security to already cash-strapped cities and states that are "still reeling from federal and state tax cuts that primarily benefit the wealthy"; moreover, the administration forced a $2.5 billion cut for homeland security efforts while congressional Republicans cut an additional $1 billion from homeland security, and now contemplates the elimination of over 1,200 FBI agents.

A year and a half after 9/11/01, we read:

> Among the biggest challenges facing Tom Ridge, the homeland security czar, is protecting America's privately owned infrastructure from terrorist attack – its power plants, pipelines, shipyards [and chemical plants]. . . . Mr. Ridge has said, and a new report by the General Accounting Office confirms, that most of these facilities are vulnerable. One would expect President Bush to put the safety of these plants at the top of his list. But so far the administration has offered no legislation to address the issue. . . . [P]rotection is spotty at best, and no substitute for an industry-wide strategy (*New York Times*, 2003b, p. 22).

A month after that, in May of 2003, we find that a bill has been submitted by the Bush administration, ostensibly to protect against chemical security breaches. The U.S. has 15,000 chemical plants and other sites that store large amounts of hazardous materials; we also have over one hundred "sites where toxic gases released in a terrorist attack could kill or injure more than a million people" (*New York Times*, 2003c, p. 26). The administration's bill, though, does not require the most dangerous plants to submit plans for security to the Homeland Security Department for review. The reason given by the administration is that the Department doesn't have the resources for review; thus the bill, as put forth by the administration, "asks nothing particularly creative of industry" (p. 26).

Also lacking are biodefense specialists, a vital resource needed to fight bioterrorism (Fox, 2003). We have a dearth of such qualified people anyway, with many of those planning to retire, and those with the right skills haven't been recruited to replace them, "leaving the federal government, and the nation, vulnerable." According to the report, issued by Partnership for Public Service and cited by Fox, "If a major biological attack occurs, . . . the vitality of our biodefense corps will spell the difference between bad outcomes and catastrophic ones."

In an example of how security funds, scarce though they are, were used for non-terrorism purposes is the failed attempt on the part of Texas Republican Representatives to round up absent Democrats for a vote. The Department of Homeland Security was used as "patronage police" in tracking down Democratic members of Congress who fled their state in order to stop the voting on a re-districting plan that would favor Republicans in future elections. So the Republican whip of the House of Representatives, Tom DeLay, used Homeland Security funds and personnel (1,000 hours and 54 Security officers) to bring them back (*New York Times*, 2003d).

Perhaps the most telling indicator of our ill-preparedness and the frustrations of those aware of our failure to provide security is the resignation of a top White House counterterrorism advisor, Rand Beers, in June of 2003. Mr. Beers resigned because, as he stated, "The administration wasn't matching its deeds to its words in the war on terrorism. They're making us less secure, not more secure" (quoted in Blumenfeld, 2003). So he has left his post as National Security Council special assistant to the president for combating terrorism, as a result of seeing "the things that weren't being done" (Blumenfeld, 2003).

The lag time for security measures to be put in place has not been a matter of lacking expertise, materials, or money. Money for security is not scarce; it is simply not distributed, remaining in the hands of ultra-wealthy individuals and corporations, who, if forced to pay taxes, could easily cover the cost of "homeland security" (Ivins, 2003). For instance, at a time of dismal "budget realities," the right-controlled Congress has decided on a major dividend tax cut for the wealthy. Or, as Dionne (2003) writes:

> Politicians might find the courage to get serious about the nation's fiscal condition if they simply noted that the president is willing to do all he can to fight the war on terror – except for anything that might inconvenience the high-end taxpayers who form his political base. Here he is, after all, calling for large increases in military spending, preparing for an expensive war in Iraq and saying he will do all he can to defend the homeland – while also proposing to reduce government revenue (p. 27).

Paul Krugman (2003) goes further to say that "politics trumps national security" when he writes that, "the Bush administration isn't serious about protecting the homeland. Instead, it continues to subordinate U.S. security needs to its unchanged political agenda" (p. 23). Immediately after 9/11, Krugman reminds us, Democrat and Republican bipartisanship fell prey to traditional conservative-right suspicion of any funding for programs other than the military. Plus there is the right-wing adoration of the "heartland," by which Krugman means the Bush administration's refusal to protect large urban areas, like New York City, and states with large urban populations that, significantly, did not vote for Bush in 2000. The result is that the Department of Homeland Security "spends [seven] times as much protecting each resident of Wyoming as it does protecting each resident of New York" (p. 23).

Invitation to Terrorism. Before and since the U.S. has gone to war in Iraq, the Homeland Security chief, Tom Ridge, has warned the U.S. public that we can expect more terrorist attacks *because* of the U.S. preemptive attack against Iraq. Indeed, the U.S. preemptive strike on Iraq has angered Al Qaeda to the point that our actions have provided a recruiting tool for Al Qaeda (*New York Times*, 2003e; Van Natta & Butler, 2003). Similarly, the director of the Central Intelligence Agency, George Tenet, warned Congress in the Fall of 2002 that "there was only one circumstance in which the U.S. need worry about Iraq sharing weapons with terrorists: if Washington attacked Saddam" (Dowd, 2003, p. 31). This implies that either the U.S. attacked Saddam in order to be attacked in consequence or that the Bush administration did not care if we were attacked in retaliation. In support of the proposition that our administration invites terrorism, *The Guardian* headlines:

"US Buoyant as Saddam urges Jihad" (2003a). We might interpret this to mean that the U.S. (meaning the Bush administration, not the U.S. public) is happy that Saddam Hussein ordered his people to engage in a holy war against us. In other words, the Bush administration seems to have known that starting a war with Iraq would increase the chances of the U.S. being attacked and they did it anyway.

To make matters stranger still, the administration's stated purposes for attacking Iraq were to find Iraqi weapons of mass destruction (WMD) and to rid Iraq of Al Qaeda terrorists. However, as Giacomo (2003) reports, after the U.S. invasion and war, there has been no sign of Hussein's suspected weapons of mass destruction, and even if WMD were discovered, global skepticism would abound that the U.S. planted them to justify its war. To date (Fall of 2003, months after the US-led strike and continuous searches), no WMD caches have been discovered. As to the supposed Al Qaeda link, the repeatedly- and dramatically-stated connection between the 9/11 attacks and Saddam Hussein has not been supported: the UN Security Council, responsible for tracking Al Qaeda, has "found no evidence linking Al Qaeda to Saddam Hussein's administration in Iraq" (O'Brien, 2003, p. 12). The Council's report did find, though, that *a new generation* of Qaeda-trained terrorists are insurgent and threatening to the global community.

It is becoming clearer that the objective of the Bush administration's "war on terrorism" is not security. Instead, the objectives seem to be to maintain public fear by repeated warnings of attack, to keep terrorism at the forefront of our imaginations, and to actually increase the likelihood of terrorism. Kellner (2003) goes further to describe the Bush regime as terrorists, combining the Bush administration with the Taliban, bin Laden, and Al Qaeda as "reactionary forces" (p. 22). He finds that the Bush policy, as put forward in The National Security Strategy of the United States of America, "portends a militarist future and an era of perpetual war in which a new militarism could generate a cycle of unending violence and retribution" (p. 21). The "Bush administration reactionaries and Al Qaeda," continues Kellner, "could be perceived as representing complementary poles of a reactionary right-wing conservatism and militarism" (p. 22). So, scarily, it has been proposed that the Bush administration would benefit from further terrorist attacks on the U.S. and, thus, this administration discourages any effective prevention and control strategies. As is now becoming inescapable, the generally belligerent U.S. rhetoric and actions toward any society that is "against us" could well create a groundswell of new terrorists. We can expect "blowback and reprisal" (Kellner, 2003, p. 2) because our war-like behavior has "produced more enemies than friends in the Arab and Muslim world, and thus [we] have increased the potential for the rise of future terrorist Islamist cadres" ready and willing to attack us (Kellner, p. 3). Or, as put succinctly by Chalmers Johnson (2000), empire has its costs.

PLAYING ON FEAR, DIVERTED PUBLIC ATTENTION, AND RIGHTS ABUSE

Fear. Perhaps the most prominent fear, on the topic at hand, is fear of an unknown and unpredictable terrorist attack. There are also fears of being accused of being unpatriotic, thus creating fear of reprisals from one's own people. But fear of "the other," the outsider-terrorist, seems to be taking precedence in the U.S. presently.

The *Chicago Tribune* reports in a headline that "Bush taps America's new fear" and goes on to say that "President Bush has marshaled the argument for war with Iraq many ways and many times, but it can still be reduced to a single word: Fear" (2003a). In *The Progressive* editor's note entitled "A Drumbeat of Fear," Matthew Rothschild wonders about Bush's fear rhetoric and his need to make the U.S. public feel fearful. He interviewed Mark Crispin Miller, author of a book about Bush, who states that the "notion of unprecedented vulnerability is absolutely crucial to the Bush team's anti-constitutional program" (Rothschild, 2003, p. 4). When Bush emphasizes fear and warns the U.S. public to be afraid, what he really means (Miller believes) is: "We were safe, now we're in danger, and the danger is so severe that you must give me all possible power" (p. 4).

Klein (2003) describes the marketing of fear in terms of protectionism and isolationism. She finds that a "growing number of free-market economists, politicians and military strategists" are pushing for a fortress mentality and accompanying practices including a continental security perimeter from Mexico to Canada. This fortress mentality relies on "a useful hoax, helping U.S. citizens to see how unsafe they really are" (p. 10).

The instillation of fear in the U.S. public by the right-wing is replete with vivid images of outside threats, violent reactions by the U.S. to those threats, and promised protection from those threats. Powerful, right-wing political leaders, while expressing tremendous rage at "evildoers," promise relief from fear in exchange for reliance upon them, the terrorism warriors. We are to believe that we will be protected if we unquestioningly surrender our lives to their control.

Distractions. Our fear of being attacked diverts us from domestic program (environmental, economic, health care, and so on) erosion; in addition, the right-wing administration's show of force itself serves as a distraction. Combining public fear and the promise of security, the results have included invasions, war, and a costly and ineffective missile shield program. In December of 2002, the Bush administration delivered on earlier promises to begin building missile defenses "based on the present unreliable technology" (*New York Times*, 2002, p. 32). The reality is that "the Pentagon does not yet have a missile defense technology reliable enough to protect American cities" with the ground-based defensive systems failing in test runs and costing billions of dollars. Rushing into a missile defense strategy knowing that its underlying technology does not operate as advertised make no sense. So why do it? Perhaps because it makes us as a nation seem mighty and because it distracts us from what the administration is not doing: peace-keeping and real public protection.

The Loss of Liberty. Since George W. Bush took office and particularly since 9/11, human rights violations are in abundance. The loss of rights is not limited to terrorism issues, per se. While we have been preoccupied with the "war on terrorism," we have experienced a reduction of minorities' (notably women's) rights, as a covert by-product of this "war." More directly relevant to the war on terrorism, we find the oppression of U.S. and non-US citizens through civil rights elimination, unlawful detention, being named as enemy combatants, and so on.

Infringements upon civil liberties will likely prove self-defeating. The *Chicago Tribune* (2003b) notes that: "By embracing repressive regimes and ignoring legal standards in its treatment of suspects and prisoners, the Bush administration is undermining its own war against terrorism." David Cole (2002) describes a more specific liberty-loss via FBI snooping on citizens as time-wasting, constitutional-rights-violating, and ineffective in fighting crime. Cole is referring to Attorney General John Ashcroft's amending FBI guidelines to allow FBI spying against people involved in civil rights groups, anti-war groups, and other "dissident" organizations and movements that do not support a neo-conservative agenda. Ashcroft's new guidelines, Cole finds, "are virtually certain to deflect the attention of law enforcement from stopping terrorist acts toward policing lawful political activities" (p. 23).

Whether or not civil rights reduction will prove counterproductive to the war on terrorism, right-wing policies nevertheless are massively encroaching on civil liberties under the auspices of public protection. One strategy is to loosely define "enemy combatants" and detain those so defined without trial or legal representation. A case in point is Yasser Esam Hamdi, the American-born Saudi who was captured in Afghanistan and has been held in a military brig for over a year, showing that "Unlike wars that begin with declarations and conclude with treaties, America's 'war on terror' may become permanent if the White House so decides" (*New York Times*, 2003f, p. 24). In another case among many, an Iraqi scientist was arrested by the U.S. military in May of 2003 on suspicion that she is a key figure in Iraq's alleged bio-weapons program. In fact, she wrote a book entitled *Toxic Pollution, the Gulf War, and Sanctions*; the publisher (South End Press) is trying to win her release (Del Castillo, 2003).

Under the Bush doctrine (discussed below), American citizens are being held indefinitely, on little evidence, without access to lawyers or the outside world, without being charged with a crime, without seeing a judge, without being interrogated, and are being held in solitary confinement as "enemy combatants."

It is unknown how many Americans have been held without charges in terrorism investigations since September 11, partly because the U.S. Justice Department won't divulge that information (Egan, 2003). In the 11 months since 9/11/01, the Justice Department has detained about a thousand noncitizens in connection with terrorism inquiries, many for illegally entering the country or overstaying visas. These detainees have suffered a pattern of physical and verbal abuse: some are held in lockdowns for 23 hours a day; only taken outside their cells in handcuffs, leg irons, and heavy chains; slammed against walls; and being subjected to such verbal taunts as, "You're going to die here." The Justice Department has offered "no apologies for finding every legal way possible to protect the American public from further terrorist attacks" even though there is no indication that these detentions protect us (*New York Times*, 2003g, p. 30). Nor are children exempt from preventive detention as "enemy combatants." *The Guardian* (2003b) reported that the "US military has admitted that children aged 16 years and younger are among the detainees being interrogated at its prison camp in Guantanamo Bay, Cuba." A U.S. military spokesperson would not say how many of these young people are being held, nor would he give the age of the youngest of these teenagers, who are captured and held "as active combatants against U.S. forces."

Overall, the U.S. record on human rights, since the right took power in 2001, has undoubtedly been damaged. The Human Rights Watch (HRW) has reported that "Many countries resent or are reluctant to join the U.S. war on terrorism partly because of the government's tendency to ignore human rights in its conduct of the war" (*Associated Press*, 2003a). The HRW report went on to say "even rhetorical U.S. support for human rights has been rare" and that the Bush administration's "tendency to ignore human rights in fighting terrorism is not only disturbing in its own right, it is dangerously counterproductive" since it generates terrorist recruits. A strong human rights culture would be an effective antidote to terrorism pathology but the Bush administration "sees human rights mainly as an obstacle to its goals" (*Associated Press*, 2003a). The United States is indeed "undermining its own war on terror by violating human rights standards" (Doyle, 2003). Besides suppressing prisoners' rights at the U.S. military base in Guantanamo Bay, Cuba, the U.S. discourages popular support for its aims by supporting oppressive regimes in, for instance, Pakistan and Saudi Arabia. In this odd way, the U.S. is reinforcing the logic of terrorists themselves – namely that ends justify violent means.

TERRORISM AND THE FAR RIGHT

Right-wing ideology and behavior – by elected and appointed officials or by those more commonly thought of as terrorists – serve similar goals. Both embrace coercion, both encourage public fear and, more covertly, both are concerned with maintaining their long-held (usually majority, male, propertied) privileges.

Let me first distinguish the merely conservative right from the far right, and then distinguish the two forms of the U.S. far right. The conservative right are not rabidly or radically right. They, as a public or as a group of political figures, share right-leaning views such as states' rights vs. federal control, low taxes coupled with reduced social services for the needy, protection of gun ownership, and the like. The far right are more extreme in that their views, and the policies and practices reflecting those views, are highly exclusionary (sexist, racist, anti-immigrant, homophobic, etc.), bluntly-stated, and violently destructive on a social as well as a global level. The U.S. far right, can be divided into, for lack of better terms (a) the formal or legitimized far right and (b) the informal or non-legitimized far right. The formal far right have been legally sanctioned and are highly organized. They cater to the conservative needs of wealthy corporate owners who serve as contributors to their political organizations; but knowing that they need a broader constituency to stay in power, they voice fringe, extremist social views and support fringe, extremist social policies in order to gain fringe, extremist votes. The formalized far right are dependent upon both sets of people (wealthy corporate structures and the rabidly socially intolerant) to maintain power. A large segment of the post-Reagan Republican party represents this form of the far right.

The informal, non-legitimized far right are far less organized, less skilled (usually) in voicing their demands, less financially-endowed, and thus less powerful and less influential.[1] This form of the far right is represented by the survivalist right – a broad category including militias (for instance, the Militia of Montana), the Ku Klux Klan, white supremacists (for example, White Aryan Resistance, Aryan Nation), the Posse Comitatus, and others. They support the policies of the formal far right but also sometimes engage in more direct, unsophisticated violence such as murder and bombings. The two far right factions, formal and informal, have longstanding, mutually-supportive relationships and their memberships overlap to some degree (Berry, 1999). Scholars and social commentators have written about the similarities between the survivalist right and the formal political right. For good overviews of the informal far right, see Stern (1997), Lamy (1996), Coates (1995), and Aho (1995); for commonalities across the formal and informal far right, see Levitas (2002), Bennett (1995), and Bellant (1991).

The far right globally – U.S. formal and informal far right, the Taliban, Al Qaeda, and others – share important traits. Generally, they are sexist, fundamentalist in religion, nationalist, moral-absolutist, intolerant of relativist thinking and alternative viewpoints, and concrete thinkers. They display a high degree of overt emotions, sans intellectualism, fiercely expressing religious fundamentalism and stating their *beliefs* (avoiding documented evidence) in strict, absolutist terms. Their expressed high emotion can be used for destructive purposes as when they incite a population to feel fear, revenge, and other emotions. As an aid to whipping up support, they also readily construct enemies.

Sociology of the Enemy. The sociology of the enemy is an area of study unto itself, describing the social process of artificially constructing enemies, creating an "other" for socially functional purposes (Aho, 1994). An important function of enemies is that they provide a rallying point, a point upon which to focus hatred and rally in "defense" against. The construction of enemies gives us a dividing line between "us" and "them," with "them" determined to be inferior and deserving of unequal treatment. All forms of the far right utilize the concept of the enemy, marginalizing people who are different from them and thus determined to be "evil." The U.S. far right deny or hope to deny rights to whole categories of people worthy (in their minds) of oppression: women, non-whites, non-native-born, non-Christian, homosexuals, and so on. Privileges should be restricted to them alone (right-leaning, white, straight, Christian, US-born males). If enemies (such as Muslims) can be successfully socially created, oppression is justified.

Enemies can be created on the smallest of differences, as we have seen recently in the creation of enemies who disagree politically with the far right but otherwise are indistinguishable demographically (white, US-born, etc.). Peace activists have been met with aggression, profanity, derision, and obscene gestures from pro-war activists (Murphy, 2003; Wong, 2003). Of far greater consequence, though, is the formal far right's creation of "evildoers," an "axis of evil," and Middle Easterners as presumably terrorists by virtue of birthplace.

Religion. Religion is a staunch underlying justification for far right actions and philosophies (Lears, 2003). A common theme across the U.S. formal far right and the informal far right is the focus on fundamentalist Christianity as the *only* religion and as the only guide for morality. Since their religion is the only legitimate one, it can be imposed on others; uncooperative others do not have the right to their own beliefs or non-beliefs.

Herbert describes Bush's "messianic vision of himself" as a warrior for good vs. evil (2003, p. 31). The president issued his call to arms in theological language: "The term 'axis of evil' was coined to give the war on terrorism a religious edge" and the war is viewed as a "spiritual battle" (Ritsch, 2003, p. 22). The president refused to meet with the National Council of Churches to discuss the moral issues of going to war, a war which the churches opposed. Finally, Ritsch (a Presbyterian pastor) reminds us that, "In a nuclear age, American triumphalism is not only spiritually bereft, it is, quite possibly, apocalyptic in its implications" (p. 23).

Speaking of the apocalypse, Carver (2003) describes how, after 9/11/01, Bush discovered his "life's mission." Bush "became convinced that God was calling him to engage the forces of evil in battle," with the U.S. being the definer of good and evil. In this battle, the U.S. is placed firmly on the side of the angels, which, in truth, represents a minority viewpoint. Nearly all mainstream U.S. churches opposed going to war against Iraq, and the "concept of placing America in God's camp sticks in the throat of a lot of American clergy." However, Bush's religious rhetoric does ring true for some religious zealots: About one-third of U.S. Christians are evangelicals. Most evangelicals believe in the second coming of Christ, and that the second coming will take place in the Middle East after "a titanic battle with the Anti-Christ." And who would be the anti-Christ? Saddam Hussein. In short, these far-right Christians and Mr. Bush may see the battles in the Middle East as part of Armageddon, as described in the Bible's Book of Revelations. For them, stark talk of good vs. evil is founded in their fundamentalist beliefs, and the U.S. war in the Middle East is "divinely ordained" (Carver, 2003).

Jackson Lears (2003) discusses Bush's war on Iraq as a "crusade," a set of events guided (Bush believes) by "the hand of a just and faithful God" (p. 29). Lears writes, "From the outset [Bush] has been convinced that his presidency is part of a divine plan, even telling a friend while he was governor of Texas, 'I believe God wants me to run for president.' This conviction that he is doing God's will has surfaced more openly since 9/11" with his self-presentation as the leader of a global war against evil. Pointing to the obvious danger signs, Lears writes:

> The belief that one is carrying out divine purpose can serve legitimate needs and sustain opposition to injustice, but it can also promote dangerous *simplifications* – especially if the believer has virtually unlimited power, as Mr. Bush does. The slide into self-righteousness is a constant threat (p. 29, emphasis added).

Absolutisms, Concreteness and Simplicity. An important trait of the right-wing is their inability or unwillingness to see things from an alternative viewpoint. Relativity is seen as a sign of weakness. Since cultural relativity is not something they are interested in or willing to consider, the right-wing are sometimes surprised at reactions from others who don't think like they do. Mackey (2003) describes the wrong-headedness of the U.S. military action that killed Saddam Hussein's sons (on July 22, 2003). The U.S. military seemed to think the Iraqis would be pleased, but the Iraqis were disappointed that they did not get to exact revenge themselves. It would have been far better, she says, if the sons had been captured, put on trial, and punished because Iraq is a "society that rejects authority and thrives on conspiracy theory" (p. 23). It is a culture with "a deep-seated need for revenge" (p. 23). These are traits that the U.S. authorities overlooked.

In another example of unwillingness to think in relative terms, Filkins (2003) describes combat scenes of U.S. marines battling Iraqi fighters who sometimes mix with (and become indistinguishable from) civilians. One marine, in describing their work, said, "We had a great day. We killed a lot of people" (p. 1). Some of the killed, as it turns out, were civilians. The Bush administration hawks view any attacks on U.S. troops as cruel, unfair, and as war crimes while not viewing our similar treatment of Iraqi civilians as cruel, unfair, or as war crimes. From a warrior's or a terrorist's point of view, it may be acceptable to hurt or kill "others," even if they are noncombatants, and call it "collateral damage." Yet our own innocents, as in the 9/11 victims, are worthy and valuable.

On the whole, the far right show an incapacity to view social phenomena, people, cultures, etc. in relative terms. They seem unwilling to imagine how others feel and think, to be empathetic to "outsiders." Their explanations are simplistic and absolutisms are pronounced in black-and-white, concrete terms. It is true for the Taliban, with their strict views on grooming, women's roles, recreation, and indeed all aspects of social life. It is also true for the U.S. right-wing. A phrase we will long remember from this time period is the president's remark: "You're either with us or against us."

SUMMARY

In support of the proposition that the right-wing in the U.S. government is not interested in controlling terrorism, I offer the following: (a) Attention to terrorism serves as a distraction from severe social, economic, and environmental problems in the US; (b) Fear of terrorism serves to increase support for bad policies and bad policymakers, due to the public need for protection and false assurances from the administration that we will be protected; and (c) The right-wing appears reluctant to discourage terrorism and instead has engaged in some activities (notably the invasion of Iraq) that seem to encourage it. Also discussed are the overlaps across terrorists of several stripes – formal far right U.S. political parties, informal far right U.S. organizations, and far right terrorists who wage jihad against the U.S. (for example, Al Qaeda). These far right factions, U.S. and non-US, share important common behavior and beliefs: religious fundamentalism, simplistic interpretations of complex social phenomena, and violence to enforce their demands for public cooperation.

Focusing on the U.S. formal far right, John Le Carre (2003) lists the reasons he believes that the U.S. has gone mad. The evidence he cites includes: human rights reduction, secretive media and corporate behavior, distraction from the botched 2000 presidential election, the Enron fiasco, tax cuts for the rich, environmental destruction, trashed international treaties, the emphasis on fear, the focus on enemies, the predominance of religion, our keen oil interests, absolutism, and distraction from the real purpose of the war (corporate accumulation of wealth rather than freedom and democracy). The U.S. reaction to 9/11, Le Carre says, has been erosion of freedoms that once were "the envy of the world," a compliant media that does not dare say what the Bush administration does not want them to say, and vested corporate interests deeply tied to right-wing politics. Le Carre couches his conclusions in terms of *deflection* when he writes, "Bush and his junta succeeded in deflecting America's anger from bin Laden to Saddam Hussein"; and he refers unflinchingly to the U.S. preemptive strike on Iraq as a "surreal" act of terrorism. All the while, the American public are not only misled but are being "browbeaten and kept in a state of ignorance and fear." A clear message is, those of us who are not with the president are against him, worse, we are *the enemy*. Relying on religious justification, the right-wing administration determines what is absolute good and absolute evil, when the true meaning of the delineation is that one must be on their side . . . or else.

CONCLUSIONS

The war on Iraq, continued terrorism, and the repressive reaction by the Bush administration was made possible, or certainly made easier, by the events of 9/11. One of the most repressive outcomes of 9/11, and the public fear that followed, is the "Bush Doctrine." The Bush Doctrine is a policy paper, formally entitled The National Security Strategy of the United States of America. According to Todd Gitlin (2003), the doctrine is a heavy-handed, self-righteous, dangerous, imperialist and costly policy allowing for pre-emptive strikes against anyone at any time, without explanation. It is "a romantic justification for easy recourse to war whenever and wherever an American president chooses" (p. 35). George Packer (2003) writes similarly of the Bush doctrine, that it is "a blend of aggressive nationalism and incompetent imperialism, led by people who want dominance without responsibility" (p. 38).

The Bush strategy mobilizes fear, stoking paranoia, and linking Al Qaeda's indisputable threat after 9/11 to all societies that the Bush administration hopes to assault and conquer. At the same time, the Bush doctrine appears to guard public safety while it fails to acknowledge that "reckless swashbuckling helps recruit terrorists" and "indulges in the same drastic oversimplification that motivates the terrorists" thus supplying "a gift to anti-Americans everywhere" (Gitlin, pp. 36, 37).

Moreover, the far-right Bush administration feels no need to tell the public the truth and indeed hides the truth, as we have discovered in the Summer of 2003, with the absence of WMD in Iraq. The administration feels no compunction to say what it knows regarding terrorism, the source of this information, or how legitimate and convincing this information is (Gitlin, p. 36). Such secrecy and falsehoods may, unless checked, increase fear on the part of the public. We are fearful of Al Qaeda-type terrorists and many are becoming grossly worried about what our government will do (create enemies, encourage terrorism) and not do (protect us).

Suggestions. Since it is not unlikely that terrorism will re-visit the US, and since the right-wing appear uninterested in stopping it, the left needs to offer solutions for managing terrorism. Broadly, we need to expand political freedom globally.

More specifically, a progressive foreign policy would require more and different commitments, not just peacekeeping, but also (and very importantly) economic development, disallowing a worsening of economic inequality; economics is not merely a sideshow in the search for democracy. Aside from economic changes, democratic multilateralism would be helpful. Multilateralism would require that the U.S. allow and encourage UN peacekeeping operations, fair representation in the International Criminal Court, and the like. It goes without saying that we should avoid military interventions and should pay attention to problematic areas worldwide before they reach a crisis stage.

In addition to coordinated international efforts across humanitarian, financial, legal-judiciary, military, and political fronts, global social movements toward social justice would be most beneficial. Such global movements, Kellner (2003) advises, would require that all citizens become informed about the conflicts of the present, as well as how to deal effectively and peacefully with those conflicts.

Grassroots movements are also essential, and, luckily, we have some evidence of local defiance. Small and large cities in the U.S. are joining a rising chorus of municipalities that have passed resolutions "urging local law enforcement officials and others contacted by federal officials to refuse requests under the Patriot Act that they believe violate an individual's civil rights under the Constitution" (Nieves, 2003). These cities have passed ordinances outlawing voluntary compliance with the Patriot Act. Likewise, lawmakers and lobbyists are increasingly sounding alarms about the Patriot Act, presumably an anti-terrorism act (passed soon after 9/11), which gives the government unprecedented powers to monitor citizens. The Act allows libraries to track who borrows what books, allows bookstores to track who buys what books, asks businesses to "hand over electronic records on finances, telephone calls, e-mails and other personal data," and permits investigators to "subpoena private books, records, papers, documents and other items"... all in the name of anti-terrorism (Nieves). The Patriot Act is not going to stop terrorism; it is merely intrusive, abusive snooping on private citizens. Grassroots movements, made up of thinking citizens, are trying to stop it.

Progressive activism includes a courageous and honest return to social standards such as equality, tolerance, open-mindedness, freedom of speech, civil rights, and so on. At the same time, it must be seriously proposed that countering terrorism with an alternative, US-brand of terrorism does not reduce terrorism. A better, more effective strategy would be to talk and, better yet, listen, to other cultures on how best to contain hatred and violence through education, economic assistance, or any means necessary.

Within the US, dissemination of truth and exposure of repression would be helpful. Exposure of right-wing agendas has become more difficult of late because our media, educational systems, and other resources for dispersing facts and viewpoints have been greatly compromised by the right, and because criticism is met with punishment. It must be remembered, however, that the progressive majority have historically widened protection for those who need it, have increased security, and have expanded rights – including the right to be free from terrorism from without as well as from within.

NOTE

1. Or, as Julian Bond, NAACP executive director, says, "The average KKK member may be stupid, but the well-financed forces of the radical right are not" (*Associated Press*, 2003b).

REFERENCES

Aho, J. A. (1994). *This thing of darkness: A sociology of the enemy*. Seattle: University of Washington.
Aho, J. A. (1995). *The politics of righteousness: Idaho Christian patriotism*. Seattle: University of Washington.
Associated Press (2003a). Human rights report rips in U.S. record. *Associated Press* (http://msnbc.com) (January 14).
Associated Press (2003b). NAACP's Julian Bond raps Bush. *Associated Press* (http://msnbc.com) (July 14).
Bellant, R. (1991). *Old Nazis, the new right, and the Republican Party*. Boston: South End.
Bennett, D. H. (1995). *The party of fear: The American far right from Nativism to the militia movement*. New York: Vintage.
Berry, B. (1999). *Social rage: Emotion and cultural conflict*. New York: Garland.
Berry, B. (forthcoming). Sexual victimization by airport screeners, Post 9/11: Terrorism, sexism, and capitalism at work. In: C. T. M. Coston (Ed.), *Victimizing Vulnerable Groups: Images of Uniquely High Risk Crime Targets*. Westport: Praeger.
Blumenfeld, L. (2003). Ex-security aide blasts terror war. *Washington Post* (http://msnbc.com) (June 16).
Carver, T. (2003). Bush puts God on his side. *British Broadcasting Corporation* (http://news.bbc.co.uk) (April 6).

Chicago Tribune (2003a). Bush taps America's new fear. *Chicago Tribune* (http://chicagotribune.com) (March 18).

Chicago Tribune (2003b). U.S. rights stand called self-defeating. *Chicago Tribune* (http:// chicagotribune.com) (January 15).

Coates, J. (1995). *Armed and dangerous: The rise of the survivalist right.* New York: Hill and Wang.

Cole, D. (2002). Misdirected snooping doesn't stop terror. *New York Times* (June 4), A23.

Del Castillo, D. (2003). Publishing House criticizes U.S. Government for arrest of Iraqi scientist on "most wanted" list. *Chronicle of Higher Education* (May 13), http://chronicle.com.

Dionne, E. J. (2003). It's time to do the math. *Washington Post National Weekly Edition* (January 6–12), 27.

Dowd, M. (2003). Powell without Picasso. *New York Times* (February 5), A31.

Doyle, M. (2003). U.S. accused of human rights violations. *British Broadcasting Corporation* (http://news.bbc.co.uk) (January 14).

Egan, T. (2003). Terrorism task force detains an American without charges. *New York Times* (April 4), A14.

Filkins, D. (2003). Either take a shot or take a chance. *New York Times* (March 29), A1, B4.

Fox, M. (2003). Report: U.S. lacks bureaucrats to fight bioterror. *Reuters* (http://reuters.com) (July 8).

Giacomo, C. (2003). No sign yet of Iraqi weapons of mass destruction. *Reuters* (http://reuters.com) (March 31).

Gitlin, T. (2003). America's age of empire. *Mother Jones* (January/February), 35–37.

The Guardian (2003a). U.S. buoyant as Saddam urges Jihad. *The Guardian* (http://guardian.co.uk) (April 1).

The Guardian (2003b). U.S. detains children at Guantanamo Bay. *The Guardian* (http://guardian.co.uk) (April 23).

Herbert, B. (2003). Ready for the peace? *New York Times* (March 30), A31.

Ivins, M. (2003). Tax dodgers apply here. *The Progressive* (January), 46.

Johnson, C. (2000). *Blowback: The costs and consequences of American empire.* New York: Henry Holt.

Kellner, D. (2003). *From 9/11 to terror war: The dangers of the Bush legacy.* Lanham, Rowman & Littlefield.

Klein, N. (2003). The rise of the fortress continent. *The Nation* (February 3), 10.

Krugman, P. (2003). Red-blue terror alert. *New York Times* (April 4), A23.

Lamy, P. (1996). *Millennium rage: Survivalists, White Supremacists, and the Doomsday prophecy.* New York: Plenum.

Le Carre, J. (2003). The United States of America has gone mad. *Times of London* (http:// timesonline.co.uk) (January 15).

Lears, J. (2003). How a war became a crusade. *New York Times* (March 11), A29.

Levitas, D. (2002). *The terrorist next door: The militia movement and the radical right.* New York: St. Martin's.

Mackey, S. (2003). Better alive than dead. *New York Times* (July 24), A23.

Meeks, B. N. (2003a). Air marshals pulled from key flights. *MSNBC* (http://msnbc.com) (July 29).

Meeks, B. N. (2003b). TSA in "witch hunt," air marshals say. MSNBC (http://msnbc.com) (August 12).

Miller, L. (2003). U.S. may cut air marshals despite warning. *Seattle Post-Intelligencer* (http:// seattlepi.com) (July 30).

Murphy, D. E. (2003). Two sides on war are entrenched in spokane, but cracks show. *New York Times* (April 3), B11.

Nieves, E. (2003). Local officials defy the patriot act. *Washington Post* (http://msnbc.com) (April 21).

New York Times (2002). The rush to build missile defenses. *New York Times* (December 18), A32.

New York Times (2003a). Shortchanging security. *New York Times* (August 6), A20.

New York Times (2003b). Avoiding chemical catastrophe. *New York Times* (April 1), A22.

New York Times (2003c). Chemical security. *New York Times* (May 5), A26.

New York Times (2003d). Diverting the war on terrorism. *New York Times* (June 10), A26.

New York Times (2003e). Terrorists. *New York Times* (March 16), A11.

New York Times (2003f). Detaining "enemy combatants." *New York Times* (January 10), A24.

New York Times (2003g). The abusive detentions of Sept. 11. *New York Times* (June 3), A30.

O'Brien, T. L. (2003). U.N. Group finds no Hussein-Al Qaeda link. *New York Times* (June 27), A12.

Packer, G. (2003). America's age of empire. *Mother Jones* (January/February), 35, 38–39.

Reuters (2003a). U.S. to cut 6,000 airport screening jobs. *Reuters* (http://reuters.com) (April 30).

Reuters (2003b). Democrats fault Bush on homeland defense. *Reuters* (http://reuters.com) (January 25).

Ritsch, F. (2003). The bully pulpit: Of God, and man, in the Oval Office. *Washington Post National Weekly Edition* (March 10–16), 22–23.

Rothschild, M. (2003). A drumbeat of fear. *The Progressive* (April), 4.

Stern, K. S. (1997). *A force upon the plain: The American militia movement and the politics of hate.* Norman: University of Oklahoma.

Stern, J. (2003). How America created a terrorist haven. *New York Times* (August 20), A25.

Van Natta, D., & Butler, D. (2003). Anger on Iraq seen as New Qaeda recruiting tool. *New York Times* (March 16), A1, A16.

Vidal, G. (2002). *Dreaming war: Blood for oil and the Cheney-Bush Junta.* New York: Thunder's Mouth Press/Nation Books.

Wolf, J. (2003). U.S. starts screening all checked bags on flights. *Reuters* (http://reuters.com) (January 1).

Wong, B. (2003). Peace activists claim harassment. *Seattle Post-Intelligencer* (http://seattlepi.com) (April 2).

PART IV:
THE CONSTRUCTION AND
REALITY OF TERRORISM

SPEAKING OF EVIL AND TERRORISM: THE POLITICAL AND IDEOLOGICAL CONSTRUCTION OF A MORAL PANIC

Victor E. Kappeler and Aaron E. Kappeler

ABSTRACT

This article examines the political and ideological construction of terrorism as a moral panic in the United States. We begin by briefly recounting the general themes and patterns of constructing crime as a social problem. We then turn our attention to an analysis of the speeches used by political figures and law enforcement officials to construct the social reality of terrorism. We identify five rhetorical themes in the political discourse on terrorism: the epidemic, dehumanizing metaphors, reification of civilization, the construction of villains and heroes, and situating terrorism. After analyzing these themes in a historical and comparative cultural context, we discuss the role global ideologies play in our perception of social reality and how criminology reifies this conceptual order.

We are planning a broad and sustained campaign to secure our country and eradicate the evil of terrorism, ... We will find those who did this, we will smoke them out of their holes, we will get them running, and we will bring them to justice (U.S. President George W. Bush, September 15, 2001).

Terrorism and Counter-Terrorism: Criminological Perspectives
Sociology of Crime, Law and Deviance, Volume 5, 175–197
Copyright © 2004 by Elsevier Ltd.
All rights of reproduction in any form reserved
ISSN: 1521-6136/doi:10.1016/S1521-6136(03)05011-5

INTRODUCTION

The words "crime" and "criminal" conjure powerful images and understandings. Regardless of what country we live in, we are taught from childhood that people who are criminals live among us and that crime threatens our safety, well being, and sense of order. We learn that crime has devastating personal and social consequences. Crime is a cultural universal varying only in its social and political construction.

Because of the enormous threat crime entails, the eradication and punishment of criminal behavior is seen as a desirable and just goal. Crime control is basic social defense; "justice" requires the detection, control, and punishment of criminals. Crime control is a logical extension of good common sense. After all, crime is an attack on safety, freedom, and order that must be aggressively repelled; anything less is somehow unthinkable or even unpatriotic. To question this common sense understanding of crime is to reject a lifetime of socialization and an accumulation of almost sacred values. It is this feature of crime that makes it an essential component of constructing particular social and ideological orders. It is in the construction of what is "thinkable" and the consequences of uttering the unthinkable that crime gains its power.

The impact of some crimes is so enormous it shakes the very foundation of society and represents an attack on civilization. Acts of terrorism are crimes that the President of the United States described as "so terrible they offend humanity itself . . . aggressions and ambitions of the wicked must be opposed early, decisively and collectively before they threaten us all" (Bush, November 10, 2001).

The purpose of this article is not to assess the empirical reality of terrorism, not to make assertions from a social facts perspective, nor to be dismissive of the destructive nature of terrorism. Rather we will consider the language used in the political construction of the social problem. While terrorism certainly evokes emotionalism and calls for action, it is necessary to understand its ideological and rhetorical construction as a social and political problem. We begin by briefly recounting the general themes and patterns of constructing crime as a social problem. We then turn our attention to an examination of the speeches used by political figures and law enforcement officials in the United States to construct the social reality of terrorism. We identify five rhetorical themes in the political discourse on terrorism: the epidemic, dehumanizing metaphors, reification of civilization, the construction of villains and heroes, and situating terrorism. After analyzing these themes in a historical and comparative cultural context, we discuss the role of global ideologies play in our perception of social reality and how criminology reifies this conceptual order.

THE CONSTRUCTION OF CRIME PROBLEMS

Scholars have attributed the emergence of social problems to a variety of sources, such as the mass media (Fishman, 1998), urban legend (Best & Horiuchi, 1985), group hysteria, ideology, political power (Quinney, 1970), the agendas of governments and social control agencies (Kappeler, Blumberg & Potter, 1996) or latent social forces that direct public attention and shape the nature and character-istics of social problems. Despite differences in explaining their emergence, the construction of social problems, particularly crime problems, follow some fairly predictable themes and rhetorical patterns. These themes generate public support and attention and give crime problems a sustainable momentum.

Perhaps the most powerful and effective characterization of a crime problem is the claim that it threatens an entire society. Sustainable crime problems are characterized as an enormous threat to the physical safety of a majority of people, and claims are made that the problems are reaching epidemic proportions. The argument is made that the behavior is so widespread and frequent in its occurrence that no one is safe. This characterization builds an affinity of fear between the victims of a social problem and the audience. Thus crime problems are often constructed by claim-makers as widespread, affecting thousands and leaving no one untouched by the newly discovered evil.

The acceptability and duration of a crime problem is extended when it is con-structed as constituting not only a physical threat; but also a threat to fundamental social values. Crime is not just unacceptable behavior but it threatens women and children, families, freedom and our very way of life. Crime problems are almost always characterized as constituting a major threat to middle-class values, norms, or lifestyles. Blending crime problems with threats to religious beliefs, economic systems, sexual attitudes or orientations, the traditional family, or political preference increases the volatility of the issue. The fear generated by the confluence of the unpopular deviant, the innocent victim, and the perceived threat to tradition produces a formal and often violent social response. The argument is simple; a growing menace is plaguing society; the conduct of a deviant group, affects innocents and endangers tradition.

The idea that "normal" life might break down ensures that social institutions become involved in the reform process. The undesirable conduct is perceived as both a physical and substantial threat to existing social arrangements and institutions. Crime problems that reach this characterization become moral panics (Cohen, 1972); they clarify the moral boundaries of society and demonstrate that there are limits to what will be tolerated. Erich Goode and Nachman Ben-Yehuda (1994) assert that moral panics are "characterized by the feeling . . . that evildoers pose a threat to the society and to the moral order as a consequence of their behavior and, therefore, 'something should be done' about them and their behavior" (p. 31). Crime problems become calls to moral action.

Crime problems are often constructed with dramatic dichotomies among social actors. There are "virtuous" heroes and "innocent" victims contending with "evil" villains who pose a clear and certain threat. Those who engage in the social problem are characterized as "evil" and "different" from the audience. Groups most vulnerable to this construction are those who are easily distinguishable from the dominant social group. Distinctions are often as crude as race, color, religion, or national origin. Hate groups, pro-slavery advocates, supporters of prohibition, and advocates of the death penalty have all portrayed their adversaries as deviants – different and posing grave threats to society. The importance of this characterization of "difference" cannot be overstated, and it has been used throughout history to manipulate public sentiment.

Deviants are contrasted with an "innocent" or "helpless" victim population who bear the brunt of the newly found social evil. The more innocents perceived as being affected by the social problem, the greater the likelihood of public attention and support for the creation of policy targeting unpopular groups. Women and children are often used as the virtuous victims who suffer at the hands of the unpopular deviant. Casting victims as innocents authorizes the implementation of violent sanctions against the deviants – accompanied by feelings of moral superiority and the satisfaction of retribution. This is not to say that innocents do not suffer as the victims of crime; rather the focus is on the rhetorical construction of the innocent person victimized by the evil stranger.

These dualities of good and evil result in the emergence of brave and virtuous heroes who stand for the social values being threatened and offer protection from the onslaught of the different and dangerous ones. Heroes are often agents of social control institutions; those "men of action" place themselves in harm's way. Their virtues are extolled directly and in sharp contrast to the depraved deviants who threaten society. Dualities are used to develop crime control policy, enact criminal laws, and even bring nations to war.

The fear of physical danger associated with a crime problem is often short-lived if the problem fails to affect a significant proportion of a society or if its empirical reality is challenged. The crime problem must then be reconstituted so that it is linked to other problems. Normalizing and situating it into a web of interrelated social evils bolsters the declining problem. Drug abuse, for example, is linked to teenage pregnancy, high school dropout rates, and organized crime. The reformulation of an amalgamated crime problem is reinforced through symbolic construction; it becomes more powerful as part of a collective than it would be if viewed independently.

Terrorism is one of the most powerful contemporary constructions of a social threat. Unlike many other moral panics associated with crime, terrorism has been constructed in a global rather than a national political framework in ways that stir highly selected global ideologies. Terrorism is a powerful example of a social problem that follows the patterns of crime construction.

TERRORISM AS EPIDEMIC

Terrorism and crime respect no borders and threaten civilized countries throughout the world" (McCraw, May 20, 2003).

Like other crime problems, terrorism has been constructed by political claim-makers as epidemic in proportion. In the early stages of problem construction, statistics are often manipulated and disseminated by political officials and by the media. The frequency of the behavior and the actual number of individuals engaged in the newly discovered social evil are often exaggerated. Terrorism has been no exception to this pattern. Despite the lack of credible evidence about the actual numbers of people involved and the scope of terrorism, the behavior has been characterized as vast and global. Consider the President Bush's claims:

Al Qaeda operates in more than 60 nations, including some in Central and Eastern Europe. These terrorist groups seek to destabilize entire nations and regions. They are seeking chemical, biological and nuclear weapons. Given the means, our enemies would be a threat to every nation and, eventually, to civilization itself (Bush, November 6, 2001).

The threat is constructed as global, the deviants are said to be widespread, and they have designs to use unthinkable weapons that threaten entire nations. The President continues:

In four short months, our nation has . . . captured, arrested, and rid the world of thousands of terrorists . . . Most of the 19 men who hijacked planes on September the 11th were trained in Afghanistan's camps, and so were tens of thousands of others. Thousands of dangerous killers, schooled in the methods of murder, often supported by outlaw regimes, are now spread throughout the world like ticking time bombs, set to go off without warning . . . hundreds of terrorists have been arrested. Yet, tens of thousands of trained terrorists are still at large (Bush, January 29, 2002).

The assertion is that the threat is so vast, that deviants number in the tens of thousands. Evidence of the assertion, however, is based on the number of detentions and arrests by law enforcement officials without an adequate definition of terrorist activity. This form of claimsmaking- the failure to adequately define the threatening behavior- has been used in many moral panics, such as ritual child abuse, serial murder, missing children, stalking and juvenile crime. (Kappeler et al., 1996) When the empirical reality of these crime problems is measured, the actual number of people involved and the frequency of the behavior is often far less than the assertions of claimmakers.

Likewise all-inclusive language has constructed the number of potential victims of terrorism. The political rhetoric leaves no one safe from a potential attack. President Bush has remarked that terrorists have "mad, global ambitions" and a desire to "control every life and all of life" (Bush, November 6, 2001). These statements cast the broadest possible net of victimization ensuring that everyone is symbolically touched by the threat. The empirical reality of terrorist victimization pales in comparison to the political rhetoric.[1]

DEHUMANIZING METAPHORS

The terrorists have no true home in any country, or culture, or faith. They dwell in dark corners of earth. And there, we will find them" (Bush, October 12, 2001).

The political construction of terrorism is replete with dehumanizing metaphors that foster duality and accentuate difference. In these constructions, perhaps even more important than the language used are the associations made with other more complex and often culturally based constructions of reality. Consider President Bush's comments:

The best way to protect our homeland is to hunt the killers down one by one and bring them to justice.... This is a different kind of enemy. These are commanders who hide in dark caves, and then send youngsters to their suicidal death.... They kind of slither into cities and hope not to get caught.... And they're allusive [sic] and they're determined – but so are we. We've got a fabulous United States military, and they're on the hunt (Bush, September 5, 2002).

The metaphors used in this statement clearly construct terrorists within the confines of animalism, savagery, and a Western cultural code. The act of the "hunt" invokes not only animalism and dehumanization but brings a level of acceptance to the method and outcome of our social response to terrorism.[2] It informs us on how justice is to be actualized; casting the endeavor into a prey-predator paradigm creates a life or death inevitability to our actions.

The choice of the verb "slither" is an allusion to the biblical serpent as the embodiment of evil. The conception of the snake as a negative symbol is a western tradition. In many pre-monotheistic and new world cultures, the snake represents strength, connection with ancestors, fertility, power, and a myriad of other more positive associations.

The evildoers are situated in "dark caves" that represent danger, fear and the unknown primordial aversions that continue to motivate the urge to suppress.

The terrorists are symbolized as primitives in opposition to the heroes who are highly sophisticated, technologically savvy, and knowledgeable individuals.[3] The assertion that terrorists "send youngsters to their suicidal death" is, on the surface, the most factual statement. However, it rests on a Western cultural understanding of competency, adulthood, and deviance. The statement removes the possibility of choice from the child-actor by attributing all responsibility to the unknown deviants. This invokes the innocence strategy discussed earlier and makes the deviant's behavior even more appalling. The age of competency and the demarcation between childhood and adulthood, however, is culturally determined. By way of example, in much of the Islamic world a 15-year-old boy has reached the age of majority and is an autonomous member of society capable of making adult decisions, he is not regarded as an impressionable child. Likewise, suicide in defense of one's belief is not seen as a moral frailty or act of deviance; rather it is perceived as a soldier giving his or her life for their country. In most of the Islamic world the actors are seen as martyrs to be celebrated.

Mastery of a culture's symbolic communication allows one to manipulate the symbolic order- and is a source of great power in modern society. It can cast the villain into the role of hero; it can make the unthinkable, thinkable; and it can even bring nations to war. Terrorism is symbolically constructed from the abstract relationships that fall outside our traditional perceptions of justice. Political, legal, economic, scientific, and religious constructions all interact with impressions of crime and justice. The political views we hold and those that are expressed for us affect not only our perceptions of terrorism but also our perception of self – when we define the enemy, and we also define ourselves. The intersections between economics, religion, law, politics, and our thoughts about morality form a conceptual roadmap that guides our reading of terrorism and our response to it.

REIFICATION OF CIVILIZATION

> We wage a war to save civilization, itself. We did not seek it, but we must fight it – and we will prevail (Bush, November 8, 2001).

According to the political rhetoric, terrorism constitutes a threat to society unlike any other social problem; it threatens civilization itself.[4] This allusion is more than a way of expressing the severity of the destructive behavior and the reality of a terrorist attack. Consider the force and breadth of this assertion in the remarks of the United States Attorney General, echoed by the Secretary of State.

> The terrorist enemy that threatens civilization today is unlike any we have ever known. It slaughters thousands of innocents – a crime of war and a crime against humanity (Ashcroft, December 6, 2001).

> I think every civilized nation in the world recognizes that this was an assault not just against the United States, but against civilization (Powell, 2002).

These statements follow the pattern established in many crime panics. They assert that a new social evil has been discovered and that the evil is unlike any behavior or threat society has ever experienced. This theme has been used to construct the crimes of drug abuse, serial murder, child abuse, missing children and serial killers, all of which have clearly delineated characteristics but become during panics reconstituted forms of criminality.

When American political figures imply that a particular group of individuals threaten the foundations of civilization, they are continuing a tradition of alarmism that extends as far back as the ancient Greeks and Romans. During the Roman Empire the great intellectuals of the day, such as Tacitus, speculated that their neighbors to the north were a lower standard of human being because they refused to submit to Roman rule. The Germanic tribes' failure to learn Latin and their refusal to accept Roman ways of dress and life, combined with the Roman perception that German speech was babbling all contributed to the label of barbarian. Scholars have long observed the tendency to label groups as different. William Ryan (1976) states:

> The Different Ones are seen as less competent, less skilled, less knowing – in short less human. The ancient Greeks deduced from a single characteristic, a different language, that the barbarians – that is, the "babblers" who spoke a strange tongue – were wild, uncivilized, dangerous, rapacious, uneducated, lawless, and, indeed scarcely more than animals. [Such characterization] not infrequently justifies mistreatment, enslavement, or even extermination of the Different Ones (p. 10).

The President and the Attorney General invoked this very characterization in their speeches on terrorism.

> . . . a group of barbarians have declared war on the American people . . . . (Bush, Sept. 15, 2001).

> Some have asked whether a civilized nation – a nation of law and not of men – can use the law to defend itself from barbarians and remain civilized (Ashcroft, February 19, 2002).

The cry of alarm about barbarians at the gates has, throughout human history, been put to the service of countless national, political, religious, and economic agendas. The use of the term civilization to describe one group automatically confers subhuman character on the cultural other who is to be feared and hated for lack of development. The advanced/primitive duality is a substantive anchor in the panic over terrorism. On its face, the idea of civilization is equated with refinement, order, technology, reason and the ideals of freedom, democracy, and justice. These concepts are perceived as positive; how could anyone reject them as undesirable? This question has induced speculation that terrorists and their supporters are envious or jealous of the Western way of life, which further bolsters the correctness of the Western perspective.

> They have attacked America, because we are freedom's home and defender. They hate what we see right here in this chamber – a democratically elected government. Their leaders are self-appointed. They hate our freedoms – our freedom of religion, our freedom of speech, our freedom to vote and assemble and disagree with each other (Bush, September 20, 2001).

The construction denies the possibility of a differing perspective, asserting that freedom is the basis of the conflict rather than an opposing political-economic ideology. Consider this dismissive remark by the President.

> They don't represent an ideology, they don't represent a legitimate political group of people (Bush, September 25, 2001).

The vast majority of terrorist acts are driven by an ideology that is diametrically opposed to the ideology of these targets. The civilization embraced by those who commit terrorist acts bears little resemblance to the Western concept.

Rather than being an objectively discernable state, civilization is a set of ideological principles in staunch opposition to and rejection of other fundamental cultural and ideological patterns. The traditional formulation of civilization in Western thought is a highly stratified society with access to material resources, and a reverence for authority and the maintenance of certain norms, which buttress and facilitate these structures. By definition then, the notion of civilization rejects patterns and cultures that fall outside of these normative values. Cultures and groups of individuals who consciously reject progress, technology, innovation, and consumption are suspect. The creation of the uncivilized other has justified conquest and dominance of those who refuse to conform.

VILLAINS, HEROES AND GOOD "VOLKS"

> We cannot fully understand the designs and power of evil. It is enough to know that evil, like goodness, exists. And in the terrorists, evil has found a willing servant (Bush, October 11, 2001).

The most basic moral construction- good and evil-becomes the foundation for understanding terrorism, with powerful consequences. We construct two opposing camps: those of us who are good, law-abiding and productive members of society and those who are evil, criminal and destructive social forces. While the language of terrorism invokes simple comparisons between people and behavior, it has powerful implications for how we see ourselves and the world around us.

> They're flat evil. That's all they can think about, is evil. And as a nation of *good folks*, we're going to hunt them down, and we're going to find them, and we will bring them to justice (Bush, September 25, 2001; italics added).

As the initial duality of terrorism gathers complexity, more people are drawn into the web of terrorism's social construction. Simple distinctions are often compounded into more elaborate constructions that extend the scope of terrorism and raise the stakes of stigma. Simple constructions of terrorism can cast long shadows that extend well beyond the initial designation of criminal. The stigma of terrorism can attach to people who are unfortunate enough to have an association with a criminal.

> We're going to find those evil-doers, . . . we're going to hold them accountable and we're going to hold the people who house them accountable. The people who think they can provide them safe havens will be held accountable. The people who feed them will be held accountable (Bush, September 17, 2001).

It is, however, not just criminal behavior that falls under the shadow of stigma. The construction of terrorism stigmatizes ideologies opposed to the official construction of terrorism and the approved social response. Attorney General John Ashcroft made the following remarks to Congress about people who expressed concern over the erosion of civil rights and liberties in the wake of the terrorist attacks on the World Trade Center:

> . . . to those who scare peace-loving people with phantoms of lost liberty; my message is this: Your tactics only aid terrorists – for they erode our national unity and diminish our resolve. They give ammunition to America's enemies, and pause to America's friends. They encourage people of good will to remain silent in the face of evil (Ashcroft, December 6, 2001).

So the rhetorical duality of terrorism extends its scope to those who associate with criminals and those who question the erosion of liberty-while simultaneously amplifying the virtues of those who remain uncontaminated. President Bush defined the duality in the following terms: "Well, you've probably learned by now, I don't believe there's many shades of gray in this war. You're either with us or against us; you're either evil or you're good" (Bush, February 11, 2002). As the duality of crime extends it scope and becomes a moral script, social actors are cast into dramatic and mutually dependent roles. There are brave, crime-control heroes who "shine the light of justice" and "draw the line in the sand against the evil ones" (Bush, October 10, 2001). Their heroic nature is in stark contrast to those evil-doers who "live in the shadows, and operate under the cover of darkness . . . (Attorney General John Ashcroft, October 10, 2001).

> Today, brave men and women in uniform abroad and at home answer our President's call for justice. Sworn to defend the Constitution and our liberties, and motivated by the memories of September 11, they live each day by a code of honor, duty, and country. And they know that

they may die preserving the promise that terrorism will not reach this land of liberty again – for we are a nation locked in a deadly war with the evil of terrorism (Ashcroft, June 5, 2003).

The victims of terrorism are likewise constructed in stark contrast to the "evil ones." to enhance the emotional impact and to elicit the desired social response. The political construction of terrorism uses innocence and portrays actions in terms of protecting women and children.

We must not forget that our enemies are ruthless fanatics, who seek to murder innocent men, women and children to achieve their twisted goals (Ashcroft, June 5, 2003).

But in the long run, the best way to defend our homeland – the best way to make sure our children can live in peace – is to take the battle to the enemy and to stop them (Bush, November 8, 2001).

SITUATING TERRORISM

Just three days removed from these events, Americans do not yet have the distance of history. But our responsibility to history is already clear: to answer these attacks and rid the world of evil (Bush, September 14, 2001).

In the political construction of crime problems there are no ordinary criminals-nor is the solution merely a political response. The social response to terrorism must be constructed with the same drama and emotionalism as the portrayal of the deviant. In these simple, yet dramatic, constructions of terrorism, control is not merely an occupation or a form of social defense; it is transformed into a calling. Once again we construct our actions through the duality of good and evil, thereby defining ourselves and our actions in oppositional discourse.

This is our calling. This is the calling of the United States of America, the most free nation in the world, a nation built on fundamental values; that rejects hate, rejects violence, rejects murderers, rejects evil (Bush, October 10, 2001).

The Attorney General was even more explicit,

But the call to defend civilization from terrorism resonates from a deeper source than our legal or political institutions. Civilized people – Muslims, Christians and Jews – all understand that the source of freedom and human dignity is the Creator. Civilized people of all religious faiths are called to the defense of His creation . . .. We are a nation called to defend freedom – a freedom that is not the grant of any government or document but is our endowment from God (Ashcroft, February 19, 2002).

The religious grounding also follows a historical pattern. Politicians manufacture dichotomies that place actors either on the side of divine judgment or against it-linking the goals and objectives of a particular administration or interest group to a broader determined course of human civilization as mandated by higher powers. In the 1840s, Manifest Destiny became the slogan for American westward expansion. It provided the ideological justification for the Mexican War in which the United States hoped to gain territory in the Southwest and Midwest as part of the growing ambitions to be a world power. Contrasting the alleged underdevelopment and savagery of Native Americans and Mexicans with American civilization, linked the actions of the government with the spirit of progress. In the view of many of the day, it was simply providence from God and his will that the United States extend its borders to the Pacific Ocean-supplanting or displacing, if necessary, existing cultures and populations.

Similarly Ashcroft's comments link the United States with righteousness and portray it as the appointed defender not only of civilization, but the whole of creation. These rhetorical devices imply that the American ideological paradigm is in effect the only one that will insure the continuance of freedom, morality, security and ultimately our very reality. Our actions are not merely a social aim or form of defense, they are transformed into a divine calling.

The policies of the Bush administration's predecessors against fundamentalist organizations, theocratic governments, and secular nationalists have culminated today in the war against terrorism, which is constructed in nearly the same way as America's conquest and subsequent mastery of the western frontier. The refusal of fundamentalist Islam to accept Western values and the central place of free market-capitalism stands as an impediment to the course, which must be accepted by all peoples of the world.

> When it comes to the values we hold dear, we will be strong, and we'll be steadfast. And when it comes to enforcing doctrine, when I said, either you're with us or against us, they understand. And when I said, if you're going to harbor one of those terrorists, you're just as guilty as the terrorists – thanks to the United States military, thanks to our coalition, the world now knows what we mean (Bush, May 10, 2002).

The United States perceives itself as global policeman and defender. It is obliged to sweep away this new threat, as it did the indigenous peoples who refused to share in the vision for a continental empire. The use of force always useful in the "civilizing process" is only one essential part of achieving control. It must be tempered with the assertion that the United States is prosecuting its current war to grant freedom, democracy, peace and all the material comforts of our way of life to the nations of the middle east.

The handling of the "uncivilized" has always been a "*Verbindung*" (loose coupling) of mystification, justification, and the realities of coercion. The concept of "Lifting up the noble savage," dates at least to the eighteenth century and was predicated on the belief that Colonialism could bring about the improvement and salvation of Africans, Native Americans, and other "primitive" peoples. By introducing the newly conquered to the ideas of science, rationality and the Enlightenment, the Europeans believed they could save other races from their sub-human condition. The true nature of Colonialism, however, calls into question the altruistic ethos espoused by thinkers such as Jean-Jacques Rousseau. Consider one example of how dominant socio-economic norms of the West have been presented: an American marine shouts to a crowd of Iraqi demonstrators, "We're here to give you your fucking freedom . . . now back off!" (CBS News, 2003).

> We are confident, too, that history has an author who fills time and eternity with his purpose. We know that evil is real, but good will prevail against it. This is the teaching of many faiths (Bush, November 10, 2001).

> Our alliance of freedom is being tested again by new and terrible dangers. Like the Nazis and the communists before them, the terrorists seek to end lives and control all life. And like the Nazis and the communists before them, they will be opposed by free nations and the terrorists will be defeated (Bush, November 23, 2002).

The war against terror takes on a new meaning within the context of other past battles and protracted conflicts. The war against terror like the struggle against Nazism and Marxism is as much as anything else an ideological struggle for the hearts and minds of people around the world. The worldview of the Muslim fundamentalist is as antithetical to the American socio-economic and political agenda as were the previous competitors of fascism and international socialism.

NORMALIZING TERROR AND BOLSTERING CRIME PROBLEMS

> Terrorism and crime are inextricably linked. International and Domestic Terrorism Organizations and their supporters engage in a myriad of crimes to fund and facilitate terrorist activities. These crimes include extortion, kidnapping [sic], robbery, corruption, alien smuggling, document fraud, arms trafficking, cyber crime, white collar crime, smuggling of contraband, money laundering and certainly drug trafficking (McCraw, May 20, 2003).

After September 11, 2001, the Bush administration used the issue of terrorism to rekindle the drug war, and to cast drug users into the role of enemies of freedom. In press conference after press conference, Attorney General John Ashcroft informed the public and law enforcement community that there was a direct link between terrorism and drug use.

> . . . the lawlessness that breeds terrorism is also a fertile ground for the drug trafficking that supports terrorism. And the mutually reinforcing relationship between terrorism and drug

trafficking should serve as a wake-up call for all Americans. When a dollar is spent on drugs in America, a dollar is made by America's enemies.... The Department of Justice is committed to victory over drug abuse and terrorism, and the protection of the freedom and human dignity that both drug abuse and terrorism seek to destroy (Ashcroft, March 18, 2002).

Although the Attorney General did not provide any evidence of the link between drug use and terrorism he repeatedly made the following remarks, "The attacks of September 11 demonstrated in dramatic fashion the need to pay attention to all facets of our national security. Would-be terrorists, drug smugglers and other illegal migrants pose continuing threats to the health and safety of our nation and its people" (Attorney General John Ashcroft, January 17, 2002). Individual drug users were characterized as contributing to terrorism.

The bottom line is that terrorists and terrorist groups will resort to any method or means to fund and facilitate their terrorist agendas. As state sponsorship of terrorism has come under greater international condemnation, the tremendous profit potential associated with drug trafficking make it attractive from the perspective of terrorist groups. This is further evidence that the prospect of terrorist-related drug trafficking represents a continuing and significant threat to our national security (McCraw, May 20, 2003).

Narco-terrorist organizations ... generate millions of dollars in narcotics-related revenues to facilitate their terrorist activities .... The War on Terror and the War on Drugs are linked, with agencies throughout the United States and internationally working together as a force-multiplier in an effort to dismantle narco-terrorist organizations. Efforts to stop the funding of these groups have focused on drugs and the drug money used to perpetuate violence throughout the world. International cooperative efforts between law enforcement authorities and intelligence organizations are critical to eliminating terrorist funding, reducing the drug flow, and preventing future terrorist attacks (Casteel, May 20, 2003).

This process of situating terrorism within the cultural stock of previously constructed crime problems makes the collective ideology more powerful and understandable. The media official alerts, in nightly news sound bites the media are a conduit for political rhetoric and the claims of law enforcement officials. Terrorism has found a place in the public explanation for crime-reinforcing other previously constructed social problems.

IDEOLOGY AND CONCEPTUAL SPACE

The words we actually speak or write are not merely the products of an unlimited number of choices; rather, they are guided by our ideological understanding of the world. This does not mean that we do not have the ability to choose between words or to curtail our comments. It does mean that the direction our conversation takes is influenced by the arrangement of ideologies we have learned.

The distinctions between social, political, legal, economic, religious, and scientific spheres of thought are artificial. Politics, economics, law, and religion share a unified purpose when they intersect with crime and justice. Our justice system is inextricably bound to these ideologies. While we may comfort ourselves with the familiar assertions that the police are free from politics, crime control policy is not affected by religion, or the administration of justice is not based on economic considerations, these are largely mystifications. We may even find comfort in relying on scientific studies of crime hoping that they too are free from the influence of politics and economics. These mystifications are created by highly selective and refined manipulations of ideological space.

Global ideologies are broad systems of ideas that inform narratives, discussions and even social policy. Ideologies justify or legitimate a narrative by appealing to a reader's own encyclopedic knowledge of the world. We might not even be aware that we hold a particular ideology until we are exposed to a narrative or discussion that strikes a dissonant note. Sometimes this recognition is merely a vague sense that what the writer or speaker is saying is wrong. We might find it difficult to articulate exactly what is wrong, but we have an uneasy feeling about the direction of the dialogue. Other times we might feel that the writer has "hit the mark" and is on target with an idea, but we are not really sure why the idea resonates. A narrative that meshes with a reader's ideological understanding provides a level of comfort and affinity with a narrative or discourse. Conversely, a narrative situated outside the reader's ideology or understanding can create confusion and resistance to the message. When discussions of crime are constructed within conforming and comforting ideological frameworks they seem natural and make sense to us. When they are constructed in frameworks that are foreign, they can be disturbing, seem non-sensical, and even contrived.

Some of us might remember being taught never to engage in discussions of religion or politics in social settings because these discussions might offend our guests or lead to conflict. When we consider this childhood lesson we might think of the difference between Democrats and Republicans or perhaps liberals and conservatives. This childhood example illustrates two points. First, people have strong beliefs about certain ideological domains-particularly religion and politics. Remarks that are contrary to an audience's ideological sense of the world can offend, while those that are consistent can bond the speaker and audience. Second, the example shows how the ideological domain of politics is shaped and limited in American thought.

Certainly the Democrat/Republican dichotomy relates to the ideological domain of politics, but it is a much narrower construction than a global ideology. It represents a particular arrangement within an ideological domain rather than the entire realm of politics. Why did we think of Democrats and Republicans rather than the conservative or labor parties or Maoists and Social Democrats? This is because our understanding of an ideological domain is often limited by the way the domain has been constructed and presented in the past. The narratives we have been exposed to in our readings and conversations all determine what comes to mind when we speak or read about politics. The same can be said for economics, religion, and even science. What distinctions come to mind when we think of crime; murder, robbery, rape or perhaps terrorism? What about political, police, environmental, white-collar crime, and state terrorism?

Almost daily we are exposed to highly selective constructions of global ideologies. These constructions often represent mere slices of an ideological domain. How many times has CNN interviewed a Maoist or member of the British Labor party? How many times have you seen a member of the House of Commons on "Crossfire," even though CNN is your international source for news and world events. Seldom are we exposed to the entire range of an ideological domain. These observations suggest that we are exposed to only a small slice of the full breath of political ideology. As a result when we write or speak about politics, our remarks are guided by our limited exposure and understanding. Our discussions often fall between the ideological markers that have been created for us by family, teachers, the media, political leaders and an abundance of literature we have been exposed to over the course of a lifetime. So it seems perfectly natural that when we think of politics we think of Democrats and Republicans and when we think of crime we think of murder, robbery and rape; detection, control and punishment.

Rarely do we write or speak from a single ideological domain. Our ideological constructions are much more complex. Most of the narratives to which we are exposed- especially when we speak of crime and justice-involve a number of domains. When we debate what police practices are acceptable in a democratic society to protect citizens from property crime, we are drawing not only from the domain of politics but also from the economic and legal domains. We assume for example that a democratic society is a capitalist society and that these societies embrace civil rights and liberties, the private ownership of property, and a desire to restrict police power. We can also be blinded to the fact that many democratic societies are not capitalist and that many capitalist societies are not so democratic. We might not even think that property could be conceptualized outside the framework of private ownership because of our legal understanding of property.

Thinking about the acceptable limits of police practice then, is guided by several ideological domains arranged such that the answers to our question are essentially predetermined. If a proposed police practice interferes with the possession of personal property, it is likely to meet resistance regardless of its efficacy. The direction or trajectory the discussion takes and our response to the debate is a product of our arrangement of ideological domains. We might not even be aware that we embrace or reject a crime control reform because of our ideology rather than the merits of the proposal. Interweaving these selected perspectives creates global ideologies.

Discourses that are constructed based on selective use of ideological domains can steer us away from or create barriers to alternative choices, directions and thought patterns. By managing conceptual space, we bracket out ideas and force the audience down a path that ends in a predetermined destination.

Global ideologies are often constructed from limiting domains. We are often unaware that the domains of politics, economics, religion, law, and science are interrelated and interdependent. If presented for discussion, the domains are conceptually severed, giving the impression that they do not depend on one another and that changes in one domain do not have consequences for others. When theorists speak of the political economy they do so to capture the interrelationships between politics and economics rather than to foster false dichotomies. However, the construction of global ideologies creates false dichotomies between domains and social experience.

Likewise, differing ideological positioning, within a single domain are hierarchically ordered into bundles of oppositional knowledge, with some ideologies being preferred and others being cast into the role of opposition. In discussions of economics this is often to distinguish between capitalism and socialism as two clearly distinct economic systems. In reality no state operates under either a purely capitalist or socialist economic system. Capitalist systems have features of socialism, and socialist systems have features of capitalism. Global ideologies are distortions in that they can never truly exist in their isolated and oppositional forms. No state is purely socialist or capitalist. No government is purely democratic or solely authoritarian. Global ideologies present a vision of the world from the perspective of those who control ideology-whether it is political, economic, social, religious or scientific. By casting ideologies as oppositional one, is forced to choose among false dichotomies and in doing so the interrelations as well as the potentialities among constructions are muted.

Ideological domains can also be fused together in highly selective narratives. One of the most popular of these constructions is the fusion of democracy and capitalism. In many narratives, democracy is equated with capitalism if not constructed as being dependant on it. Alternatives to capitalism are therefore constructed as undemocratic, even though most socialist states have democratic features. By wedding a clearly acceptable or desirable ideological construction like democracy with a more vulnerable construction like capitalism, a stronger and more complex ideology emerges. The complex arrangement is difficult to disaggregate and creates the impression that they are both popular and vital components of a desired state of reality. These constructions become even more powerful when they are linguistically linked to other desirable states of being. Freedom is linked to the capitalist-democratic construct; free trade is said to promote democratic ideals. The police protect our freedom, in fact they serve and protect our freedom, property and civil rights in a democratic society, but they restrict, control, and oppress in socialist societies. To challenge the police in a democratic society is to challenge freedom, democracy and capitalism. To support the police in a socialist society is to support oppression, control of property and restrict freedom. These constructions develop despite the fact that the police in any society largely operate to support and reproduce social and moral order determined by those with power. Crime is an essential component of this construction because it s the ideological construction by linking it to an objective material reality.

A CONCLUDING NOTE ON THE ROLE
OF CRIMINOLOGY

All constructions of realities are not created equal. Some language, imagery and thought are given a privileged place in our culture. Some symbolic depictions of reality become so accepted, commonplace, and powerful that they seem natural and not in the slightest way contrived, manipulated or constructed. These privileged representations of reality exist at the expense of suppressed alternative representations of reality.

Our understanding of crime and justice is determined by a coherent and elaborate code created by the manipulation of ideology, signs, images, words, and metaphors. This code allows us to write, talk, and think about issues of crime and justice within a cultural framework. Absent a code "there is no intelligible discourse" (Hall, 1980, p. 131). The crime code organizes single texts, speeches, and dialogues by linking them together into a meaningful system that guides interpretation. The crime code fuses political, scientific, religious, and economic ideologies "by its coherence, its homogeneity, its systematicity, in the face of the heterogeneity of the message, articulated across several codes" (Heath, 1981, p.129). The code maintains ideological order by pulling together language in a way that fosters highly selective representations of reality.

We learn the code of crime by embracing the values, assumptions and ideologies it contains. In this learning process, we, are often unaware that what the code symbolizes is a construction. The nature and power of the code can be highlighted by comparing it to other cultures and ways of thinking that reveal the hidden nature of values and ideologies. Illustrating codes therefore is a comparative and relational endeavor that requires privileged codes to be compared to those of lesser privilege. The language of terrorism is no exception; it invokes a highly selective ideology. Criminology, too, plays an important role in the continuance of privileged codes.

Students soon learn the complexity of crime when they begin studying criminology. They learn that there are various schools of criminological thought and that these schools can be contrasted by their positions on the causes of crime. They may learn that criminological theory can be divided into schools that assert criminal behavior is the product of free will or those that stress behavior is determined by social, biological or psychological factors. Some students may even learn that theories of crime can be sliced into those that focus on social structure and those that focus on social processes that contribute to criminality. Criminological theory can even be forced into distinctions between consensus and conflict or macro and micro theories. In the best of educational experiences, students begin to question these simple distinctions by seeing a little conflict in consensus, by sensing that social structure and process may be interdependent, or even by arguing that there might be some determinism in free-will arguments. After all, what allows us to make all those rational choices so necessary to rational choice theory? What determines what behaviors are rational and irrational?

This learning experience, however, does not stray too far away from the simplistic dichotomies of good and evil, criminals and law-abiders, and punishment and correction. In fact, the core of many criminological theories, and most applied criminology depends on these simple dualities. At the core of most criminological theories is the attempt to distinguish between criminal and law-abiding behavior. Rarely does one run across a theory of crime or a test of a criminological theory that questions these basic distinctions. The criminological enterprise reinforces these oppositional distinctions because they are the foundation of criminology and the construction of crime.

Criminology proper, the formal scientific study of crime, has historically concerned itself with overt manifestations of crime and social activities. That is to say, traditional approaches to the study of crime focus on the behavioral, procedural, or structural aspects of crime and justice. Because of this focus, criminology proper is concerned with how crime is structured and arranged in its most overt manifestations – what we can see and count. Whether our inquiry surrounds police practice, court decisions, the efficacy of punishment, or terrorism, criminology has focused its attention on actions and activities rather than the ideological and symbolic constructions that are the backdrop for giving crime its meaning.

This is not to say that criminology is atheoretical. The formal study of crime has yielded an array of theories about the overt causes of crime and even the less concrete aspects of crime like social structure and justice processes. The centrality of logical positivism, however, has held criminology's gaze to the manifest and measurable proprieties of crime, whether they are evident in social structure or the justice process. Seldom does it question its own dualistic construction of crime or the ideological choices inherent in the techniques and methods used to study crime. In fact, criminology masks its ideological nature with the pretense of objectivity. As a consequence, criminology has been blind to the ways in which symbolic codes fashion our constitution of social structure and process and the subsequent reification of that symbolic constitution. Our thoughts, language, and imagery dictate the questions we ask and the methods we use to measure results. The implication in the lack of critical examination of the ideological and conceptual underpinnings of criminology is that a critical examination of how criminology is constituted, how its methods and techniques are designed, and the consequences of its theories and findings are less important than the study of criminal behavior. In this sense, criminology proper has become a method of objectifying a unified reality of crime that fits well into the accepted web of political, scientific, economic, social, and moral order.

Criminology as manifested in its theories and applied studies has failed to make meaningful progress in understanding crime, justice, or even terrorism. By failing to analyze the abstract codes and modalities of ideological and symbolic production, the discipline has expanded the production of crime control ideology and reinforced its power. The same ideological constructions that create our reality of terrorism guide the course of criminological thought and practice. This lack of critical reflection renders criminology another articulation of ideological processes, rather than an investigation of the reality of crime. Rather than lifting the veil, criminology and its bounded logic has created another layer of obfuscation. Criminology serves as a form of intellectual domination by contributing to the ideological code of a symbolic superstructure that masks contradictions. This confining view has restricted a critical examination of the very essence, function, and meaning of crimes like terrorism.

NOTES

1. According to the F.B.I., between 1980 and 2000 there were an average of about 4.4 domestic terrorist acts in the United States each year. Domestic acts account form about

75 percent of all suspected acts of terrorism in the United States. These acts include both terrorist acts and those merely suspected of being terrorist acts. The behaviors ranged from vandalism to bombings, were often carried out by lone individuals, and many were the results of rightwing extremists (see FBI, 1998; Watson, February 6, 2002).

2. The hunt metaphor surfaces in numerous speeches. "They will try to hide, they will try to avoid the United States and our allies – but we're not going to let them. They run to the hills; they find holes to get in. And we will do whatever it takes to smoke them out and get them running, and we'll get them . . ." (Bush, September 15, 2001); "We've got better intelligence-gathering, better intelligence-sharing, and we're on the hunt. And we will stay on the hunt. The threat that you asked about, Steve, reminds us that we need to be on the hunt, because the war on terror goes on" (Bush, July 30, 2003).

3. The "shadows" and "caves" metaphors appear in numerous speeches. "We hunt an enemy that hides in shadows and caves" (Bush, November 6, 2001); "We will flush them out of their caves, we'll get them on the run, and we will bring them to justice" (Bush, May 2, 2003).

4. The civilization metaphor has been used in numerous political speeches to construct potential victims and to characterize potential offenders. In a speech, Vice President Cheney stated the armed services are defending "civilization and human values." The implication is that the values of the opposition are less than human. "No nation can be neutral in this conflict, because no civilized nation can be secure in a world threatened by terror" (Bush, November 6, 2001). Law enforcement officials also repeat assertions that terrorism threatens civilization.

REFERENCES

Ashcroft, J. (2001). Attorney General announcement with President Bush, Secretary of State Powell and FBI Director Mueller. FBI Headquarters (October 10).

Ashcroft, J. (2001). Testimony before the Senate Committee on the Judiciary, Washington, DC (December 6).

Ashcroft, J. (2002). Remarks before the National Religious Broadcasters Convention Nashville, Tennessee (February 19).

Ashcroft, J. (2002). Remarks of Attorney General John Ashcroft, U.S. Border Patrol-Native American Border Security Conference (January 17).

Ashcroft, J. (2002). Transcript News Conference – FARC, DOJ Conference Center (March 18).

Ashcroft, J. (2003). Testimony of Attorney General John Ashcroft U.S. House of Representatives Committee on the Judiciary (June 5).

Best, J., & Horiuchi, G. (1985). The razor and the apple: The social construction of urban legends. *Social Problems, 32*(1), 488–499.

Bush, G. W. (2001) Address to the nation and joint session of Congress (September 20).

Bush, G. W. (2001). "No Nation Can Be Neutral in This Conflict." Remarks Made by the President to the Warsaw Conference on Combatting [sic] Terrorism (November 6).

Bush, G. W. (2001). Guard and Reserves "Define Spirit of America," Remarks by the President to Employees at the Pentagon, The Pentagon (September 17).

Bush, G. W. (2001). Homeland Security In Address to the Nation World Congress Center, Atlanta, GA (November 8).

Bush, G. W. (2001). President Pays Tribute at Pentagon Memorial Remarks by the President at the Department of Defense Service of Remembrance The Pentagon, Arlington, VA (October 11).

Bush, G. W. (2001). President: FBI Needs Tools to Track Down Terrorists Remarks by the President to Employees at the Federal Bureau of Investigation FBI Headquarters (September 25).

Bush, G. W. (2001). President's Remarks at National Day of Prayer and Remembrance, The National Cathedral Washington, DC (September 14).

Bush, G. W. (2001). Radio Address of the President to the Nation (September 15).

Bush, G. W. (2001). Remarks by the President at the Pentagon (October 12).

Bush, G. W. (2001). Remarks by the President During Announcement at the Federal Bureau of Investigation, FBI Headquarters, Washington, DC (October 10).

Bush, G. W. (2001). Remarks by the President to United Nations General Assembly, U. N. Headquarters. New York, NY (November 10).

Bush, G. W. (2002). Remarks by the President at Scott Mccallum for Governor Reception, The Pfister Hotel Milwaukee, Wisconsin (February 11).

Bush, G. W. (2002). Office of the Press Secretary (January 29).

Bush, G. W. (2002). Remarks by the President at Taft for Governor Luncheon, Hyatt Regency Hotel Columbus, Ohio (May 10).

Bush, G. W. (2002). Remarks by the President to the Citizens of Vilnius, Rotuse Vilnius, Lithuania (November 23).

Bush, G. W. (2002). Remarks made at a roundtable with small business leaders at the Broadbent Arena. Louisville, KY (September 5).

Bush, G. W. (2003). Excerpts from President's Remarks in Santa Clara, California (May 2).

Bush, G. W. (2003). Remarks by the President, Press Release. Office of the Press Secretary (July 30).

Casteel, S. W. (2003). Narco-Terrorism: International drug trafficking and terrorism – a dangerous mix. DEA Congressional Testimony, Statement of Assistant Administrator for Intelligence Before the Senate Committee on the Judiciary (May 20).

CBS News (2003). This isn't liberation this is conquest. *Socialist Worker* (April 18), 1.

Cohen, S. (1972). *Folk devils and moral panics: The creation of the Mods and Rockers.* London: MacGibbon & Kee.

F. B. I. (1998). Terrorism in the United States, 1998: Counterterrorism Threat Assessment and Warning Unit National Security Division. Washington, DC: U.S. Department of Justice.

Fishman, M. (1998). Crime waves as ideology. *Social Problems, 25*(5), 531–543.

Goode, E., & Ben-Yehuda, N. (1994). *Moral panics: The social construction of deviance.* Cambridge: Blackwell.

Hall, S. (1980). Encoding/decoding. In: Centre for Contemporary Cultural Studies (Ed.), *Culture, Media, Language: Working Papers in Cultural Studies, 1972–1979* (pp. 128–138). London: Hutchinson.

Heath, S. (1981). Metz's Semiology: A short glossary. In: M. Eaton (Ed.), *Cinema and Semiotics (Screen Reader 2)* (pp. 125–137). London: Society for Education in Film & Television.

Kappeler, V. E., Blumberg, M., & Potter, G. W. (1996). *The mythology of crime and criminal justice.* Prospect Heights, IL: Waveland Press.

McCraw, S. C. (2003). Assistant Director, Office of Intelligence Federal Bureau of Investigation on International Drug Trafficking and Terrorism, Testimony Before the Senate Judiciary Committee Washington, DC (May 20).

Powell, C. (2002). Remarks by the President, Secretary of State Colin Powell and Attorney General John Ashcroft, Camp David, Thurmont, MD (September 15).

Quinney (1970). *The social reality of crime*. Boston: Little, Brown.

Ryan (1976). *Blaming the victim*. New York; Vintage Books.

Watson, D. (2002). Statement for the Record of Dale L. Watson Executive Assistant Director Counterterrorism and Counterintelligence Federal Bureau of Investigation on The Terrorist Threat Confronting the United States Before the Senate Select Committee on Intelligence Washington, DC (February 6).

PUNISHMENT & VIOLENCE

THE CHALLENGE OF TERRORISM TO FREE SOCIETIES IN THE GLOBAL VILLAGE

Paul Leighton

ABSTRACT

After 9–11, 110 Nobel laureates released a statement saying "The only hope for the future lies in cooperative international action, legitimized by democracy. . . . To survive in the world we have transformed, we must learn to think in a new way." This chapter argues for criminologists contributing and thinking in a new way by returning to and updating the notion of The Challenge of Crime in A Free Society. It reviews present challenges from terrorism and criminology's shortcomings, explores implications of the new conception, and highlights difficulties in studying anti-American terrorism as well as continued attention to domestic terrorism.

INTRODUCTION

The FBI's Uniform Crime Reports (FBI, 2002a) for 2001 registered an increase in homicides of 2.5%, notable as an end to the decade long drop in crime rates just as criminology produced the first book on the topic (Blumstein & Wallman, 2000). Interesting in their absence are all the victims of September 11 terrorism from the categories of murder, assault and hate crimes. While airplane-into-skyscraper is not what comes to mind when thinking about the "crime problem," mass murder

Terrorism and Counter-Terrorism: Criminological Perspectives
Sociology of Crime, Law and Deviance, Volume 5, 199–217
© 2004 Published by Elsevier Ltd.
ISSN: 1521-6136/doi:10.1016/S1521-6136(03)05012-7

is still murder – and the UCR has "explosion" as a subcategory of homicide that has even been used for past terrorism victims.

Excluding 9–11 victims is not based on uncertainty as to how many deaths occurred: for New York, the FBI notes there are 2,830 homicides and 7,233 aggravated assaults that it didn't count. The assaults are excluded because of a "Hierarchy Rule of Summary" which requires that "only the most serious offense in an incident is reported" (FBI, 2002b, p. 7). The homicides are then excluded "because they are statistical outliers that will affect current and future crime trends" and "they are different from the day-to-day crimes committed in this country" (FBI, 2002a, p. 303). So, the all important "trend data" – used for reports, articles and textbooks – excludes victims of Sept. 11 terrorism, who are relegated to special section of the UCR. However, the UCR will not contain a special section for sniper killings around Washington, DC in the fall of 2002, which were not 'day to day crimes; although the Olympics are held every four years and rotate countries, there was no special section for Eric Robert Rudolph, bomber of the 1996 games in Atlanta. While serial killers frequently populate the media, their victims are still infrequent enough to pose the question of why their victimization (such as those cannibalized by John Wayne Gacey) is accepted as "day to day" crime.

The six victims of the first World Trade Center bombing were included in that year's UCR without comment. But Ramzi Yousef, one of those ultimately convicted, wanted to kill 250,000: "Yousef would explain [it was] the number killed by the American atomic bombs dropped on Hiroshima and Nagasaki. If he could murder on that scale, he believed, he would teach the United States it was in a war" (Benjamin & Simon, 2002, p. 7). His plan was to cause an explosion that would make one tower fall and knock over the other one. While the ultimate damage was not on the order Yousef expected, six deaths, more than a thousand injured, and $500 million in damage – "the worst terrorist act" in the nation's history, according to prosecutors (Kittrie & Wedlock, 1998, p. 761) – is not day to day crime.

Further, the 168 victims of Oklahoma City bomber Timothy McVeigh are included in the UCR, with a note in the state data to explain the dramatic increase in Oklahoma's homicide rate (FBI, 1996, pp. 64, 78). McVeigh was an enthusiastic reader of the *Turner Diaries* (MacDonald, 1980), a fictional account of Earl Turner's resistance to the "Zionist Occupied Government" that had overtaken the U.S. and was mistreating white citizens, including through disarming them. Turner starts by passing out leaflets, but by the novel's end becomes a suicide terrorist flying an aircraft loaded with a nuclear weapon in a morning mission to the Pentagon. McVeigh did not have the resources of his fictional hero, but his revenge for the government's killing of citizens at the Branch Davidian compound in Waco (Hamm, 1997) was the "deadliest terrorist attack in United States history" (Kittrie & Wedlock, 1998, p. 776). The incident is not day to day crime, but the UCR's Index Crime section recorded that murder by explosion increased from 10 in 1994 to 190 in 1995 (FBI, 1996, p. 18).

The attacks of 9–11 are larger in scale, but it hardly makes sense for the UCR to include relatively smaller acts of terrorism when they are the "worst in history," and exclude larger ones. According to the FBI, the UCR's "primary objective is to provide a reliable set of criminal justice statistics for law enforcement administration, operation and management" (2002, p. 2). If so, then it should show what criminal justice professionals already know – that Sept. 11 changed their mission and jobs. The FBI now has agents at 46 locations around the world, and "plans to open offices in Kabul, Jakarta and eight other foreign capitals as part of a decade long overseas expansion that officials say is crucial to meet the global threat of al-Qaida and other terrorist groups" (Anderson, 2003). The UCR notes its 70 year history is based on "law enforcement agencies voluntarily reporting crimes that were a product of society of the time. However, that society has evolved into a more complex, global society of the twenty-first century that is faced with fighting crimes that previously had been unimaginable" (FBI, 2001, p. 302). The FBI may be opening field offices in Uzbeckistan, Afghanistan, Malaysia and Yemen, but rather than also updating this important statistical reference, the FBI clearly thinks that it is better for the UCR and the mindset of all who depend it on it for information, to be firmly grounded in a simpler era not concerned with global terrorism.

Adding in all the World Trade Center victims of 9–11 does add an outlier to crime data, creating difficulties in analyzing issues like the impact of community policing on violent crime. But since the number of September 11 victims is known exactly, individual researchers can "correct" for the impact of terrorism after justifying to themselves and the readers that it is necessary to make the research more "meaningful." Such data correction will be legitimate for many projects, but there is value in the making the researcher justify removing it and in the process be introspective about the continued significance of the research question in light of "unimaginable" new crimes. By including the 9–11 victims, people using the UCR would have a visual reminder of the event because the spike in the homicide graph becomes a memorial – a simple and odd memorial, but one which has great power to engage the thoughts of anyone reading official publications and their derivatives about the nation's "crime problem." Remembering 9–11 would be a regular occurrence exerting an ongoing push on the discipline. Instead, the UCR sets up a model for criminology that continues its disciplinary status quo, which is a "grudging acceptance of terrorism" (Rosenfeld, 2002, p. 1).

The problems with not conceptualizing terrorism as crime ultimately go beyond consistency or integrity with the UCR, or even the effects on criminology. Acknowledging the tragic events as crime would require more emphasis on criminal procedure and individual rights enshrined by the Constitution. Negating

September 11 victims from "day to day" crime signals that they are outside traditional notions of a rule of law and supports Presidential assertions about the propriety of unprecedented power; it becomes easier for the administration to set up what have been called "legal black holes" like Camp X-Ray at Guantanamo Bay where the detainees (including several children) are not recognized as criminal defendants or Prisoners of War. Excluding 9–11 victims undercuts the growing need to further develop international law and stronger institutions of international justice for a shrinking global village. Three decades of wars on crime and drugs have already eroded many procedural safeguards important to a democratic society, and the war on terrorism has created further shortcuts in the freedoms that the U.S. is allegedly trying to protect. This is important not just to those whose rights are immediately affected, but also – because contrary to the facile notion that the terrorists "hate us because we're free" – the Pew Center's Global Attitudes project found "a pattern of support for democratic principles combined with the perception that their nation is currently lacking in these areas is characteristic of many Muslim nations" (Pew Center, 2003, p. 40). Thus, championing democracy in deeds as well as rhetoric is crucial both to preserving the core values of the nation and to U.S. moral leadership in the world.

When the Directors of the Bulletin of the Atomic Scientists moved the hands of its "Doomsday Clock" from nine to seven minutes before midnight, they noted the terrorist acts should have been a global wake-up call: "Moving the clock's hands at this time reflects our growing concern that the international community has hit the 'snooze' button rather than respond to the alarm." The Board went on to "fully support" this warning signed by 110 Nobel laureates: "The only hope for the future lies in cooperative international action, legitimized by democracy . . . To survive in the world we have transformed, we must learn to think in a new way" (Atomic Scientists, 2002). However, since that time, the U.S. pursued a unilateralist war on Iraq, unsupported by the United Nations and without meaningful international cooperation. Disturbingly, the Pew Center found that America has lost much of the goodwill it gained after the attacks of 9–11: "The bottom has fallen out of support for America in most of the Muslim world" (2003, p. 3).

In the face of this dire situation, the question is, Can criminology be a constructive influence for thinking in cooperative, democratic and new ways? Will the discipline instead follow the UCR in keeping the pre-9–11 mentality with its implicit repudiation of the rule of law? If criminologists can overcome disciplinary inertia, what could they contribute?

This chapter argues that criminology can and should make a contribution to the pressing problem of terrorism and in doing so make long overdue disciplinary changes by becoming more global and as interested in topics like ethnic cleansing as serial killers. However, the criminal justice system has spent three decades fighting wars on crime and drugs – efforts that at best have been marginally successful despite enormous expense, and have increased racial tension because of disproportionate minority involvement with the criminal justice system. A War on Terrorism that follows the model of the War on Crime and War on Drugs would be catastrophic.

In order to overcome problems associated with the "law and order" perspective guiding the destructive War on Crime, this chapter argues for embracing a new guiding framework based on a return to – and update of – *The Challenge of Crime in a Free Society* (Report by the President's Commission on Law Enforcement and Administration of Justice, 1967). The argument is not for a literal rereading of the report, but for criminologists to develop research agendas around the Challenge of Terrorism to the Free Societies of the Global Village. This conception is consistent with statements by the Atomic Scientists and Nobel Laureates; it helps criminology be relevant to the problems of the complex 21st Century global village and will equip students with an understanding of democratic freedoms rather than knee-jerk patriotism. The first section below elaborates on the depth of the current challenge from terrorism, anti-Americanism, and the inadequacies of contemporary criminology. The subsequent section explores the new "paradigm" and its implications for research agendas. The final section provides a preliminary discussion of the challenges posed by studying anti-Americanism, the limits of understanding it, and the importance of not creating "Islamicterrorist" to go with the "criminalblackman" (Russell, 1998) bogeyman.

THE CHALLENGE

Emphasis on the free society is not meant to minimize the threat posed by terrorists or anti-Americanism. Al Qaida has been disrupted, but the string of bombings so far in 2003 show it is still a potent force.[1] President Bush declared after September 11 that he wanted mastermind Osama bin Laden "dead or alive," but attention shifted to Iraq and on the second anniversary of 9–11, observers wryly comment "Osama bin Forgotten." Less humorously, the war in Iraq "widened the rift between Americans and Western Europeans, further inflamed the Muslim world, softened support for the war on terrorism, and significantly weakened global support for the pillars of the post-World War II era – the U.N. and the North Atlantic alliance" (Pew Center, 2003, p. 1).

Even without the war on Iraq, the problems raised by September 11 are formidable. The global village – "a stepchild of technology, not the flowering of community" (Johnson, 2001) – gets smaller. Issues of oil, geo-politics, deeply ambivalent reactions to hegemonic American culture, along with a variety of other factors, play into terrorism; and a failure to understand the root causes of terrorism guarantees its perpetuation. Conflicts with parts of the Muslim population are likely for the near future and "top Bush aides have begun to talk about a long and expensive U.S. presence in the Middle East, a generational commitment akin to the half-century presence in Europe during the Cold War" (Milbank & Allen, 2003, p. A01). On the eve of the second anniversary of 9–11, a video of bin Laden has surfaced, in which his top deputy says the United States has so far experienced "just the first skirmishes" and "the real battle has not started yet. Prepare yourself for the punishment for your crimes" (CNN, 2003).

Sadly, even after the 9–11 crisis, American interest in foreign news is low, with the number who follow international news "somewhat closely" unchanged from before 9–11. The "modest increase" in those who follow foreign news "very closely" "comes from the ranks of those who are already interested in international news" (Kutz, 2002, p. A13). In spite of low interest in information about the world, Americans are willing to back extreme measures to the fight the war on terror: "one in 3 could accept government-sanctioned torture of suspects" and "27% could support using nuclear weapons, compared with just 10% for use of chemical or biological weapons – even though nuclear weapons are typically far more destructive" (McLaughlin, 2002). [Readers who have forgotten why Yousef was bombing the trade center the first time should reread that section.]

Perhaps such attitudes are lapses from the broader economic and democratic ideals promoted by the U.S. that receive widespread support in the world (Pew Center, 2003). But the inconsistent and partial application of those principles causes tension not only with Arab nations, but also European allies and thus both inflame the Arab world and make cooperative action with European allies more difficult. Real and imagined grievances surround both U.S. support for dictatorial Arab regimes and a close strategic alliance with Israel, which has a long history of abuses in its intense conflicts with Arab nations. The "legal black holes" established by the U.S. mostly ensnare Muslims, which furthers the belief that America selectively targets Islam, evidence for some of an enduring Crusader mentality.

The possibility of military tribunals handing down death sentences offended many in Europe as well as the Middle East. Camp X-Ray in the Guantanamo Bay legal black hole holds citizens from several European nations, which have expended great effort to ensure access to diplomatic counsel and promises not to seek the death penalty. Success by European nations and the failure of Arab states to achieve the same furthers the perception of double standards and persecution of Muslims. In addition, the situation creates a strong rift with European states that have all abolished capital punishment, even for war crime and genocide, because it "has no place in the penal system of modern civilized societies" (in Grant, 1998, p. 20). In contrast, the U.S. is steadfast in the face of United Nations criticism of its frequent executions for day to day crimes. America has even executed foreign nationals who had not been notified of the right under the Vienna Convention to contact their embassy for assistance – and one such execution proceeded in violation of a stay ordered by the International Court of Justice (Grant, 1998).

More generally, the U.S. demands that other countries extensively revise their laws and legal system to comply with human rights treaties, while it reserves the right to continue executions of juveniles and the mentally retarded. The War on Terror exacerbates existing tensions over capital punishment, which are symbolic of larger skepticism over U.S. moral leadership on human rights and its separatism within an international legal order at a time when the emphasis needs to be on democratic actions and international cooperation.

Although criminology can not be responsible for the full range of challenges outlined above, its own shortcomings should be acknowledged before advocating an expansion into new areas. Feagin, in the published version of his American Sociological Association Presidential Address, has a major heading: "Be More Self-Critical" (2001, p. 13). In the spirit of "accelerated self-reflection" it is important to note that "crime" is generally limited to "[American] [street] crime." American criminology tends to be about as interested in international and global issues as Americans in general are in international news, with a survey of comparative criminal justice courses concluding "in spite of the rhetoric, not much real progress has been made since the first report on this issue [in 1983]" (quoted in Barberet, 2001, p. 3, bracket provided by Barberet). Michael Tonry concludes that the U.S. is "curiously impervious" to ideas and sentencing innovations from abroad (ibid.) and Elliott Currie (1999) describes a problematic "new triumphalism" based on the "American model" of crime reduction.

Americans, including criminologists, do not tend to believe that genocide has happened in the U.S. (Churchill, 1997; Johnson & Leighton, 1999), so topics related to terrorism – ethnic cleansing, massacres, human rights, etc – are typically not seen as "relevant." Thus, homicide is a central topic for criminology, serial killers are trendy, but genocide [from the Greek work *genos* (race or tribe) and the Latin *cide* (kill)] is not what "real" criminology is about (Barak, 1998, p. 39). Even though "war crimes" has the word "crime" in it, the topic and related issues like the International Criminal Court are rarely discussed in criminology's main journals or conferences. International Law and human rights are likewise marginalized, largely through the impact of political decisions:

> The set of [Reservations, Understandings and Declarations] which the Senate has attached to each human rights treaty on ratification has prevented the treaty's provisions from having any direct effect through U.S. courts and from giving individuals justiciable rights. This is one of the principle reasons why international human rights law is so little known, or used, by U.S.

lawyers and civil rights advocates and why human rights treaties have remained essentially "off shore," and have had little visible impact on U.S. law or practice (Grant, 1998, p. 26).

The U.S. and other democratic counties thus face the threat of terrorism for the foreseeable future. Besides understanding this violence, key challenges lay in protecting the freedoms that make the U.S. respected round the world and engaging international law in a way that does not undermine our ability to (as the Atomic Scientists put it) pursue "cooperative international action, legitimized by democracy." Criminology has some potential to contribute to these pressing problems, but the discipline requires long overdue changes to make it more worldly and intellectually consistent. If September 11 does not prompt change, then it is difficult to imagine what must happen for criminology to stop being parochial or limited by questionable political decisions defining crime and justiciable issues.

CRIME (AND TERRORISM) IN A FREE SOCIETY (GLOBAL VILLAGE)

In order to reveal the wealth of criminological issues raised by terrorism, a new organizing framework or paradigm is useful. It should embrace democracy, be global and not replicate the iatrogenic problems of the War on Crime and Drugs.[2] Going back to a time before the various "law and order" campaigns, the President's Commission on Law Enforcement and Administration of Justice issued a report entitled, *The Challenge of Crime in a Free Society* (1967). The Commission disregarded what Packer (1967) calls the President's "embarrassingly naïve" questions (which are not even quoted in the final report) and set off on its own agenda. The Commission included four members from the police and prosecution, but no criminal defense attorneys, and still managed to highlight the importance of freedom: "Our system of justice deliberately sacrifices much in efficiency and even in effectiveness in order to preserve local autonomy and to protect the individual" (1967, p. 7).

In the next sentence, the Commission states that "sometimes it may seem to sacrifice too much," and noted the limited success in fighting organized crime. One could replace the Commission's reference of "Cosa Nostra-type criminal organizations" with "al Qaida and terrorist networks" and capture current sentiments, just as enemies prior to the Commission (Communism, etc) also created concern about excessive individual rights. However, in reviewing situations going back to Colonial times, former Supreme Court Justice Douglas notes:

Short cuts are always tempting when one feels his cause is just. Short cuts have always been justified on the grounds that the end being worthy, the means of reaching it are not important.

Short cuts, however, are dangerous. If they can be taken against one person or group, they can be taken against another. Our greatest struggle has been to provide procedural safeguards that will protect us against ourselves and make as certain as possible that reason and calm judgment will not be swept away by passion and hysteria" (1954, p. 69).

Overall, Packer (1967) rightly criticizes the Commission's report for avoiding fundamental questions in favor of a public education document awash in "particularism" with recommendations that are "unexpceptional" and "mechanical" ("more money, more people, more research"). Embracing *The Challenge of Crime in A Free Society* is thus not a call to reread the report, but to recognize the Commission had a productive guiding framework. The ensuing decades focused on "order" rather than freedom, and the threat of terrorism creates further temptations to sacrifice freedom (even in the name of protecting it). Thus, a new conception should return to embracing freedom, be updated to include terrorism and recognize that technology has made the world so interconnected as to give the globe the feel of a village. Although the entire field of criminology need not take up such questions, criminologists should consider using 9–11, its anniversaries and related events as time for introspection about whether to devote some of the energy to *The Challenge of Terrorism for the Free Societies in the Global Village*.

For those studying terrorism and related issues, this conception helps to guard against further unnecessary erosions in the democratic freedoms the country is ultimately trying to protect. For criminology, this framework has implications both for the subjects within the disciplinary boundaries and for what Quinney has termed "Criminology as Moral Philosophy" (2003). In both cases, the goal is to avoid the type of self-criticism Feagin had for sociology when he noted that in their quest for detached, objective research the major journal in their field from the 1920 to the 1940s published "remarkably few" pieces on "the growing fascist movements in the United States and Europe, some of which would soon help generate a catastrophic war" (2001, pp. 8–9).

The Challenge of Terrorism for the Free Societies in the Global Village has several important implications for the subject matter of criminology, including its study of violence, criminal procedure, and international law (including human rights). Terrorism builds on the study of violence and hate crimes, which should be supplemented with additional attention to massacres, genocide and mass killings like ethnic cleansing. (These topics, in turn, involve greater exposure to human rights and international law, which are also salient topics in their own right in the global village.) Barak (2003) does an admirable job examining interpersonal, institutional and structural violence, and their relationships across many types of violence; he even manages to connect these to "pathways to nonviolence" through his reciprocal model. Interestingly, he notes that in response to the terrorists flying suicide missions with airplanes, one enraged man committed a hate crime by driving his car at high speed into a mosque. The behaviors are not identical but highlight the continuity of new research questions from ones firmly within the disciplinary boundaries.

Extending current criminological topics like community policing and criminal procedure also open up the discipline to new areas. Someone not familiar with the discipline would be unsure if "Community Policing in Battle Garb" (in Kraska, 2001, p. 82) described the task of U.S. soldiers in Iraq trying to do peacekeeping in communities (trying to prevent violence and looting) or the efforts of domestic officers doing community policing in hostile inner cities as part of the war on crime. Indeed, Packer discusses "the war between the police and urban poor," who "see the police more as destroyers than protectors" (1967); contemporary observers comment on police as an "occupying army" in some neighborhoods. Again, the two are not identical and shaped by different rules of engagement, but greater attention to international laws like the Geneva Convention and International Humanitarian Law helps illustrate the continuity of the criminological issues. More generally, the phenomenon discussed by Kraska, *Militarizing the American Criminal Justice System* (2001) is a trend that the PATRIOT Act greatly accelerated by blurring criminal justice and national security intelligence gathering. The mixing of functions and expanding police powers are important issues in trying to strike the balance between the threats of terrorism and the threat from Big Brother's surveillance (Reiman, 2001). But the blending of criminal justice and military functions also means that a greater range of "military" and human rights issues are also issues for criminology.

Beyond the implications of the PATRIOT Act, and even war crimes, the "legal black holes" are important subjects for criminological attention and as signals about the health of democratic freedoms that justice Douglas noted should not be swept away by passion or hysteria. For example, Jose Padilla, accused of plotting to use a radiological ("dirty bomb"), was declared an "enemy combatant" and taken to a military facility, raising the "pivotal question": "Can an American citizen, arrested on U.S. soil, be held incommunicado in a military prison indefinitely – without being charged with a crime, without access to a lawyer?" (Span, 2003, p. A01). President Bush claims Padilla is not a Prisoner of War or held under the terms of regular criminal procedure – but in either case, the political decision removing Padilla from the criminal justice system does not remove this issue from the scope of criminology.

The last paragraph hints at the second major set of implications, which have to do with the moral and political stance to the topics. Explicit within *The Challenge of Terrorism* is a concern for democratic freedoms, which in turn is grounded in a conception advanced by Feagin (2001, p. 6) and Quinney (2003) that the discipline needs to advance the social good and social justice. Quinney conceives of "Criminology as Moral Philosophy" (2003, p. 355), similar to Postman's view that all social science is moral theology in that it strives "*not*, obviously, to contribute to our field, but to contribute to human understanding and decency" (1988, p. 17). Quinney adds the "Criminologist as Witness," by which he means criminology should be a "stance for the witnessing of contemporary history" (2003, p. 366). Witnessing is not just a passive act but also includes the critique, for example of shortcuts in democratic freedoms, violations of international law (especially when they undermine the potential for international cooperative action), and U.S. refusal to recognize "the political culture of Texas is no less exempt from human rights scrutiny than that of Tehran or Badhdad" (Grant, 1998, p. 29).

The previous paragraphs are meant to be more illustrative than definitive about the impact of a new guiding framework. Although it is not suggested as The Paradigm for all criminology, seeding classrooms with these issues and framework will help students see that criminology is relevant to what's on the nightly national news and not just the crime reported on the local evening news. Many of the students will be domestic criminologists or criminal justice practitioners, but criminology can still play a role in preparing them to be citizens of a global village, and hopefully ones who have reverence for democratic freedoms instead of blind patriotism.

THE CHALLENGE OF STUDYING TERRORISM: ANTI-AMERICANISM, ANTI-SEMITISM AND "CHRISTIAN TERRORISM"

Serial killers seem to be chic; they are the object of cultural fascination and attract numerous students to be psychological profilers, like the "mindhunters" in true crime books and myriad popular media. The passion for learning how to think like a serial killer does not apply to getting inside the head of a terrorist, so there's much more interest in understanding Ted Bundy or even Jack the Ripper than Osama bin Laden. Investigating serial killers tends to be an exercise in abnormal psychology, drawing mostly from individual biography. Understanding terrorism requires confronting the disturbing conclusion that people responsible for mass violence are in many ways normal,[3] at least in the sense that people with diagnosable personality disorders tend not to work well in teams or organizations. Indeed, in an extensive literature review, Hudson (1999) concludes that "there is little reliable evidence to support the notion that terrorists in general are psychologically disturbed individuals."

Further, while the motivations of serial killers are personal, terrorism involves political violence, which frequently requires knowledge of politics, world history or international news. More problematically, terrorism related to 9–11 requires an appreciation of intense anti-American sentiments, a topic difficult at the best of times and perilous during the outpouring of patriotism following a crisis. While the mind hunters of serial killers get widespread admiration and respect, those trying to understand anti-American terrorism are frequently derided as unpatriotic or worse. For example, one university that simply wanted to require all incoming freshmen to read a book about Islam found itself "besieged in federal court and across the airwaves by Christian evangelists and other conservatives" (Cooperman, 2002, p. A01). Fox News Network's Bill O'Reilly compared the assignment to teaching "Mein Kampf" in 1941 and questioned the purpose of making freshmen study "our enemy's religion" (ibid.). [However, one freshman, demonstrating a much better grasp of the issues, commented: "After the terrorist attacks, I was so angry that I really didn't care to learn anything about Muslims. But I know now that refusing to learn is what causes more anger and confusion" (Johnson, 2002, p. A02).]

Many criminologists have critiqued the War on Crime without being anti-police and while maintaining supportive professional relationships with students working in the system, so there should be a basis for critiquing the War on Terror – including military actions – without being "anti-troop" or unpatriotic. Strong emotions mean the logical argument might be hard to get across, but the author of the book required by the university (previous paragraph) underscored the larger point:

> There's a large undercurrent out there that did not believe President Bush when he said Islam is not our enemy. We don't need to condemn those people, or dismiss them. We should talk with them and really talk this thing through, because we're going to be involved in conflicts in areas with largely Muslim populations for the foreseeable future (Nightline, 2002).

Indeed, the magnitude of the problem with Muslim countries and anti-Americanism is underscored by the Pew Center's Global Attitudes Survey, which asked people in different countries about their confidence in different leaders to "do the right thing regarding world affairs" (2003). Osama bin Laden came out ahead of President Bush in several countries whose combined population approaches a half billion people (see Table 1). This survey, done after 9–11, is consistent with earlier information that "scores of Pakistanis have named their newborn sons Osama," highlighting that the terrorists may be on the fringe "but those who applaud are the disenfranchised Muslims everywhere" (Reeve, 1999, p. 203).

Some of the foreign policy issues underlying anti-Americanism are beyond criminology, but the "terrorist as hero" motif builds on *Criminals as Heroes* (Kooistra, 1989), which examines the celebrity status accorded wild west outlaws and 20th Century gangsters. Hero status occurs when an audience finds "some symbolic meaning in his criminality" (1989, p. 152), for example when substantial segments of the public feel " 'outside the law' because the law is no longer

Table 1. Percent of People Expressing Confidence in Bush or Osama Bin Laden to "Do the Right Thing Regarding World Affairs."

Country	Bush	Bin Laden	2003 Population
Indonesia	8	58	234.89 million
Jordan	1	55	5.46
Morocco	2	49	31.69
Pakistan	5	35	150.7
Palestinian authority	1	71	3.3
Turkey	8	15	68.11
Total			494.15 million

Note: Indicates percent expressing "A lot" or "some" confidence.
Source: Pew Global Attitudes Survey (2003), Topline Results pp. 154–155, 158. Population Data from U.S. Census, International Data Base, available: http://www.census.gov/ipc/www/idbsum.html. Data for Palestinian Authority for 2001, from Jewish Virtual Library, American Israeli Cooperative Enterprise. Available: http://www.us-israel.org/jsource/arabs/palpop01.html.

seen as an instrument of justice but as a tool of oppression wielded by favored interests" (1989, p. 11). At such times, or among groups with this perception, there is a "market" for symbolic representations of justice and "a steady need for the production of celebrities" (Kooistra, 1989, p. 162). (This analysis indicates an issue going beyond individual terrorists and suggests that disenfranchisement is a more fruitful avenue than the more simplistic question of whether poverty causes terrorism.)

Although anti-Americanism is an important issue, there are also significant limitations on its ability to explain terrorist attacks perhaps directed at Western targets but that kill large numbers of Arabs and fellow Muslims. Hoagland notes: "Events since [9–11] have shown that [why do they hate us?] was too self-centered and exclusionary a reflex. Those who hate in this way hate much more than us" (2003, p. B07). Their project is ultimately much larger than anti-Americanism because "the radicals have an entire world to destroy before their apocalyptic design of restoring the Islamic caliphate can be realized" (ibid.). The caliph is "an integral part of Islam's glory," a "divinely mandated leader whose forces led a lightning conquest of much of the known world for the faith" (Benjamin & Simon, 2002, p. 47). Restoring the caliphate is a reference to the dream of a multi-nation Islamic superpower ruled under sharia or Islamic law.

Making sense of this part of bin Laden's quest involves an examination of the influence of medieval Muslim theologian ibn Taymiyya. In contrast to the religious-scholarly establishment of the time, he believed in a personal engagement with holy writ and is thus akin Martin Luther (Benjamin & Simon, 2002,

p. 46). Issues of statecraft and governance were central to ibn Taymiyya's writings, especially the secularization of government and the consequent subordination of religion to the state. Rulers needed to enforce sharia and exhibit personal piety: "To obey a leader who violated the percepts of Islam would be to reject the word of God and be guilty of apostasy oneself" (Benjamin & Simon, 2002, p. 48). Ibn Taymiyya wanted to purify Islam and a crucial aspect of this task was jihad, holy war – and not the "inner" jihad or individual struggle to become more devout. Jihad was against enemies, but not just the ones at the political borders: "By asserting that jihad against apostates within the realm of Islam is justified – by turning jihad inward and reforging it into a weapon for use against Muslims as well as infidels – he planted a seed of revolutionary violence in the heart of Islamic thought" (Benjamin & Simon, 2002, p. 50).

In a rich and readable chapter, Benjamin and Simon trace this current of thought from ibn Taymiyya through the Crusades, the humiliating rise of European ascendancy, down to bin Laden. Along the way are figures like prison author Sayyid Qutb, who "for better or worse, is the Islamic world's answer to Solzhenitsy, Satre and Havel, and he easily ranks with all of them in influence" (2002, p. 62). He saw "virtually every confrontation between the worlds of Islam and the West [as] a repetition" of the Crusades, which are "an ancient and perpetual antagonism, unconfined by specifics of time and place (ibid., p. 66).

The many strains of thought converge in bin Laden, who asserts his own right to interpret religious doctrine and views less militant interpretations as coming from the paid lackeys of apostate leaders bought off by the U.S. Indeed, such governments tend to be more Western, secular and thus not only place human judgment over the divine but lead Muslims away from the true faith. For bin Laden, the overthrow of such governments is an important step to securing rule by those such as the Taliban, who govern in accordance with Islamic law. The ultimate goal, however, is to create an Islamic superpower and resurrect the glory days where Islam was a powerful force, united under a divinely appointed ruler. To this end, bin Laden has released a fatwa (religious decree, even though technically he does not possess the authority) about the "Zionist-Crusader Alliance" and elsewhere has indicated that acquiring a nuclear weapon is a religious duty (Benjamin & Simon, 2002, pp. 140, 160).

Bin Laden's fatwa highlights the importance of anti-Semitism *and* anti-Americanism; it also connects al Qaida with domestic terrorists reading the *Turner Diaries* (MacDonald, 1980) and identifying with the characters' struggle against Z.O.G., the Zionist Occupied Government. Israel is viewed with hostility in much of the Arab world because of its treatment of Arabs, especially Palestinians. In addition to being a close ally of Israel, the U.S. is also perceived to mistreat Arabs and have double standards for enforcing human rights, especially when it comes to Israel. Within the U.S., many on the survivalist right see Israel as dominating the United Nations, the "New World Order" and/or the U.S. government, with mass media ("Jewsmedia" rather than "newsmedia") being the propaganda arm of ZOG (Ezekiel, 1995; MacDonald, 1980; Ridgeway, 1995). Among those on the survivalist right who see the U.S. government as having lost legitimacy, the strikes on the Pentagon, World Trade Center and a heavily Jewish town like New York City were not cause for anger or patriotism, but respect at a successor to McVeigh (Hamm, 1997). (Remember that the FBI still does not know if the anthrax attacks on the media and Congress were from al Qaida or a domestic terrorist with is own anti-government agenda.)

Aside from concerns about U.S. and foreign terrorists working together, the larger point is not to get so focused on al Qaida as to forget about domestic threats. Russell argues that black men and crime are so closely linked and so strongly embody white America's fear of crime as to warrant using "criminalblackman" (1998). This focus on street crime, especially by racial minorities, helps deflect attention from a great deal of white collar and corporate crime (Enron, etc.) that is far more harmful (Reiman, 2004). "Islamicterrorist" should not blind people to the threats of domestic terrorism or the value in studying it. Further, imagine calling someone like Randolph, the Atlanta Olympic bomber, a "Christian terrorist" because he declared

> total war on the ungodly communist regime in New York and your legislative [sic] bureaucratic lackey's in Washington. It is you who are responsible and preside over the murder of children and issue the policy of ungodly preversion thats [sic] destroying our people (in Cooperman, 2003, p. A03).

As Aho notes, most mainstream Christians would consider Randolph's version of Christianity ("Christian Identity") to be a heresy: "If Christians take umbrage at the juxtaposition of the words 'Christian' and 'terrorist,' he added, 'that may give them some idea of how Muslims feel' when they constantly hear the term 'Islamic terrorism' " (in Cooperman, 2003, p. A03; see also Aho, 1990).

Further, most people assumed the perpetrator of the federal building in Oklahoma City attacked was Middle Eastern, yet it turned out to be McVeigh. When the World Trade Centers and Pentagon were hit, people again assumed the perpetrator was Arab. This time, they were right, but *The Turner Diaries* (MacDonald, 1980) ends with a nuclear suicide mission into the Pentagon; the "great Houston bombings" occur in the novel on September 11, "which left more than 4,000 persons dead and much of Houston's industrial and shipping facilities smoldering wreckage" (MacDonald, 1980, p. 94). Additional commonalities in the thinking of domestic and international terrorist include Earl Turner's fictional group The Order favoring multiple simultaneous attacks (MacDonald, 1980, p. 62), much like al Qaida.

Bin Laden believes that if he can weaken the U.S. economically, it will not have resources to enslave others (Benjamin & Simon, 2002, p. 156). The Order starts out by trying to cause trouble so that the government will become repressive and people will rise in revolt. However, the Order realizes that people will not revolt as long as they have a paycheck, color TV and a full belly (1978, p. 101) – so the emphasis shifts to undermining infrastructure:

> power stations, fuel depots, transportation facilities, food sources, key industrial plants. We do not expect to bring down the already creaky American economic structure immediately, but we do expect to cause a number of localized and temporary breakdowns, which will gradually have a cumulative effect on the whole public (1978, p. 102).

Other ideas involve counterfeiting, hitting a nuclear reactor and finally stealing nuclear missiles. By the novel's end, The Order launches nuclear weapons, killing millions and causing genocide in an effort to "liberate" first the U.S., then the planet: "we will liquidate all the enemies of our people, including in particular all white persons who have consciously aided those enemies" (1978, p. 181; see also discussion of "slaughter of innocents," p. 195 ff). Substituting "Islam" for the "White Race" that Turner fights for would reveal a proximate outline of bin Laden's "apocalyptic design of restoring the Islamic caliphate" that might claim large numbers of Muslim lives. Believers in either are dangerous and similar in at least some important ways.

CONCLUSION

Realizing that an unknown number of people harbor fantasies of mass nuclear annihilation is disturbing – even more so when one considers the popularity of bin Laden or the *Turner Diaries*. There's a temptation to find topics that don't keep one up at night and that make better polite conversation when people ask about what you study. Criminology journals are likely to remain receptive to unimaginative and marginally relevant but technically well executed quantitative pieces over an extended treatment of issues raised in this chapter. While not all criminologists should take up these topics, more should – and professional introspection should be widely encouraged.

Researchers who investigate genocide note that they risk displacing economics as "the dismal science," and studying terrorism is a step in that same direction. But there are also risks in *not* moving in that direction, of rearranging deck chairs (or regression models of deck chair theft) and neglecting the big threats. Friedrichs, "as someone who has co-taught a course on the Holocaust for quite a number of years" had "long wondered what German criminologists were doing in the 1930s, while their state was in the process of implementing one of the great crimes in human history" (2002). Obviously they were not addressing Nazism and he asks, "What the Hell were they thinking?"[4] Many continued to study conventional forms of criminal behavior, which some imbued with the racist, biogenic approach of the government. While not trying to compare the U.S. to the Nazis, the point is to ask about the judgment of history at an important juncture: will future generations ask of criminology, "What were they thinking?"

NOTES

1. Elsewhere, I have created an extensive web page that discusses the string of terrorism attributed to Al Qaida, as well as links discussing the group's intensive efforts to acquire Weapons of Mass Destruction. This page is part of Mark Hamm and Paul Leighton (Eds), *Teaching and Understanding September 11*, the full contents of which are freely available through http://stopviolence.com > September 11 contents. For the bin Laden page, check in the "Photo" section of the main table of contents. Other sections include syllabi and writings on: terrorism and political violence; Mid East, Islam and anti-Americanism; and Law and International Justice. This project is part of an effort to think in a new way and is explained in the original (2002) full introduction, available from the main contents page.

2. Iatrogenic is a medical term related to injury or illness that result from medical treatment, such as getting an infection from an operation. Within the drug war, the harm reduction approach blames current policies for infections and HIV because clean needle exchanges are not legal; one effect of mass incarceration is to weaken informal social controls like family and community (Clear, 2002). President Bush went into Iraq supposedly to prevent terrorism, but at this point the chaotic situation may be a breeding ground for terrorism and anti-Americanism.

3. In an often quoted passage, Arendt remarks that six psychiatrists certified Nazi Eichmann

as 'normal' – 'More normal, at any rate, than I am after having examined him,' one of them is said to have exclaimed, while another had found that his whole psychological outlook, his attitude toward his wife and children, mother and father, brothers, sisters, and friends, was 'not only normal but most desirable' (1964, pp. 25–26).

4. He used this more pointed language in a discussion we had at the first American Society of Criminology meeting after 9–11.

REFERENCES

Aho, J. (1990). *The politics of righteousness.* Seattle: University of Washington Press.

Anderson, C. (2003). FBI planning offices in foreign capitals. Available, http://www.onlineathens.com/stories/032903/war_20030329104.shtml (Accessed 28 June 2003).

Arendt, H. (1963, 1964). *Eichmann in Jerusalem: A report on the banality of evil* (revised and enlarged edition). New York: Viking Press.

Atomic Scientists (2002). From the board of directors: It's seven minutes to midnight. *Bulletin of the Atomic Scientists* (27 February).

Barak, G. (1998). *Integrating criminologies.* Boston: Allyn & Bacon.

Barak, G. (2003). *Violence and nonviolence.* Thousand Oaks: Sage.

Barberet, R. (2001). Global competence and American criminology – An expatriate's view. *The Criminologist, 26*(2).

Benjamin, D., & Simon, S. (2002). *The age of sacred terror.* New York: Random House.

Blumstein, A., & Wallman, J. (Eds) (2000). *The crime drop in America.* Cambridge: Cambridge University Press.

Churchill, W. (1997). *A little matter of genocide.* San Francisco: City Lights Books.

Clear, T. (2002). The problem with 'addition by subtraction': The prison-crime relationship in low-income communities. In: M. Mauer & M. Chesney-Lind (Eds), *Invisible Punishment: The Collateral Consequences of Mass Imprisonment.* New York: New Press.

CNN (2003). Al-Jazeera airs purported bin Laden tape (September 10). Available: http://www.cnn.com/2003/WORLD/meast/09/10/binladen.tape/.

Cooperman, A. (2002). A timely subject – and a sore one: UNC draws fire, lawsuit for assigning book on Islam. *Washington Post* (August 7).

Cooperman, A. (2003). Is terrorism tied to Christian sect? Religion may have motivated bombing suspect. *Washington Post* (2 June).

Currie, E. (1999). Reflections on crime and criminology at the millenium. *Western Criminology Review, 2*(1). Available: http://wcr.sonoma.edu/v2n1/currie.html.

Douglas, W. (1954). *An almanac of liberty.* Garden City, NY: Doubleday & Co.

Ezekiel, R. (1995). *The racist mind.* New York: Viking/Penguin.

Feagin, J. (2001). Social justice and sociology: Agendas for the twenty-first century. *American Sociological Review, 66*, 1–20.

Federal Bureau of Investigation (1996). *Crime in the United States, 1995.* Washington, DC: Government Printing Office.

Federal Bureau of Investigation (2002a). *Crime in the United States, 2001.* Washington, DC: Government Printing Office.

Federal Bureau of Investigation (2002b). Crime trends, 2001 preliminary figures. Available, http://www.fbi.gov/ucr/01prelim.pdf.

Friedrichs, D. (2002). September 11th and its aftermath. In: M. Hamm & P. Leighton (Eds), *Teaching and Understanding September 11.* Available: http://stopviolence.com.

Grant, S. (1998). A dialogue of the deaf? New international attitudes and the death penalty in America. *Criminal Justice Ethics, 17*(2).

Hamm, M. (1997). *Apocalypse in Oklahoma.* Boston: Northeastern University Press.

Hoagland, J. (2003). Fighting for the soul of Islam. *Washington Post* (13 July), B07.

Hudson, R. (1999). *The sociology and psychology of terrorism: Who becomes a terrorist and why?* Washington, DC Federal Research Division, Library of Congress and U.S. Dept of Commerce, National Technical Information Service. (A short excerpt bearing directly on the question of mental illness is available through http://stopviolence.com > Sept. 11 Contents.)

Johnson, R. (2001). Village life. Poem available in Sept. 11 section of: http://stopviolence.com.

Johnson, D. (2002). N.C. university students discuss readings in Islam: Christian group sought to bar assignment on Koran. *Washington Post* (August 20).

Johnson, R., & Leighton, P. (1999). American genocide: The destruction of the black underclass. In: C. Summers & E. Markusen (Eds), *Collective Violence: Harmful Behavior in Groups and*

Governments Lanham: Rowman & Littlefield. (A shorter version of this article is available through http://paulsjusticepage.com.)

Kittrie, N., & Wedlock, E. (Eds) (1998). *The tree of liberty: A documentary history of rebellion and political crime in America. Volume 2: Cold war to new world order* (rev. ed.). Baltimore: Johns Hopkins University Press.

Kooistra, P. (1989). *Criminals as heroes: Structure, power and identity.* Bowling Green: Bowling Green State University Popular Press.

Kraska, P. (2001). *Militarizing the American criminal justice system.* Boston: Northeastern University Press.

Kutz, H. (2002). Despite Sept. 11, interest still low in foreign news. *Washington Post* (June 10), A13.

MacDonald, A. (1980). *The Turner diaries* (2nd ed.). New York: Barricade Books.

McLaughlin, A. (2002). How far Americans would go to fight terror. *Christian Science Monitor* (November 14). Available: http://www.csmonitor.com/2001/1114/p1s3-usju.html.

Milbank, D., & Allen, M. (2003). Security may not be safe issue for Bush in '04. *Washington Post* (August 22).

Nightline (2002). Koran dispute: Students discuss Islamic holy book analysis after a court fight to block it (August 25). Available: http://abcnews.go.com/sections/nightline/DailyNews/koran020824.html.

Packer, H. (1967). Copping out. *New York Review of Books*, 9(6).

Pew Center (2003). View of a changing world. Washington, DC: The Pew Research Center for The People and The Press. Available: http://people-press.org/reports/display.php3?ReportID=185.

Postman, N. (1988). "Social Science As Moral theology" in *Contentious Objections.* New York: Vintage/Random House.

President's Commission on Law Enforcement and Administration of Justice (1967). *The Challenge of Crime in a Free Society.* Washington, DC: U.S. Government Printing Office.

Quinney, R. (2003). Criminology as moral philosophy, criminologist as witness. In: D. Hawkins, S. Myers & R. Stone (Eds), *Crime Control and Social Justice.* Westport: Greenwood.

Reeve, S. (1999). *The new jackals: Ramzi Yousef, Osama bin Laden and the future of terrorism.* Boston: Northeastern University Press.

Reiman, J. (2001). Driving to the Panopticon: A philosophical exploration of the risks to privacy posed by the highway technology of the future. In: P. Leighton & J. Reiman (Eds), *Criminal Justice Ethics.* Upper Saddle River: Prentice-Hall.

Reiman, J. (2004). *The rich get richer and the poor get prison* (7th ed.). Boston: Allyn & Bacon.

Ridgeway, J. (1995). *Blood in the face: The Ku Klux Klan, Aryan Nations, Nazi Skinheads, and the rise of a new white culture* (2nd ed.). New York: Thunder's Mouth.

Rosenfeld, R. (2002). Why criminologists should study terrorism. *The Criminologist: The Official Newsletter of the American Society of Criminology*, 27(6).

Russell, K. K. (1998). *The color of crime: Racial hoaxes, white fear, black protectionism, police harrassment, and other macroaggressions.* New York: New York University Press.

Span, P. (2003). Enemy combatant vanishes into a 'legal black hole'. *Washington Post* (July 30).

SUBJECT INDEX

SET UP A CONTINUATION ORDER TODAY!

Did you know you can set up a continuation order on all JAI series and have each new volume sent directly to you upon publication. For details on how to set up a continuation order contact your nearest regional sales office listed below.

To view related Sociology series,
please visit

www.ElsevierSocialSciences.com/sociology

30% DISCOUNT FOR AUTHORS ON ALL BOOKS!

A 30% discount is available to Elsevier book and journal contributors ON ALL BOOKS plus standalone CD-ROMS except multi-volume reference works.

To claim your discount, full payment is required with your order, which must be sent directly to the publisher at the nearest regional sales office listed below.

ELSEVIER REGIONAL SALES OFFICES